The *New*
Washington One-Day Trip Book

*For my Dad, Harry Ockershausen,
who taught me to notice the wonder
of the world!*

The New Washington One-Day Trip Book

101 Offbeat Excursions in and Around the Nation's Capital....

JANE OCKERSHAUSEN

EPM

Publications, Inc./McLean, Virginia

Library of Congress Cataloging-in-Publication Data

Ockershausen, Jane.
    The Washington one-day trip book: 101 offbeat excursions
in and around the Nation's Capital / Jane Ockershausen.—4th
ed.
        p.   cm.
    Includes index.
    ISBN 0-939009-59-5
    1. Washington Region—Guidebooks.   I. Title.
F192.3.025   1992
917.5304'4—dc20   91-46710
                                                               CIP

EPM Publications, Inc., 1003 Turkey Run Road,
    McLean, Virginia 22101

Printed in the United States of America

Cover and book design by Tom Huestis

Cover photo: Navy-Marine Memorial in the
    Lady Bird Johnson Memorial Grove
Credit: Bill Clark, Courtesy of National Park Service

Contents
THE WASHINGTON ONE-DAY TRIP BOOK

═══════════════════════WINTER═══════════════════════

Helpful Telephone Numbers for Travelers

Virginia Traveler Information Service	(804)786-4484
Delaware Tourism Office	(800)441-8846
Maryland Travel Information	(800)543-1036
West Virginia Travel Information	(800)225-5982
Pennsylvania Travel Information	(800)237-4363
Washington, D.C. Convention & Visitors Bureau	(202)789-7000

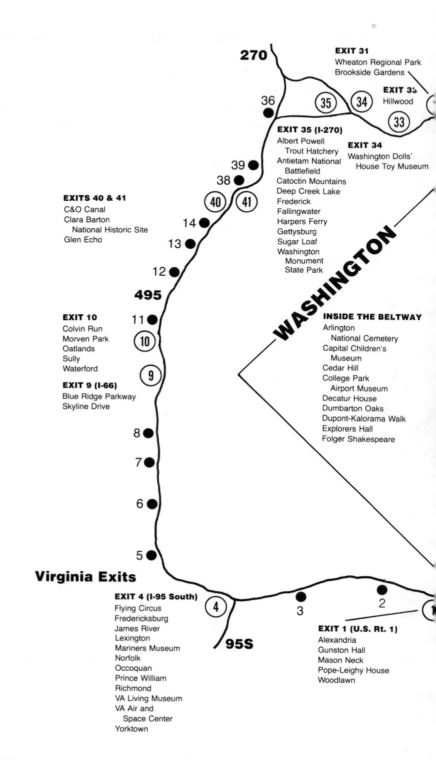

270

EXIT 31
Wheaton Regional Park
Brookside Gardens

EXIT 33
Hillwood

36

35 34 33

EXIT 35 (I-270)
Albert Powell
  Trout Hatchery
Antietam National
  Battlefield
Catoctin Mountains
Deep Creek Lake
Frederick
Fallingwater
Harpers Ferry
Gettysburg
Sugar Loaf
Washington
  Monument
  State Park

EXIT 34
Washington Dolls'
  House Toy Museum

39
38

40 41

EXITS 40 & 41
C&O Canal
Clara Barton
  National Historic Site
Glen Echo

14
13
12

495

WASHINGTON

EXIT 10
Colvin Run
Morven Park
Oatlands
Sully
Waterford

11
10
9

INSIDE THE BELTWAY
Arlington
  National Cemetery
Capital Children's
  Museum
Cedar Hill
College Park
  Airport Museum
Decatur House
Dumbarton Oaks
Dupont-Kalorama Walk
Explorers Hall
Folger Shakespeare

EXIT 9 (I-66)
Blue Ridge Parkway
Skyline Drive

8
7
6
5

Virginia Exits

EXIT 4 (I-95 South)
Flying Circus
Fredericksburg
James River
Lexington
Mariners Museum
Norfolk
Occoquan
Prince William
Richmond
VA Living Museum
VA Air and
  Space Center
Yorktown

4 3 2 1

95S

EXIT 1 (U.S. Rt. 1)
Alexandria
Gunston Hall
Mason Neck
Pope-Leighy House
Woodlawn

Maryland Exits

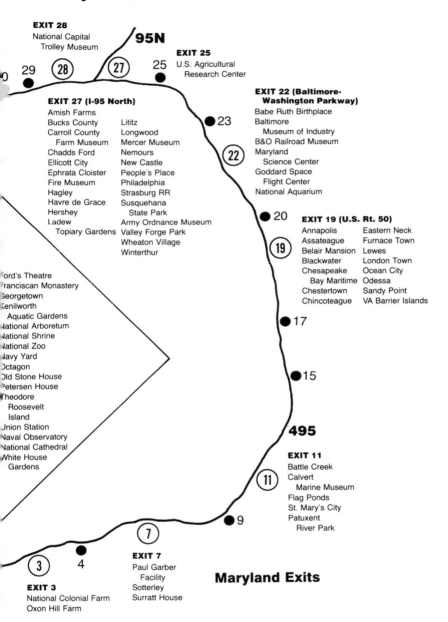

95N

EXIT 28
National Capital
Trolley Museum

EXIT 25
U.S. Agricultural
Research Center

29 28 27 25

EXIT 27 (I-95 North)
Amish Farms
Bucks County
Carroll County
 Farm Museum
Chadds Ford
Ellicott City
Ephrata Cloister
Fire Museum
Hagley
Havre de Grace
Hershey
Ladew
 Topiary Gardens

Lititz
Longwood
Mercer Museum
Nemours
New Castle
People's Place
Philadelphia
Strasburg RR
Susquehanna
 State Park
Valley Forge Park
Army Ordnance Museum
Wheaton Village
Winterthur

23
22

**EXIT 22 (Baltimore-
Washington Parkway)**
Babe Ruth Birthplace
Baltimore
 Museum of Industry
B&O Railroad Museum
Maryland
 Science Center
Goddard Space
 Flight Center
National Aquarium

20
19

EXIT 19 (U.S. Rt. 50)
Annapolis
Assateague
Belair Mansion
Blackwater
Chesapeake
 Bay Maritime
Chestertown
Chincoteague

Eastern Neck
Furnace Town
Lewes
London Town
Ocean City
Odessa
Sandy Point
VA Barrier Islands

Ford's Theatre
Franciscan Monastery
Georgetown
Kenilworth
 Aquatic Gardens
National Arboretum
National Shrine
National Zoo
Navy Yard
Octagon
Old Stone House
Petersen House
Theodore
 Roosevelt
 Island
Union Station
Naval Observatory
National Cathedral
White House
 Gardens

17

15

495

EXIT 11
Battle Creek
Calvert
 Marine Museum
Flag Ponds
St. Mary's City
Patuxent
 River Park

11

9

7

EXIT 7
Paul Garber
 Facility
Sotterley
Surratt House

3   4

EXIT 3
National Colonial Farm
Oxon Hill Farm

Maryland Exits

═Explore Your World!═

I began writing the first edition of *The Washington One-Day Trip Book* twenty years ago. In the early seventies most families did their traveling during an annual two-week vacation. One-day trips were not as widely popular as they are today. Changing vacation habits have put new emphasis on day-tripping and weekend excursions. In the intervening years I have written six additional One-Day Trip Books for the mid-Atlantic region.

My two decades of research have taken me to hundreds of historic homes, museums and other sites. I find that at each spot visitors learn or see something new. Day-tripping is an enjoyable way to learn. Travelers gain insights into American history, get a hands-on introduction to transportation as it developed in this country, learn about horticulture, viticulture and astronomy. Whatever your interest there are places to visit that can enhance your knowledge and appreciation.

I have also discovered that everything changes, museums expand, new programs are introduced and new information uncovered. I encourage you to revisit spots you toured years ago. I did during the year and a half I spent revising this book and found that many of my favorite attractions like the Yorktown Victory Center and Mariners' Museum were better than ever.

The title of this book, *The New Washington One-Day Trip Book*, calls attention to the fact that it is an entirely new edition. You'll find old favorites from earlier editions, but information about each site is updated and revised. Roughly a third of the selections are new to the book. You'll find more Washington attractions in this edition because I included some that can be enjoyed during a long lunch break or on an afternoon foray into the city. Listings of Christmas tree farms, pumpkin patches, vineyards and white-water rafting outfitters that were once part of the text are now listed in special interest sections.

This book will tell you how to tour spots that you may pass everyday on your way to work—the Anderson House, the U.S. Naval Observatory, the Goddard Space Flight Center or the U.S. Agricultural Research Center in Beltsville. The sites are arranged according to the best season to visit. The right time of year can transform an otherwise ordinary hillside into a truly breathtaking vision as happens when Forsythia Hill blooms at Dumbarton Oaks or the azaleas flower at the National Arboretum. Special events make Waterford special in October and Chestertown in May. Migration of Canada geese makes the fall the best time to visit Blackwater, Eastern Neck National Wildlife Refuge or Merkle Wildlife Refuge.

Whatever your special interest the topical cross reference shows, at a glance, all the selections that relate to it. The map at the front of the book combines excursions geographically. For example, if you are heading for Chadds Ford, you also can include a stop at Longwood Gardens, Hagley Museum, Winterthur or Nemours.

If you are staying home with young children you will find many of these excursions in your neighborhood or within a short driving distance. Brief trips provide a welcome respite and are easier for young children than overnights. A stop at Oxon Hill Farm, Wheaton Regional Park or Glen Echo is fun for preschoolers and needn't involve the whole family. Check the topical listing for other spots with special appeal for children. If you take along a picnic lunch these excursions are economical and educational getaways.

The book also contains a descriptive list of annual events to help plan your outings to include festivals and fairs. Some daytrippers prefer to avoid crowds when visiting sites, and for them these popular annual events are occasions to avoid. These 101 excursions are unusual, enjoyable, economical and educational. Even though the trips are arranged seasonally, many of the sites can be visited at any time of the year. It's always a good idea to read all the information about an excursion and to call ahead before starting out. One-day trips provide enrichment for the whole family and create experiences that children will long remember.

I hope your one-days are fun days!

J.O.

Spring brings a glorious show of floral color to the gardens of
the Henry Francis du Pont Winterthur Museum, Delaware. Entrance door and window of west facade date from 1762. Courtesy
Winterthur Museum.

Spring

Babe Ruth Birthplace and Baltimore Orioles Museum

In a League by Himself

Spring means baseball to a large percent of Americans. But this national passion is in season year-round at the **Babe Ruth Birthplace** and Baltimore Orioles Museum.

The Babe, at least a realistic life-size facsimile, is back in the rowhouse where he was born on February 6, 1895. The house at 216 Emory Street, seven blocks from the Inner Harbor, was slated for demolition in 1967. Baseball fans, civic leaders and community residents joined to save the Babe's birthplace and the adjacent houses, which now serve as a museum.

Young George Ruth spent only a short time at his grandmother's house after his birth before his parents moved into their own place. This is, however, the only surviving house linked with the Babe's Baltimore childhood. The mementoes of his eventful life fill all the available space in the 12-by-60 foot house, and other baseball memorabilia spill over into the houses on either side.

George's parents owned a tavern, and although it no longer stands, a recent archaeological dig unearthed artifacts from it. The museum displays these mementoes. While his parents worked all day and late into the night, George fended for himself and developed some bad habits and wild ways.

But things changed radically when George was eight and began attending St. Mary's Industrial School for Boys, part orphanage and part reform school. He didn't like the school, but it was at St. Mary's that George discovered baseball.

One of the museum's most delightful items is a hymnal that supposedly belonged to George. The inscribed flyleaf signed by George reads: "World's worse (sic) singer—world's best pitcher."

Those with a sketchy knowledge of baseball think of Ruth as the Sultan of Swat, but real fans remember that he first won fame as a pitcher. He peaked at the 1918 World Series, just four years after he started playing with the major leagues. On the mound for the Boston Red Sox, he pitched 29¼ consecutive scoreless innings. It wasn't until 1961 that Whitey Ford broke his record.

The Babe earned most of his records as a hitter. In 1927 he hit

60 homeruns. This record also held until 1961 when Roger Maris hit 61. During his entire career Ruth hit 714 homeruns, a feat topped only by Hank Aaron with 755. If you like detailed stats the museum has a Home Run Club Room with a plaque for each of the Babe's homeruns. You also can read up on the 14 other players to hit 500; the most recent was Mike Schmidt.

This museum is a hit with fans from the moment they enter and read the sign: "Baseball Spoken Here." "Spoken" is an accurate way to describe many of the exhibits. There are recorded interviews with Babe Ruth's family, Mike Wallace narrates a 20-minute film on the Babe, and fans and teammates talk about this baseball legend.

Not all the items are behind glass; you can handle a collection of bats, balls and gloves. Young fans enjoy seeing old equipment like the 1879 single-stitched baseball and the 1910 finger glove. It brings a lump to the throat to see the Babe's old Louisville Slugger.

Local fans are justifiably proud of the collection in the museum's Maryland Hall of Fame Room. Here you see career information on outstanding players from the state. Highlighted are the six local players inducted into the Baseball Hall of Fame at Cooperstown, New York: Babe Ruth, Lefty Grove, Al Kaline, Judy Johnson, Jimmy Foxx and John Franklin "Home Run" Baker.

This local boosterism extends to the collection designated as the **Baltimore Orioles Museum**. A continuing video shows the high spots of more than 54 years of Orioles' play. Vince Bagli narrates a Maryland baseball overview called "Hard Shell, Hard Ball." Yet another video focuses on great moments of play by each member of the Baltimore Orioles' Hall of Fame.

While in the Baltimore area, there is another rite of spring to explore. An ideal place to seek fresh flowers, fruits and vegetables is **Lexington Market** at Lexington and Eutaw Streets. The sign over the door invites you to visit "World Famous Lexington Market." Though it hardly rivals the Los Angeles Farmers Market, this Baltimore landmark is a thriving example of an old-fashioned market. It opened in 1782 when farmers started bringing their produce into town and is now one of the country's oldest continuously operated markets.

Today the market spreads through three-block-long buildings with stalls for more than 130 merchants. A wide variety of meat, poultry and fish is available, and butchers cut to order. Some stands offer prepared food, so you might want to visit around lunchtime and try some Sicilian pizza, Polish sausage, hot soft pretzels, barbecued chicken or steamed crabs.

The Babe Ruth Birthplace and Baltimore Orioles Museum is open April through October from 10:00 A.M. to 5:00 P.M. daily.

November through March it closes an hour earlier. Admission is charged. The Lexington Market is open at no charge Monday through Saturday from 8:30 A.M. to 6:00 P.M.

Directions: From the Beltway I-495/95 take the Baltimore-Washington Parkway into Baltimore. The Parkway becomes Russell Street and then becomes S. Paca. The Babe Ruth Birthplace is two blocks south of Pratt Street and the University of Maryland Hospital on Emory Street.

B&O Railroad Museum

Birthplace of the American Railroad

Charles Carroll, the oldest surviving signer of the Declaration of Independence, laid the cornerstone for the nation's first long distance railroad, the Baltimore and Ohio at Mount Clare in West Baltimore on July 4, 1828. At the celebration, Carroll said, "I consider this among the most important acts of my life, second only to the signing of the Declaration of Independence, if second even to that."

It is noteworthy that on the same day just outside Washington, D.C., President John Quincy Adams, the son of another signer, was turning over the first shovel of soil for the construction of the Chesapeake and Ohio Canal (see selection).

Since the story of railroading in America began at Mount Clare, it is appropriate that the nation's oldest railroad station is the repository for the world's most comprehensive railroad car collection. The passenger car roundhouse is still filled with cars. The **B&O Railroad Museum** has more than 100 locomotives and full-size models. Many of the cars are displayed on the 22 separate spoke-like tracks surrounding the original wooden turntable of the roundhouse.

You can see a replica of the historic car that Peter Cooper built at Mount Clare in 1829. He called his engine the Teakettle, but others called it the Tom Thumb. It was this car that had the legendary race with a horse—and lost! There are many tales told about this race, but historians now believe the train lost the race because a fan belt broke. No horse could have beaten the engine's normal running time of 26:22 minutes for the 13-mile trip between Mount Clare and Ellicott City. Trains began making this journey on May 24, 1830. Before Peter Cooper's engine, horse-drawn train cars ran from Mount Clare Station to the Carrolton Viaduct for ten cents a ride.

Besides the Tom Thumb, Mt. Clare's tracks have the 1856 4-4-0 locomotive known as the William Mason, (which has been used in movies and TV programs), the Freedom Train used during the 1976 Bicentennial celebration, and the Allegheny with its massive 600-ton engine.

The variety in style and design of the plush passenger cars is astonishing. The 1930 Imperial Salon coach is considered by many as the most luxurious coach car ever operated in America. There are also Pullmans, diners, observation cars and specialized cars like the tunnel-gauging porcupine car and the molten steel-carrying submarine car, so named because it resembled an underwater sub.

The museum contains railroad memorabilia and examples of other early forms of transportation such as the Conestoga wagon. In the adjoining **Annex** there is the museum gift shop and a HO gauge model layout that runs on the half-hour from 10:30 A.M. to 3:30 P.M. The Annex also has a small theater that shows movie shorts on railroading. The railroad cars, locomotives and engines overflow to the yards, both in front and in back of the museum. You can take a photograph of your youngster playing conductor on one of these old engines.

The B&O Railroad Museum is open Tuesday through Sunday from 10:00 A.M. to 4:00 P.M. During June, July and August the museum stays open until 8:00 P.M. on Thursdays. Admission is charged.

Local landowners and businesses either donated or sold for a nominal price the land to build the Baltimore & Ohio Railroad. These entrepreneurs wanted to get their cargo to important Ohio River territories. James MacCubbin Carroll sold the ten acres on which the Mount Clare Station was built for one dollar. After your visit to the museum you can visit Carroll's nearby family home, **Mount Clare Mansion**.

Carroll's home is the oldest in Baltimore. It dates back to 1756. This pre-Revolutionary Georgian mansion was built by Charles Carroll, the Barrister, who is noted for his work in drafting the Declaration of Rights for Maryland and the Maryland State Constitution. He is not, however, the Charles Carroll who signed the Declaration of Independence. The house is furnished with Carroll family pieces. Tours are given Tuesday through Saturday from 11:00 A.M. to 4:00 P.M. and Sunday 1:00 to 4:00 P.M.

Directions: From the Beltway I-495/95 take Exit 22, the Baltimore-Washington Parkway to Baltimore. Turn left on Lombard Street. Continue on Lombard to Poppleton and turn left. The B&O Railroad Museum is located at 901 W. Pratt Street. For the Mount Clare Mansion continue on Pratt Street to Martin Luther King Boulevard and turn right. Turn right on Washington Boulevard and continue to the mansion in Carroll Park.

Belair Mansion and Stable Museum

Lots of Horsing Around

Why is it that although we explore exotic ports of call with thoroughness and unflagging energy, we all too often ignore attractions in our own neighborhoods? Spring is a good time to remedy this oversight and get to know the attractions—historic and scenic—of one of Washington's largest bedroom communities, Bowie, Maryland.

Belair Mansion, "The Home of the Early Maryland Governors," was once a showpiece of colonial grandeur. Its history goes back more than 230 years. The central portion of the mansion was built in the 1740s by Benjamin Tasker, for his son-in-law Samuel Ogle who was honeymooning in England with Tasker's daughter, Anne. Ogle had raised colonial eyebrows when at age 47 he married the 18-year-old Annapolis belle.

In addition to planning the house, Benjamin Tasker, between 1752 and 1760, planted an "avenue of tulip trees" starting at the mansion entrance and continuing down the hill to Old Annapolis Road. Many of the trees here are of interest. In addition to the tulip poplars, one of which is more than 200 years old, other noteworthy specimens on the grounds include *magnolia acuminata*, or cucumber tree, that is the National Champion—the largest of its kind in the nation. Another tree, the *ailanthus*, is the State Champion.

The interior of the house is undergoing substantial restoration, so the free tour has been temporarily suspended. You can see the grounds and the exterior. For details on the reopening, call Bowie City Hall at (301)262-6200.

In addition to its distinction of having been home to five Maryland governors, Belair Mansion is also known as "The Cradle of American Racing." At the Belair Stable Museum, listed on the National Register of Historic Places, you can enjoy a free tour covering over 200 years of American thoroughbred racing, which began in 1747 when Samuel Ogle brought home from his honeymoon some of the most valuable race horses from England: a stallion, Spark, and a filly, Queen Mab. The acquisition of Spark was through the good graces of Charles Calvert, the fifth Lord Baltimore. Calvert, who was a Gentleman of the Bedchamber in the service of Frederick, Prince of Wales, was given the stallion by the Prince. Calvert then gave Spark to Samuel Ogle.

Another famous British horse, Selima, was brought to the Belair stables by Benjamin Tasker, Jr., when he took over the management of the Belair estate. Selima was a champion racehorse in her day. When William Woodward purchased the Belair Mansion in 1898, he placed a plaque on the stable wall honoring Selima and her equally famous offspring, Selim.

It was William Woodward who added the hyphen and wings to the mansion, giving it the exterior appearance it has today. Woodward also added the stone stables and continued the tradition of horse racing at Belair. Three great horses would be stabled here—Gallant Fox (1930) and Omaha (1935), both winners of the Triple Crown, and Nashua (1955), one of the great money earners of his day.

While touring the historic sites of Bowie don't miss scenic **Allen Pond.** During the summer, boats are available, and youngsters can fish from the bank while families enjoy a picnic. Well-placed benches invite visitors to sit and enjoy the day. Be sure to walk as far as the gazebo and watch the swallows sweeping and gliding by.

The Belair Stable Museum is open on Sundays from 1:00 to 4:00 P.M. in May, June, September and October.

Directions: From the Beltway I-495/95 take Route 50 east for about seven miles to Bowie. Then take Collington Road for roughly 1¾ to Route 450 and make a right. Take Route 450 to the light immediately past Bowie High School. At the light make a right on Belair Drive. The stables are on the left. To reach the mansion turn right on Tulip Grove Drive, and you will see it on your left.

Chadds Ford

Wyeth Not?

If you think you have to head for a big city to enjoy a one-day outing that includes art, history, nature, gardens, crafts, a winery and a colonial inn, think again. **Chadds Ford** in the Brandywine Valley, two hours from Washington, offers just such a mixture.

The scenic rolling hills and farmlands make the drive alone worthwhile. This is the countryside that inspired the Wyeths, one of America's most prominent family of artists. The work of three generations of Wyeths—Andrew, N.C, Jamie and other family members—are on display at the **Brandywine River Museum**, a work of art itself.

Housed in a renovated 19th-century gristmill, the museum has two glass towers that add a picturesque grace note and give visitors a glimpse of the slow-moving Brandywine River from each floor. The Andrew Wyeth Gallery has a state-of-the-art skylight that fills the room with natural light. Andrew's wife, Betsy, hangs all the work in here. N.C. Wyeth was a noted illustrator, and his work for such classics as *Treasure Island* and *Kidnappped* is displayed. Jamie Wyeth's famous pig portrait is part of the museum's permanent collection.

The galleries not only display work in the Brandywine tradition, they also sell prints, framed or unframed, in a wide range of prices. The museum shop offers an excellent selection of books on art, natural history and conservation.

A part of the **Brandywine Conservancy**, the museum participates actively in the conservation of natural resources. A mile-long nature trail begins at the museum and meanders along the river. Elevated walks cross marshy sections and helpful trail markers broaden visitors appreciation of the plants and natural features encountered along the way. A visit in the spring is particularly enjoyable because wildflowers bloom along the woodland trail. Volunteers at the Brandywine Conservancy have planted wildflowers around the museum, blue flowers predominating in spring, and yellow in summer and fall. At Christmas time there is an exhibit of trees decorated with ornaments made from dried plants. A large working O-gauge railroad runs during the holiday season.

The Brandywine River Museum is open daily (except Christmas Day) from 9:30 A.M. to 4:30 P.M. The museum has an attractive restaurant that is open from 11:00 A.M. to 3:00 P.M. A nominal admission is charged.

For a wide selection of handcrafted items, head up Route 1 just a short distance to the **Chadds Ford Barn Shops**. Browse through the quaint collection of craft and specialty shops and enjoy lunch or dinner in an inn where George Washington's troops supped before the Battle of Brandywine. The 18th-century stone Chadds Ford Inn has wooden-pegged floors. The walls are now hung with Wyeth prints, and the menu is continental (215)388-7361.

If you want to spend more than a day in the area, the Brandywine River Hotel that sits behind the Chadds Ford Inn is a marvelous getaway. Many of the rooms have fireplaces and Jacuzzi baths (215)388-1200. There also are numerous bed-and-breakfast spots. For a complete listing contact the Brandywine Valley Tourist Information Center at (215)388-2900. This center, in a 1855 Friends Meeting House that is listed on the National Register of Historic Places, is located at the entrance to Longwood Gardens (see selection).

For history buffs the **Brandywine Battlefield Park** is a *must* stop. Here on September 11, 1777, the English won the battle that enabled them to capture Philadelphia, the colonial capital. Faulty intelligence contributed to the American defeat, although Washington might have felt "intelligence" wasn't the right word for the information he received about the British troops.

Landing in Maryland with 15,000 men, General Howe began his march towards Philadelphia. First reports indicated he had divided his force. Thinking the British would be outnumbered, Washington sent 14,000 men under General Greene to attack. A second report came in, saying that Greene faced the entire British force. Washington quickly sent a message telling Greene to retreat across the Brandywine River. Still a third report arrived. This one said that the British force was divided. Such confusion contributed to the colonists' defeat.

Misinformation, ammunition shortages and British superiority in experience and numbers all contributed to Washington's loss at Brandywine. The Americans paid a high price for their defeat: The British wintered in comfortable quarters in Philadelphia while the Americans were consigned to the misery of Valley Forge (see selection).

At the Brandywine Visitor Center there are maps and exhibits detailing battle. You'll also see how the encounter at Brandywine fits into the total story of the American Revolution. Within the park you can visit the restored headquarters of General Washington and that of his aide, General Marquis de Lafayette. The exhibit buildings are open weekends only from October to May from 10:00 A.M. to 4:30 P.M. During the summer they are open daily from 10:00 A.M. to 5:00 P.M. and on Sundays from NOON to 4:30 P.M. No admission is charged.

The Brandywine Valley area is also noted for a trio of garden estates unrivaled in beauty in the country. Longwood Gardens, Winterthur, Nemours and Eleutherian Mills (now part of Hagley Museum) are a 15- to 30-minute drive apart. They are all du Pont family showplaces (see selections).

Families on budgets can picnic at Brandywine Battlefield Park or enjoy the mushroom specialties at the unpretentious Hugo's Inn on U.S. 1 near **Phillips Mushroom House**. Since this area is the mushroom capital of the world, Phillips is the place to discover how mushrooms are grown and harvested. It's also a good spot to purchase fresh or preserved mushrooms. Wine lovers should stop in for a tour and tasting at the Chadds Ford Winery near the Brandywine River Museum.

Directions: From the Beltway I-495/95 take I-95 north to the Wilmington, Delaware area. Exit on Route 202 and continue to the intersection with Route 1. Turn left on Route 1 and travel a short distance to the Brandywine Battlefield Park on the left. One more mile will bring you to Chadds Ford. The Brandywine River Museum will be on your right, and up the road a bit the Chadds Ford Barn Shops will be on the left.

Chestertown and Eastern Neck National Wildlife Refuge

It's Tea Time

There is a standing invitation to tea on the Saturday before Memorial Day at **Chestertown**, Maryland. This is not an ordinary tea party in a stuffy formal parlor; this party takes place in the town harbor as part of the annual re-enactment of the "tea party" that occurred in 1774.

Nearly everyone knows at least some of the story of the Boston Tea Party. On the night of December 16, 1773, Boston radicals disguised themselves as Indians, crept aboard three British ships, and dumped 342 chests of tea into the harbor. This dramatic protest of the hated tea tax was widely reported and cheered. Less than six months later the action shifted south to Chestertown for a less famous tea party.

The Maryland patriots wore no disguises, nor did they wait for the dark of night. On May 23, 1774, angry patriots headed down to the harbor, climbed aboard the brigantine *Geddes* and threw the cargo of tea into the Chester River. According to some reports they even tossed a few of the crew overboard. Each year this spirited protest is recaptured, with colonially attired merchants once again gathering at the Town Park. They vigorously debate the issue of British rule and the pros and cons of the tea tax with the predictable result of yet another tea party. This festival is a sure-fire way to get young children interested in U.S. history.

Whether you come for the festival or when the streets are quiet and filled only with the ghosts of the past, be sure to take a walking tour of Chestertown. There are 24 locations marked on the town's walking tour map. The town was one of the colonies' most prosperous ports, a major stopover for travelers from Virginia to Philadelphia. The 1746 Customs House, at Water and High Streets, handled goods from around the world. Overseeing the transactions was William Geddes, Collector of Customs for the Port of Chestertown.

If you visit Chestertown from May through October you can tour William Geddes's house, now called the **Geddes-Piper House**, at 101 Church Alley. It is the town's only example of a Philadelphia townhouse. Since it was Geddes's ship that was the target of the town's tea party, it is appropriate that one of the decorative touches in this house is William Geddes's collection of teapots. The house is open weekends from 1:00 to 4:00 P.M.

Also open during those hours is the **Buck-Bacchus Store**, Queen and High Streets. This 18th-century store illustrates the dual nature of the many in-town properties that served as both a business and a home. The restoration re-creates an 18th-century living area and a 19th-century general store.

Many visitors find the town's gracious Georgian homes along the Chester River so appealing that they return in September for the Candlelight Tour. This is the only time Chestertown's private homes are open to the public.

If you're in town in late afternoon you can follow in George Washington's footsteps and enjoy the hospitality of the **White Swan Tavern** at 231 High Street. English tea is served daily from 3:00 to 5:00 P.M. This is also a charming bed-and-breakfast with comfortable rooms filled with antiques including huge tester beds. Reservations are essential; call (410)778-2300.

If the colonial era is evoked at White Swan, it's the Victorian era that comes to life at the beautifully restored and refurbished **Imperial Hotel** at 208 High Street. The Imperial Dining Room features American and French cuisine.

While in the area be sure to stop at the nearby Eastern Neck **National Wildlife Refuge**. This is a spot for those who like their wildlife wild. This island retreat in the Chesapeake Bay is connected to the mainland by a bridge. There is no visitor center or obtrusive exhibit boards. Only wooden walkways and an observation platform were added to make the marsh area more accessible to bird watchers. Nature reigns supreme.

The best time to visit Chestertown is spring, but the best time to visit Eastern Neck is autumn when thousands of Canada geese stop on their migration south. It is a good idea to bring binoculars for a close look at these majestic birds. When there is a large flock of geese at the refuge the noise sounds like thousands of people cheering, something like the crowd at a football game. The birds fly out of the refuge in early morning to forage and return at sunset. The sight and sound of these geese on the wing is a phenomenon you will long remember.

A substantial number of geese winter over at this refuge, so consider visiting on a pleasant day in January or February. Canada geese are not the only migratory birds that stop here. You might see flocks of white whistling swans from Alaska, as well as snow geese and ducks. Because the refuge is a mixture of marsh and woodlands, you are also likely to spot deer, squirrels, rabbit and other wildlife. It is interesting to reflect that the first white men visited this area in 1650 and that the wildlife they encountered was much like what you'll see.

The 2,285-acre Eastern Neck National Wildlife Refuge is open daily at no charge. If you visit in the spring and supply your own canoe, you can crab. Crabbing, a popular summer activity for locals, is done along the mud flats of the Ingleside Recreation Area. This recreation area is the only part of the refuge that closes (from October through April). If you don't have a canoe, try wading out with a net and bushel basket. Old-timers suggest balancing the basket in an inner tube. Blue crabs can be caught as early as May, but July is the high season for crabbing.

Directions: From the Beltway I-495/95 take Route 50 across the Chesapeake Bay Bridge. When Route 301 splits from Route 50 take Route 301 north, then turn left on Route 213 for Chestertown. To continue on to Eastern Neck take Route 213 to the intersection with Route 20 and turn left. Continue to Rock Hall and go south on Route 445 to Eastern Neck National Wildlife Refuge.

Colvin Run Mill and Sully Plantation

Everything is Grist to the Mill

The old **mill at Colvin Run** was built sometime close to 1820, but not as early as 1794, the date inscribed on the mill's east wall. Located near Difficult Run off Leesburg Turnpike on land once owned by George Washington, the mill stands on what was a major artery connecting the rich farming valley of the Shenandoah to the busy port of Alexandria. Colvin Run was a merchant mill engaged in buying, selling and grinding grain.

A 20-foot water wheel powers the gristmill, which was constructed in the manner prescribed by Oliver Evans (1755–1819). Evans's book *The Young Millwright and Miller's Guide* revolutionized milling. Before Evans all the mill operations except turning the millstone were performed by hand. Evans redesigned mills so that each floor served a specific function. A canvas-belted elevator carried the grain from floor to floor. With the new arrangement, a miller's duties were reduced to weighing the grain, checking the equipment, starting the water wheel and receiving money.

Colvin Run has been carefully restored to operating conditions. The American Institute for Architects awarded Colvin Run Mill first prize for excellence in historic architecture. On your visit you can see grain being ground into flour and cornmeal and buy samples at the General Store, which also sells handcrafted items and other merchandise.

Situated on a hill just above Colvin Run Mill is the Miller's House, circa 1820. On the grounds there is also a 19th-century dairy barn. The Fairfax County Park Authority offers interpretative exhibits and special programs at this historic property.

Colvin Run Mill is open daily (closed on Tuesdays) 11:00 A.M. to 5:00 P.M. March through December. During January and February it is open on weekends only. Admission is charged.

Not far from Colvin Run Mill there is another Fairfax County site you should explore—**Sully Plantation**. This house, built by Richard Bland Lee in 1794, is interesting because it combines two distinct architectural styles. It uses the popular Georgian colonial plantation style favored in Virginia and the Philadelphia-style frame exterior Lee learned to like while serving in that city as northern Virginia's first congressman.

The plantation house along with the kitchen-laundry, smokehouse and stone dairy have been restored. The plantation looks as it would have during the 1795–1842 period. The furnishings are of the Federal period. There is also a kitchen and formal garden plus an archaeological site. Special educational programs are scheduled at Sully throughout the year.

Sully is open from 11:00 A.M. to 5:00 P.M. daily except Tuesdays from March through December. In January and February it is open on weekends only. Admission is charged.

Directions: For Colvin Run take Beltway I-495/95, Exit 10W, then Route 7 (Leesburg Pike) for five miles. The mill is on the right. For Sully Plantation take Exit 9 off the Beltway, Route 66. Take Route 66 to Route 50 and then proceed west for 5.5 miles to Route 28. Bear right and proceed three-fourths of a mile to Sully Plantation.

Deep Creek Lake

Dam Fun

Your access to the Beltway will determine how much time you can spend at this delightful lake resort area. In fact, if you are too far from the northwestern end of the Beltway it would be unwise to plan this as a one-day foray. It is worth the trip, however, whether it is for a day, weekend or week-long getaway. Surprisingly, many people don't know about the unspoiled charm of this man-made lake created when a dam was erected in 1923–25 for a hydroelectric project.

The 3,900-acre lake, Maryland's largest freshwater lake, has 65 miles of shoreline, most of which is privately owned. You do have access, however, to an 800-foot public beach at **Deep Creek Lake State Park.** Swimmers use the sunny beach, and picnickers cool off at tree-shaded tables. Five nature trails offer a distinctly different appeal in each season: in the spring wildflowers bloom; summertime provides intriguing views of the pleasure boats on the lake; in autumn the leaves add color to the mountainside, and in winter the trails are used for cross-country skiing.

Sports equipment for just about any activity you want to pursue is for rent. Call the Garrett County Promotion Council at (301)334-1948 for a listing of current suppliers. There is no road that follows the irregular shore line around the entire lake, so the only real way to explore is by boat. You can combine water skiing and fishing with your exploring.

The lake provides a challenge to fishermen year-round, whether they try their luck from boats or chop a hole in the ice for the challenge of winter fishing. The lake occasionally freezes enough for skating, but the ice is pretty rough. Skaters will find smoother conditions at the 13-acre lake at New Germany State Park or at the 53-acre lake at Herrington Manor State Park. Both parks have trails for cross-country skiing. Garrett County has more than 70,000 acres of public land, and many of the state parks convert their hiking trails to cross-country skiing in the winter.

One trail you should walk is at Swallow Falls State Park. It is worth the time and effort to see the 64-foot **Muddy Creek Falls** that resemble a crystal frieze. The park, boasting three waterfalls, is a scenic spot year-round. Henry Ford, Thomas Edison and Harvey Firestone camped overlooking the falls and lovely vistas in 1918 and again in 1921 when they were joined by naturalist John Burroughs.

Skiing and hiking are done under your own power; if you want some real horsepower check out the riding stables in the area. They offer trail, overnight and winter rides. If you want to really increase the horsepower, then rent a snowmobile and zip through this winter wonderland.

The Deep Creek Lake area is a treat in any season. The county will soon have to change its slogan, however, because it's unlikely to remain "Maryland's Best Kept Secret."

Directions: From the Beltway I-495/95 take Exit 35, I-270 west past Frederick to Hancock. Take Route 40 west to Cumberland. Continue on Route 40/48 to Keysers Ridge, Exit 14, then take Route 219 south to the Deep Creek Lake area.

Fredericksburg Foray

Original Americana

Fredericksburg, Virginia, founded in 1727, has figured prominently in our nation's history from its earliest days. Many well-known figures of our past lived along these tree-lined streets: James Monroe, Fielding Lewis and his wife Betty (George Washington's sister), and, a few blocks away, Mary Washington, George and Betty's mother. George himself was a frequent visitor, and his brother Charles owned a tavern in town. Later, during the Civil War, the Fredericksburg area was the scene of some of the war's most devastating battles. Some 100,000 men lost their lives in the battles of Fredericksburg, Chancellorsville, the Wilderness and Spotsylvania Court House.

To begin your journey into the past, stop at the Fredericksburg Visitor Center at 706 Caroline Street for a free audio-visual orientation. If you plan to visit all six major historic sites you can purchase a Hospitality Pass at less cost than the combined individual admission fees. The six sites, all (except the last) within walking distance of one another, are the Hugh Mercer Apothecary Shop, the Rising Sun Tavern, the James Monroe Museum and Memorial Library, the Mary Washington House, Kenmore and Belmont.

Follow the map provided at the Visitor Center down Caroline Street to the **Hugh Mercer Apothecary Shop**, which is open daily 9:00 A.M. to 5:00 P.M. In colonial days the practice of medicine and the mixing of prescriptions were not separate professions. Dr. Mercer practiced medicine in this shop from 1771 to 1776 when he left to fight in the Revolution. He died at the Battle of Princeton. His office and sitting room, where his friend George Washington often conducted business while in Fredericksburg, have been restored to their original appearances.

A few blocks down Caroline Street you'll find the **Rising Sun Tavern,** also open daily 9:00 A.M. to 5:00 P.M. (closes 4:00 P.M. November–March). This spot, like much of the town, has a connection with the Washington family. The tavern was built in 1760 by George's youngest brother, Charles. Many of the early patriots gathered here: Patrick Henry, Thomas Jefferson, George Mason, John Marshall, the Lee brothers and, of course, the Washingtons. Today only spiced tea is served; the costumed tavern wenches do, however, give guests the recipe for such 18th-century favorites as "stewed quaker."

Follow the map to 908 Charles Street and visit the **James Monroe Museum and Memorial Library**, which is open daily except Christmas from 9:00 A.M. to 5:00 P.M. It was in Fredericksburg that our fifth president began the practice of law in 1786. The Monroe furnishings exhibited in the museum were the first to be used in the White House after it was burned by the British during the War of 1812. The Monroes purchased the furniture in France in 1794 when Monroe served as Minister. One noteworthy piece is the Louis XVI desk that Monroe used in 1823 when he signed the message to Congress that became known as the Monroe Doctrine. A secret compartment in the desk that was not discovered until 1906 contained letters to Monroe from Alexander Hamilton, Benjamin Franklin and other statesmen. Perhaps the most popular exhibit is the one of elegant gowns Mrs. Monroe wore to formal functions in Paris and in Washington.

The Mary Washington House is at 1200 Charles Street; open daily 9:00 A.M. to 5:00 P.M. (closes at 4:00 P.M. March–November). George Washington's mother, living on her isolated farm as the war approached, was reluctant to move to the city, but George feared for her safety. He bought this town house for her in 1772. She spent the last 17 years of her life here, albeit reluctantly and with many complaints. Before she died in 1789 she planted part of the English garden behind her house. Mary Washington is buried in Fredericksburg, and there is a monument at her gravesite on Washington Avenue.

About a block away on 1201 Washington Avenue, you'll find **Kenmore**, the House of Betty Washington Lewis, George's only sister, a beautiful Georgian manor house Fielding Lewis built for her in 1752. Later, Lewis went bankrupt trying to supply weapons to the Revolutionary army and debts forced the sale of much of the furniture. Items have since been found to match the inventory taken at Lewis's death in 1781. Kenmore, more than most houses, offers a taste of the past because at the end of your tour you'll be served gingerbread and spiced tea in the kitchen dependency. This tasty cake is prepared from Mary Washington's recipe, a favorite with Betty and George. Kenmore is open daily 9:00 A.M. to 5:00 P.M., closing at 4:00 P.M. from December–February. It is closed on major holidays.

On the heights overlooking Fredericksburg stands **Belmont**, an 18th-century house that was the home and studio of the 20th-century artist, Gari Melchers. Gari's father was a German sculptor, and the younger Melchers studied in his father's studio and elsewhere in Europe. He and his wife, Corinne, spent years on the continent before moving to Virginia. Their Fredericksburg house is furnished with the fine art, porcelains and antique furnishings they acquired in Europe. Both Gari and his wife painted, and their works can be seen in the house and studio. Belmont is open Monday–Saturday 10:00 A.M. to 5:00 P.M. and Sunday 1:00–5:00 P.M.; it closes November–March at 4:00 P.M.

When in Fredericksburg you should also include the Civil War perspective by visiting **Fredericksburg National Military Park** and **Chatham**, which are on the battlefield tour. The Fredericksburg National Park Service Visitor Center is open daily 9:00 A.M. to 5:00 P.M.

Directions: From the Beltway take I-95 south to Fredericksburg. Exit on Route 3 east and follow the well-marked signs to the Fredericksburg Visitor Center. It is 50 miles from the Washington Beltway.

GEORGETOWN

Georgetown's Historic Landmarks

King George Would Love the Throngs

Georgetown was established in 1751 as a busy tobacco port and was absorbed into the fledgling federal capital when it was created in 1790. Today Georgetown is a busy center for wining, dining, shopping, exploring and people watching. Elegant private residences of the rich and famous, boutiques, antique shops, eateries, exclusive hostelries, and its promimity to the Potomac River attract crowds to Georgetown. While it is fascinating to stroll along the busy streets, it is worth taking time to explore a trio of historic houses.

Reflecting the early years is the **Old Stone House**, the oldest building in Washington, D.C. Begun in 1764 by Christopher Layman, who built the ground floor as a shop for his cabinetmaking business, the Old Stone House was used as both a home and business—reflecting the dual nature of Georgetown, both then and now.

Christopher Layman purchased one of the 80 lots in the original 60 acres of Georgetown. His lot was on the main street. Georgetown developed rapidly after a local warehouse was designated as an official tobacco inspection site and became one of the most important tobacco markets along the Atlantic seaboard. The hilly main road was once used for rolling hogsheads of tobacco down to ships on the Potomac River.

In 1765, after Layman's death, his widow sold the house to Cassandra Chew, a prosperous businesswoman who added the north wing in the 1770s. When you visit the Old Stone House you will see five family rooms carefully restored to represent a middle-class dwelling in the 1700s. The cabinetmaking shop and the kitchen on the ground floor were the main centers of daily life for the busy family. The women did most of their household work in front of the kitchen fireplace. On the first floor there is a decorated dining room with fine wood paneling, an inviting parlor and a servant's bedroom. The main bedroom space is in the attic. There is also a small 18th-century English garden. The Old Stone House at 3051 M Street is open at no charge Wednesday through Sunday from 8:00 A.M. to 4:30 P.M.

A relatively new house museum in Georgetown, **Tudor Place**, opened in 1988. The oldest sections of the house, the east and west wings, were built in 1796. The center section was built for Thomas Peter whose father, a successful Scottish tobacco merchant, was the first mayor of the port of Georgetown. Thomas Peter married Martha Custis, granddaughter of Martha Washington. It was Peter's bride who purchased the block-long Tudor property with an $8,000 legacy she received from George Washington. The center section of this neoclassical mansion was de-

31

signed by William Thornton whose most noted work is the United States Capitol. One of Tudor Place's most arresting architectural features is the circular, domed portico. The house was completed in 1816.

The Custis-Peter family and their descendants lived at Tudor Place until 1983 when Armistead Peter III died. Furnishings and art objects collected by six generations of the family fill the house. Martha Custis Peter brought many family pieces from Mount Vernon. The estate was called the "jewel of Georgetown Heights."

Tudor Place still has its expansive green lawns. The sloping South Lawn was planted with specimen trees in the early 19th century. English boxwood create a border in the formal North Garden. There is an intricate Flower Knot and a collection of period flowers and shrubs. Here too, 180 years of family contributions are reflected; the fountains and garden structures were added by the last owner.

Tudor Place is open by appointment only Tuesday through Saturday. Tours are given at 10:00 and 11:30 A.M. and 1:00 and 2:00 P.M. The tour entrance is at 1644 31st Street at the intersection of Q and 31st Streets. To arrange a tour, call (202)965-0400.

The third house—not in terms of when it was built, but rather when it achieved prominence—is **Dumbarton Oaks**. From August to October 1944, world leaders met at this elegant Georgetown mansion to lay the groundwork for the United Nations. Their plans, submitted to the San Francisco Conference in April 1945, evolved into the United Nations Charter.

Dumbarton Oaks is more than a historical footnote; it is a gracious mansion surrounded by one of the loveliest formal gardens in the country. The 16 acres of gardens were first landscaped in 1922 by Beatrix Ferrand. Its European style is epitomized in the perfect symmetry of the Pebble Garden and the Ellipse. Cherry Hill blooms with soft delicate pink blossoms in May. When the spring bulbs in the formal garden plots are spent, the summer annuals take their place.

The mansion contains an outstanding collection of Byzantine and pre-Columbian art as well as tapestries and antique furnishings. The estate is now a research center and museum owned by Harvard University. The mansion is open Tuesday through Sunday from 2:00 to 5:00 P.M. The gardens are open daily from April through October at the same time. Admission is charged for the gardens and donations encouraged if you tour the mansion. Dumbarton Oaks is at 32nd and R Streets, N.W. Adjacent to this private estate is **Dumbarton Park** another deligthful getaway in the spring when the wildflowers are in bloom.

There are three additional Historic Landmarks in Georgetown: the **C&O Canal** which starts one half block south of 30th and M Streets, N.W. (see selection); **Oak Hill Cemetery** at 3001 R Street, a 19th-century garden park cemetery that blends natural gardens with monuments dating from the Civil War period; and **Georgetown University**, the oldest Catholic university in the country, at 37th and O Streets, N.W.

Directions: All of these attractions are found within the Beltway, in the Georgetown section of northwest Washington bordering on the Potomac River. The Business and Professional Association of Georgetown has produced an excellent brochure and map listing historic landmarks and more than 50 recommended shopping and dining spots. You can obtain it at numerous spots in Georgetown or at the Washington, D.C. Convention and Visitors Association at 1212 New York Avenue, N.W.

Hagley Museum and Eleutherian Mills

Museum, Mansion and Mills

The **Hagley Museum** in Delaware is located on the site of the original du Pont powder works, built in 1902 by E.I. du Pont. The company founder built his home, Eleutherian Mills, overlooking the powder works to reassure apprehensive French and Irish immigrants who were reluctant to live and work close to the explosives.

Visiting Hagley Museum, you will see a re-creation of the powder works as well as the restored du Pont home. Your first stop, however, is the **Henry Clay Mill,** an 1814 textile mill, where you'll see models and dioramas of early industry along the Brandywine River—flour, paper, iron and textile mills. A talking map introduces the Brandywine region. The story of the du Pont family establishing their home and gun-powder plant completes the first floor exhibits. On the second floor are changing exhibits. If you want to do some light background reading before this day trip, read *Brandywine*, Jack Rowe's fictional account of the powder works industry.

In the restored 19th-century machine shop, a short walk (or jitney ride) from the mill, models demonstrate the step-by-step process of black powder manufacturing. The second wing of the machine shop houses a fully operational, late-1800s shop where visitors can see the old tools still being used.

There are several millraces on the museum's 232-acre property, as well as distinctively shaped granite powder mills. Walking tours of the Hagley Yard are offered, and a jitney bus transports visitors on a three-mile round trip along the Brandywine River. Outdoor exhibits include a turbine-operated roll mill, a wooden water wheel, a rare 1870s steam engine, a quarry and a restored workers' community. Wandering past the workers' homes, church and schoolhouse helps you imagine what life was like in this 19th-century community.

The lives of both workers and owner are presented because du Pont's home is also restored. **Eleutherian Mills**, the three-story wisteria-covered Georgian style home was built in 1803 by E.I. du Pont. His home overlooked the powder works in the French tradition of sharing the perils of explosions with workers. His office, from which he directed the manufacturing, was in his home. If his goal was to reassure the workers, this intention was undermined when the house suffered repeated damage from explosions. The most severe incident occurred in 1890 when the loss was so extensive the family decided not to rebuild.

The house was restored in 1923 by Henry A. du Pont for his daughter, Louise Crowninshield, who lived there only a part of each year. At her death in 1958, Eleutherian Mills became part of the Hagley Museum. The furnishings in the ten rooms open to the public span the lifetimes of five generations of du Ponts.

The mansion grounds have been reclaimed, and the lovely garden E.I. du Pont enjoyed in 1803 has been restored. There is also a stone barn filled with 19th-century vehicles including a Conestoga wagon, farm tools and weather vanes. Dependencies include a cooper shop, the first office of the du Pont Company (established in 1837), and the workshop of Lammot du Pont (used from 1831–1884).

Hagley Museum and Eleutherian Mills are open daily from 9:30 A.M. to 4:30 P.M. They may close early during the winter months and are closed on major holidays. Admission is charged. For information call (302)658-2400.

The Hagley Museum and Eleutherian Mills are located three miles north of Wilmington and a little more than a two-hour drive from the Washington Beltway.

Directions: From the Beltway I-495/95 take Exit 27, I-95. Take I-95 north to Wilmington. Take the Route 52 North exit and continue north to Route 100. Follow Route 100 to Route 141 and make a right. Stay in the left lane on Route 141 because the Hagley Museum is only a few hundred feet down Route 141 on the left.

James River Plantations

Half-Dozen Historic Homes

If your mental image of the plantations of the South is based only on *Gone With the Wind*, why not explore the real thing? Along the James River between Richmond and Williamsburg there are six gracious Southern plantations: Berkeley, Westover,

Shirley, Edgewood, Sherwood Forest and Evelynton. Each has its own intriguing history, ambience, legends and lore.

Berkeley's place in history is secured by a succession of significant firsts. According to Berkeley's records, the first Thanksgiving occurred here a year before the Pilgrims arrived in the New World and two years before the Pilgrims gave thanks for the harvest that saved them from starving.

Settlers landed at **Berkeley** on December 4, 1619, and read a message from King James I proclaiming the day of their arrival to be "perpetually keept (sic) holy as a day of thanksgiving." Each year on the first Sunday of November, this ceremony is reenacted as part of an all-day festival.

Berkeley is also one of only two houses in America (the other is the Adamses' home in Braintree, Massachusetts) that is the birthplace of a signer of the Declaration of Independence and the ancestral home of two U.S. presidents. Berkeley's historic trio consists of Declaration signer Benjamin Harrison; his son, President William Henry Harrison; and the latter's grandson, President Benjamin Harrison. Visitors are usually surprised to learn that this was where bourbon was first distilled, surprisingly by an Episcopal missionary.

During the American Revolution, Benedict Arnold's troops plundered the Berkeley estate. Then in 1861, roughly 140,000 men from General George McClellan's Army of the Potomac camped at Berkeley. President Lincoln visited twice to confer with McClellan and review the troops. Each of the first ten presidents visited Berkeley.

The estate looks serenely untouched by its tumultuous past, but it was badly damaged and in great disrepair when John Jamieson acquired it in 1907. As a young boy he had camped here as a drummer for McClellan's army. In 1917 his son, current owner Malcolm Jamieson, inherited Berkeley and embarked on his life-long efforts to restore it to its former glory. The house tour is preceded by a slide program giving the history of Berkeley. The gracious ground floor rooms are filled with period pieces collected by Grace Jamieson. After the house tour you can explore the terraced garden and enjoy lunch at the plantation's Coach House Tavern. Berkeley is open daily 8:00 A.M. to 5:00 P.M. Closed on Christmas Day. Admission is charged.

Next to Berkeley, off the same country lane, is **Westover**. The lovely brick Georgian mansion, one of the best examples of this style in the country, is not open for tours. You may explore the gardens and grounds, however, daily from 9:00 A.M. to 6:00 P.M. The estate was built around 1730 by William Byrd II, founder of Richmond.

Fortunes were made in the colony of Virginia, not from the discovery of gold but from the planting of tobacco. The Jamestown settlers soon spread out from the original settlement and established large agricultural estates. One of the earliest of these plantations was **Shirley**, first listed on the records in 1613.

The eleventh generation of the Hill-Carter family lives at Shirley now. This has been a family property for more than 300 years. The house you see today was begun in 1723 by the third Edward Hill. It was built for his daughter Elizabeth who married John Carter, the son of King Carter. The house was finished in 1738 and looked for the most part exactly as it does today.

Shirley is noted for its hospitality. On the roof there is a carved pineapple, the colonial symbol for hospitality. George Washington, Thomas Jefferson, John Tyler and Theodore Roosevelt are just a few of the historic figures who have been entertained here. Anne Hill Carter married Governor Lighthorse Harry Lee in Shirley's parlor. Their son, Robert E. Lee, spent several childhood years at Shirley.

Family pets still roam the grounds of Shirley, but none is treated quite as lavishly as Nestor, a prize-winning racehorse. Nestor had his own silver cup, now part of the silver collection in the dining room. The flatware and smaller pieces of the family silver were taken to a bank in Richmond during the Civil War. Since the banks were so packed with the belongings of fearful Southerners the larger pieces were buried in a well on the estate grounds. Those supposedly safe in the bank were lost; those hidden in the well remained secure.

Shirley is a working plantation and some of its outbuildings, like the barns, are still in use. Others like the old kitchen are filled with period utensils and tools and can be toured. The fields around Shirley are still being tilled. This is a home, not a museum, and stories about the family make this a warmly personal tour. Shirley is open daily 9:00 A.M. to 5:00 P.M. daily. Admission is charged.

Edgewood, just three miles away, is the only one of the half dozen not on the river side of Route 5. You can spend the night at this Carpenter's Gothic plantation amid a profusion of Victorian furniture, including several oversize canopy beds.

Edgewood even has a ghost, a young girl who allegedly pines for her lost love. She has been credited with moving furniture. Even if you don't overnight at this bed-and-breakfast, stop in for a look. The proprietor leads historical tours, and there is a shop in a renovated slave cabin filled with antiques. From mid-November through the Christmas season each room has at least one fancifully decorated tree. Tours are given 11:00 A.M. to 5:00 P.M. Tuesday through Sunday. For accommodation information call (804)829-2962.

Back on the river side you'll find **Sherwood Forest**, another plantation that has remained firmly fixed in the hands of one family. It is even more astounding that the present owner, Harrison Tyler, is the grandson of President John Tyler, the vice president who became the 10th president (1841-45) upon the death of his predecessor and neighbor, William Henry Harrison.

John Tyler was 68 when Lyon, his youngest son, was born. Lyon was even older when he fathered his youngest son, Harrison Tyler, at age 75. This means that for over the past century and a half Sherwood Forest has been inhabited by only three generations. The family furniture still fills the rooms, and each piece has a fascinating story attached to it. Some of the beautifully crafted pieces were used by the Tylers in the White House.

Sherwood Forest is the only James River plantation with a ballroom. It was added so that John Tyler and his guests could dance the Virginia Reel. A long hall on the other side of the main house connects the house with the kitchen making this the longest frame house in America. House tours are given by reservation only, but drop-in visitors can tour the grounds. Sherwood Forest is open 9:00 A.M. to 5:00 P.M. To arrange a house tour call (804)829-5377.

Evelynton, the latest of the gracious estates along the James River, was built in 1935 using 250-year-old bricks from an earlier house. Built in the Colonial Revival style, it looks as if it had commanded the bluff on which it stands for centuries. The house is furnished with 18th-and 19th-century pieces. This, too, is a family home and the rooms retain a comfortable look. Many of the flowers used for the arrangements that fill the house are from the estate grounds. There is a delightful gift shop in one of the outbuildings. Evelynton is open daily 9:00 A.M. to 5:00 P.M., closed on Christmas Day. Admission is charged.

Directions: From the Beltway I-495/95 take I-95 south to Richmond. Then take Route 5 east towards Williamsburg. The plantations, except for Edgewood, will be on your right. All are well marked.

London Town Publik House and Gardens

A Publik House not Known to the Public

The **London Town Publik House**, a National Historic Landmark, is all that remains of a once thriving port in Anne Arundel County, Maryland. From the 1680s to the mid-1700s, sailing vessels brought European and East Indian goods to the colonies and departed with tobacco, Maryland's popular export. In his diary for the year 1775 Thomas Jefferson mentions taking the ferry from London Town across the South River. The diaries of George Washington and Francis Scott Key also mention this ferry crossing. Colonial travelers, heading to and from Philadelphia and Williamsburg, passed through London Town, often stopping at the London Town Publik House.

On your visit you will see the same building they frequented and the same tranquil view they enjoyed of the South River. The Publik House was constructed by William Brown, a ferry master and cabinetmaker, about 1760. The inn is furnished with mid-18th-century antiques. All exterior doors, woodwork, hardware and most of the glass windows are original. The basement public rooms boast beautiful beam ceilings and brick arched doorways.

The old inn has many distinctive architectural features; of special note is the unusual way that the bricks were laid in an all-header pattern instead of the normal lengthwise fashion. The thickness of the brick wall explains why the doors are deeply inset. Several first-floor rooms are raised one step. All of these measures may have served to insulate the rooms from the winds off the river.

The 8½ acres of rolling countryside surrounding the inn have been developed into a series of natural woodland gardens. In the springtime colorful sailboats burst upon the South River like the bright flowers along the paths. There are natural groupings of holly, camellias, dogwoods, lilies of the valley and abundant wildflowers. During the summer months day-lilies bloom in profusion and the herb garden is at its peak. Waterfowl enjoy the garden pond year-round, although they are especially numerous during their autumn migration.

The London Town Publik House and Gardens are open Tuesday through Saturday from 10:00 A.M. to 4:00 P.M. and on Sunday from NOON to 4:00 P.M. It is closed on Mondays, Thanksgiving, Christmas Day and the months of January and February. The Visitor's Center has a gift shop with handcrafted items. Admission is charged.

If you're sailing or cruising in a motorboat you may want to break up your day on the water with a stop at London Town. It's a captivating trip up the South River from the Chesapeake Bay to the John O. Crandall Pier. Although there is no dockage fee it is worth noting that the depth at the pier is only five feet at high tide, too shallow for very large boats.

If you want to extend your day after a visit to London Town, continue on into **Annapolis** and head for the City Dock. At the end of the dock area is Market House, built in 1859 and restored as a bustling food emporium. You can buy the fixings for a picnic and feast *al fresco* at the waterside benches overlooking Annapolis Harbor.

If your timing is good you can take the hour-long tour aboard the *Harbor Queen* that leaves from the Annapolis dock. You can also pick up a walking-tour map of Annapolis at one of the shops in the harbor area and take a stroll through history. (See Annapolis selection.)

Directions: From the Beltway, I-95/495 take Exit 19, Route 50 east. Before you reach the Annapolis area, exit on Route 424, Davidsonville Road, heading south. This will take you past rolling corn fields and horse farms. Turn left in Davidsonville at the intersection with Route 214 and continue east for about five miles, one block past the intersection with Route 2. Take the next left onto Stepney's Lane and continue straight at the traffic signal at Mayo Road, Route 253. After crossing Mayo Road, Stepney's Lane is called Londontown Road and terminates in the London Town parking lot. If you want to visit Annapolis, retrace your steps to Route 2, head north to the intersection with Route 450 and take that into Annapolis.

Longwood Gardens

Floral Wonderland

Where would you expect to discover the finest garden estate in North America? Sunny California? Florida? Wrong! It's **Longwood Gardens** in Kennett Square, Pennsylvania, and the gardens are without equal on this side of the Atlantic.

Once they discover Longwood, visitors return to sample the pleasures of the changing seasons. Just to walk in the conservatories in mid-winter and catch the scent of the blossoms is worth the two-hour drive from Washington. January's display traditionally features hyacinths and daffodils that give a brief illusion of spring even when there is snow on the ground outside the walls of glass. The conservatory's great height is emphasized by the large columns entwined with creeping fig and bougainvillea. Hanging plant chandeliers and tall trees add to the grandeur.

Year-round favorites in this glassed-in garden are the orchids, an exhibit that changes weekly. You'll never see these rare and delicate flowers in corsages. They have an almost magical appearance. The roses here also bloom year-round. Row after row of these multi-colored beauties catch the reflected light of the winter sun. In addition, there are economic plants, succulents, house plants, bonsai and even an insect-eating plant.

In spring you can better explore the 1,050-acre park. If you had to pick just one time to see Longwood Gardens, it should be during April or May. The blossoms are breathtaking for their size and variety.

Walkways lead past formal areas planted with spring bulbs, and passing beneath the wisteria-covered arbor is a sensory treat. The path leads to a lake, and when the trees flower the quiet water of the lake reflects their pastel hues. In the spring the wide expanse near the lake explodes with brilliant daffodils. Banking the path, bright azaleas and rhododendron add their purples, pinks and oranges to the riotous scene. A filigreed gazebo is the perfect focal point for photographers.

Delight follows delight. At the far end of the lake you'll discover a charming Italian water garden, copied from the one at the Villa Gamberaia in Florence, Italy. From the bridge overlook flanked by a water staircase and rock cascade, you'll see blue-tiled pools with parallel sets of fountains, some of many fountains you'll see at Longwood.

Water, used in various ways, is a recurrent theme, and in front of the main conservatory is the largest fountain group. During the summer months there are illuminated fountain programs on Tuesday, Thursday and Saturday evenings from mid-June through Labor Day. Fireworks offer a pyrotechnical treat at selected fountain programs during the season. The colorful jets—dancing to the music while color-coordinated bursts fill the sky—are spectacular. Tickets for these special evenings must be ordered well in advance, so call early to obtain the schedule (215)388-6741. The Open Air Theater, with a six-foot-high water curtain, also has evening programs. Here too, dancing water adds another dimension to the evening concerts.

During the summer months day lilies, zinnias, artemisias, asters, helianthuses and a host of annuals bloom in profusion. June is one of the peak blooming times for the outdoor roses. The rock garden with its flowering ground cover along the hill beneath the chime tower is also a summer focal point. Ferns grow in profusion along the banks of a sparkling waterfall.

Everything seems to grow better and bigger at Longwood. The large specimens include garden cabbages as big as basketballs, brilliant blue delphiniums taller than most visitors, waterlily pads the size of truck tires and chrysanthemums as big as dinner plates.

Fall offers its own attractions: the roses put on one last show, the pumpkins hang heavy on their vines and the conservatory chrysanthemum exhibit draws many admirers. After Thanksgiving the gardens become a winter wonderland with colored lights outlining the tree branches, whimsically decorated trees in the conservatory and banks of poinsettias. The entire family will enjoy this holiday treat.

Those visitors curious to learn how this garden was created will want to tour the **Peirce-du Pont House** on the grounds. Longwood's grounds were once part of a tract purchased from William Penn in 1700 by George Peirce. Peirce's grandsons planted an arboretum of evergreen trees they called Peirce's Park. Pierre Samuel du Pont purchased the park in 1906 and added a formal garden. If you tour the garden you will see reminders of both families. The South Wing reflects the Quaker style of the Peirces while the North Wing was added in the early 20th century by the du Ponts. The estate conservatories were open to the public as early as 1921.

Longwood Gardens is open daily 9:00 A.M. to 6:00 P.M. (except the winter months when it closes at 5:00 P.M.). The conservatories are open 10:00 A.M. to 5:00 P.M. In the summer there are special five-minute daytime displays of the main fountains and the open-air theater fountains. See posted times when you arrive. During the Christmas season the outdoor lighting can be seen from 5:00 to 9:00 P.M. Admission is charged. The Terrace Restaurant, noted for its cuisine, serves local wines and uses local mushrooms in many of its selections. Indoor and outdoor dining can be enjoyed at lunch or dinner time.

Directions: From the Beltway take I-495/95 and then follow I-95 north over the Tydings Bridge. Then take Route 275/276 to the intersection with Route 1 (another option is to Route 222). Take Route 1 north to Kennett Square. The entrance to Longwood Gardens is well marked.

Morven Park and Oatlands

Southern Comfort

In the rolling countryside around Leesburg, Virginia, there are two stately colonial mansions that are at their best in the spring. Morven Park and Oatlands at first glance seem very much alike, but their differences make them an ideal double-bill.

Morven Park's white-columned portico suggests the antebellum South, but inside the furnishings remind visitors of Europe. A tour takes you through 16 rooms that range in style from a Renaissance grand hall to a Jacobean dining room and a French drawing room. The furnishings that fill the house were chosen by Westmoreland Davis, the second of two governors who owned the estate. Thomas Swann, Jr., of Maryland was the other distinguished owner. Davis and his wife found most of the exquisite antiques on their travels through Europe and Asia. The six wall-size hand-worked tapestries woven in Flanders in 1640 were among their prized possessions.

If you don't find antique furniture exciting then perhaps the 125-vehicle Windmill Carriage Collection is more appealing. You will see bygone conveyances like phaetons, landaus, sulkies and sleighs. Morven Park also has a Museum of Hounds and Hunting.

This 1,200-acre estate is always pretty in spring. Two nature trails abound with wildflowers. A formal garden, framed by box-wood, blooms with colorful bushes.

Down the road about seven miles is **Oatlands**, with a history that stretches back to the earliest days of the Virginia colony. Lord Fairfax sold the Carter family 11,357 acres. George Carter acquired the land on which Oatlands stands from his father who divided land he inherited among his ten children by lottery.

In 1803 George Carter began construction of a white-pillared Classical Revival mansion. Architectural historians consider the facade to be one of the finest in the state. The interior ornamental plasterwork is also exceptional. Here too, the furnishings reflect not only early American styles but also classic pieces from Eng-land and France. Mr. and Mrs. William Corcoran Eustis selected the furnishings. Eustis's eye for art may well have been inherited from his grandfather who founded the Corcoran Gallery, the first art gallery in Washington.

Mid-May is the best time to see Oatlands because the gardens are at their best. Mrs. Eustis restored the formal terraces laid out by George Carter and added special areas in this four-acre retreat. The wisteria walk is a fragrant delight in the spring.

Be sure to save some time to wander around Leesburg's quaint streets. The town was established in 1758 and was once a hotbed of revolutionary zeal. Residents drafted the Loudoun Resolves protesting the Stamp Act and arguing in favor of colonial rights. The town was named for Francis Lightfoot Lee, a fervid patriot and signer of the Declaration of Independence.

The colonial period doesn't seem that long ago when you stroll Leesburg's tree-lined streets. There are old stone houses that date from the late 1700s, and one log cabin dates back to the earliest days of the town. The Civil War did not ravage this community as it did so many others, primarily because the town remained in Union hands throughout the conflict.

If you want to delve into the history of Leesburg stop at the Information Center at Market Station and at the Loudoun Mu-seum. The museum shows a slide presentation on the town's history. There are also exhibits on pivotal events in Leesburg. You can follow in the footsteps of the Marquis de Lafayette and dine at the Laurel Brigade Inn. This historic spot has six antique-filled rooms for overnight accommodations (703)777-1806.

Leesburg is also noted for its antique shops. Loudoun and Market Streets have a number of small shops, and just outside the historic district there are two large emporiums. The Antique Center No. 1 is at 132 Davis Avenue. The Antique Center No. 2 is on Route 7.

Morven Park is open Saturday 10:00 A.M. to 5:00 P.M. and Sun-day 1:00 to 5:00 P.M. From Memorial Day to Labor Day weekend it is open daily except Monday. Oatlands is open Monday through Saturday 10:00 A.M. to 5:00 P.M. and Sunday 1:00 to 5:00 P.M. They are open April through November. Oatlands closes with the popular Christmas at Oatlands when the mansion is decorated to reflect styles popular in the late 19th century. Admission is charged at both estates. The Loudoun Museum is open at no charge Monday through Saturday 10:00 A.M. to 5:00 P.M. and Sunday 1:00 to 5:00 P.M.

Directions: From the Beltway I-495/95 take Route 7 west to Leesburg. Morven Park is one mile northwest of Leesburg's historic district. From Route 7 turn right and head west on Morven Park Road. Then make a left on Old Waterford Road for Morven Park. Oatlands is six miles south of Leesburg on Route 15. Loudoun Museum is in the heart of Leesburg at 16 E. Loudoun Street.

National Arboretum

Blossoms and Bonsai

Washingtonians can be classified many ways, but one distinction separates those who have never been to the **National Arboretum** and those who go regularly.

Once the arboretum is discovered it becomes a treat in all seasons of the year. It is in spring, however, that the arboretum is most floriferous. With 70,000 azaleas in bloom it becomes nature's own theme park—Azalealand. The wooded hillside paths are flanked with multi-hued blossoms. Although this spring show hardly needs a supporting cast, the peonies, flowering cherries, crab-apples and dogwood surely play important parts.

The azaleas are probably the most popular collection in the arboretum, but an earlier spring showing, the daffodils near Fern Valley, has its own fans, probably because it signals the end of winter. Another early bloomer, the camellia, has suffered from the harsh Washington winters, and the arboretum's collection is severely curtailed.

Late spring and early summer are the ideal times to explore the **National Herb Garden**. One of the three sections in this two-acre garden is the Historic Rose Garden. From the trellised overlook you can enjoy an overview of the roses. Even at that distance you will quickly discover why these old rose specimens are also designated as a Fragrance Garden. Two other areas of interest, the 16th-century English Knot Garden and the Specialty Garden, include ten individual sections. Each section has plants arranged by use—Plants in Medicine, Dye Garden, Industrial Garden, Culinary Garden, Beverage Garden and others. The New Amer-

ican Garden, another popular summer display, features peren-
nials and ornamental grasses.

Fall brings autumn foliage to the many trees in the arboretum
plus bright berries and fruits. Winter respite can be found in the
Holly Collection, National Bonsai Collection and the Penjing
Collection of Chinese-style bonsai plus a new American bonsai
collection. The **National Bonsai Collection** was Japan's $4.5 mil-
lion bicentennial gift to the United States. It is located in the
Japanese Garden and Viewing Pavilion on Meadow Road. The
53 bonsai plants range in age from 30 to 350 years. A 180-year-
old Japanese red pine, the prize of the collection, is the first
specimen from the Imperial Household of Japan to leave that
country.

Another less familiar feature of the collection are the *suiseki*,
or viewing stones. Their names reveal why they are prized by
the Japanese: Chrysanthemum Stone, Puddle Stone and Quiet
Mountain Stone.

Outdoor displays of holly and evergreen please the eye even
on crisp, cold days.

The National Arboretum is open daily, except Christmas.
There is no admission charge. Weekday hours are 8:00 A.M. to
5:00 P.M. and 10:00 A.M. to 5:00 P.M. on weekends. The National
Bonsai Collection and Japanese Garden are only open 10:00 A.M.
to 2:30 P.M.

Directions: The National Arboretum is inside the Beltway at
3501 New York Avenue, N.E. There is an entrance off New York
Avenue and another off Bladensburg Road.

Nemours

Tres Chic

Many elegant homes of the well-to-do give visitors a glimpse of
the gilded life, but few so successfully create the illusion that
you have joined that special circle as does **Nemours,** outside
Wilmington, Delaware.

Nemours is just about ten minutes from the interstate at the
Wilmington exit, little more than a two-hour drive from the
Washington Beltway. Your gracious reception will quickly erase
all the anxieties of turnpike travel. After receiving a flower from
the hostess you are served juice on the terrace and given a little
history of the du Pont family and the building of this fairy tale
estate. The main house and all the dependencies are tinted light
pink. Nestling among the 300 acres of woodland and landscaped

gardens, they blend perfectly with the pastels of spring—dogwood, azaleas, tulips and lilacs.

The patriarch of the du Ponts, Pierre Samuel du Pont de Nemours, fled from France after the Revolution. As a member of Louis XVI's cabinet, his future in France was problematic. He immigrated to America in 1799. Although he returned briefly after Napoleon's defeat and became part of the provisional government, he left again in 1815 when Napoleon returned to power.

It was his great-great-grandson, Alfred Irénée du Pont, who built this modified Louis XVI French château in 1909–1910. Throughout the 102-room house you will see reminders of Pierre Samuel du Pont and his association with Louis XVI and Marie Antoinette. Several of the decorative pieces in the house either belonged to the French king or were gifts to the du Ponts from him. The crystal chandelier in the formal dining room once hung in Schönbrunn Palace, Marie Antoinette's girlhood home in Vienna. The hall clock that plays a number of musical selections also belonged to her.

To tour Nemours is to become acquainted with Alfred Irénée du Pont, a man of incredible scope and brilliance. He was an avid hunter, sportsman, composer and inventor with over 200 inventions under patent and was interested in a multitude of other projects. Your tour shows you the informal side of his life at Nemours, including an exercise room, billiard room, bowling alley and a photographic laboratory. Spring water was pumped to another room where, at his direction, he had the water bottled as Nemours Silver Spring. This tour even shows you the boiler room, where there are two boilers and two hot-water heaters, just in case the first units should malfunction.

The gardens, included on the tour, extend for a third of a mile from the chateau. Designed in the manner of Versailles with seven man-made ponds flowing into one another and oversize sculpture and colonnades, the scene is breathtaking, particularly in the spring with the bloom of 20,000 tulips.

On your return to the Reception Center where the two-hour tour ends, you stop at the **Garage and Chauffeur's House** to see a collection of du Pont cars. Included are a 1912 Cadillac with a 1934 chassis and a second Cadillac with a 1924 body and a 1934 chassis. The latter car had no front door, and the chauffeur had to enter through the back door and climb over the front seat. You'll also see a 1960 Phantom V Towncar, a 1933 Buick Roadster and a rare collector's item—one of the ten Silver Wraith Rolls Royces made in 1951.

If you have time after your tour of Nemours, consider visiting the Hagley Museum and Eleutherian Mills just ten minutes away (see selection) where E.I. du Pont de Nemours and Company established a gunpowder mill and the family fortunes began. You can also combine a trip to Nemours with a visit to the other nearby du Pont estates, Longwood and Winterthur (see selections).

Nemours is open from May through November. Reservations are recommended for individuals and required for groups. All visitors must be over 16. Tours are given Tuesday through Saturday at 9:00 and 11:00 A.M. and 1:00 and 3:00 P.M. Sunday hours are 11:00 A.M. and 1:00 and 3:00 P.M. There are a number of steps to be negotiated on the tour, so wear comfortable shoes. Admission is charged for the tour. To make reservations write giving date and time you prefer (plus alternates) to Nemours Mansion and Gardens, Reservation Office, P.O. Box 109, Wilmington, Delaware 19899. Or call (302)651-6912.

Directions: Take the Washington Beltway I-95/495 to Exit 27, I-95 north to Wilmington. Take Exit 8 off I-95 at Wilmington. You want Route 202, the Concord Pike North ramp. On Route 202 get in the left lane so that you can turn left at the intersection with Route 141. Continue up Route 141 to the second light, Rockland Road. Turn left at Rockland Road and continue for a short distance until you see the sign for the Nemours entrance on the right. Signs direct you to the parking area and Reception Center. To reach Hagley Museum return to Route 141 and turn left, then continue for a short distance to Hagley which is on the right and clearly marked by signs.

Norfolk

Down by the Waterside

Norfolk is one waterside getaway that offers diversions, rain or shine. You don't ordinarily think of Norfolk when you think beach, but the quiet water and expansive sandy stretches at Norfolk's Ocean View beaches, paradoxically located on the Chesapeake Bay, offer sure-fire family fun. The area also offers a bustling waterfront, exotic gardens, plus an impressive glimpse of America's naval power.

It's not surfing the waves but sailing them that accounts for Norfolk's fame. The Atlantic Fleet Command at **Norfolk Naval Base** includes 126 ships. Docked along the two-mile-long harbor at the world's largest naval base are destroyers, cruisers, submarines, amphibious ships, helicopter ships, fleet oilers and tugs. The base also includes over 40 aircraft squadrons and more than 50 shore-based activities. Just about everything at this base is a record breaker: It has the largest Marine Corps barracks in the country; the Norfolk Naval Supply Center is the world's largest store; and the world's largest warships anchor here. The immense dimensions of the nuclear-powered aircraft carriers overwhelm visitors. These behemoths stretch as far as three football fields and rise as high as an 18-story building. Barring volatile international conditions the base holds open house on weekends from 1:00–4:00 P.M. At that time visitors may climb aboard two ships. Daily 55-minute tours run from 10:00 A.M. to 2:00 P.M. originating at the Naval Base Tour Office, 9809 Hampton Boulevard.

Another way to see the naval base is on one of the harbor cruises that depart from the docks at Waterside, Norfolk's festival marketplace. The cruises also pass Hampton Roads where the ironclads *Monitor* and *Merrimac* clashed during the Civil War. Your options include a two-or three-hour sail on a 135-foot three-masted Chesapeake Bay schooner, *American Rover* (804)627-SAIL, or a daytime or sunset cruise aboard the *Carrie B*, a reconstructed 19th-century Mississippi paddle wheeler (804)393-4735. *The Spirit of Norfolk* (804)-627-7771, a sleek modern cruise ship, offers dining and dancing.

From the restaurants (there are five plus a score of ethnic eateries) and decks of the Rouse-designed Waterside, you can watch the bustling activity on the Elizabeth River, milepost "O" on the Inland Waterway. This is also where you catch the ferry for the five-minute ride across the harbor to **Portsmouth**. This neighboring city has one of the state's largest concentrations of sites on the National Register of Historic Places. The Olde Town Trolley Tour's 45-minute ride glides by Federalist, Gothic and Victorian homes. The tour offers more than architectural details. You'll also hear the legends and lore of this old town, like the story of the light-fingered general and the tale of the street-sweeping minister. Call (800)338-882 for details on Portsmouth tours.

Even Norfolk's **Botanical Gardens** incorporate a nautical note—you can explore the 175-acre floral wonderland by boat. Trams also crisscross the award-winning rose garden, Japanese garden, colonial garden and the other specialty areas. Spring is the best time to visit when azaleas line the canals and tram tracks. In June more than 250 species of roses are in gorgeous bloom. The gardens are open daily from 8:30 A.M. to sunset. Admission is charged.

In inclement weather visitors explore the fascinating museums and historic houses. The **Chrysler Museum of Art** that the *Wall Street Journal* calls "one of the top 20 museums in the country" has an outstanding collection of Tiffany pieces, Chinese bronzes and paintings by Old Masters. Museum hours are Tuesday–Saturday 10:00 A.M. to 4:00 P.M. and Sunday 1:00–5:00 P.M. Donations are welcomed.

The **Hermitage**, the summer home of textile millionaire William Sloane, houses another outstanding art collection. This 42-room English Tudor mansion has bizarre decorative touches like the dark-visaged witches carved as ceiling supports, the satyrs over the library door and secret panels. As you enter the Gothic drawing room a 1935 player organ creates a ceremonial mood. Art from around the world fills each room, including the largest privately owned Oriental art collection on the East Coast. The Hermitage on North Shore Drive is open daily 10:00 A.M. to 5:00 P.M. and Sunday 1:00–5:00 P.M. Admission is charged.

Several interesting historic sites are on the self-guided Norfolk Tour, a well-marked route through the city's historic district. One attraction is **St. Paul's Church**, which survived the British bombardment of Norfolk in 1776. A cannonball fired during that siege is in the southeast wall of the church. Admission is free, and the church is open Tuesday–Saturday from 10:00 A.M. to 4:00 P.M. and on Sundays from 2:00–4:00 P.M.

In 1787 Moses Myers was the first Jewish settler in this part of Virginia. He built the house in 1792 that you will see on the Norfolk Tour, and five generations of Myers lived here. (It was enlarged in 1796-97.) The family owned more than 70 percent of the furniture; the remainder is of the period. In the dining room, considered by many architectural historians to be one of the most beautiful rooms in the South, George Washington's face gazes out from the rosette carvings flanking the fireplace. Hours: January–March, Tuesday–Saturday NOON to 5:00 P.M. Admission is charged.

The 1794 **Willoughby-Baylor House** stands at the corner of Freemason and Cumberland Streets, one of the first 20 brick houses in the city. The furniture reflects an 1800 inventory. Hours are the same as the Myers House. Also on Freemason (at 240 W. Freemason Street) is the recently opened **Hunter House Victorian Museum**. One of the last owners, Dr. J.W. Hunter, Jr., was a pioneer in the medical field. In his study you'll see an antique electrocardiograph machine. Tours are April–December on Wednesday–Saturday 10:00 A.M. to 4:00 P.M. and Sunday NOON to 4:00 P.M. Admission is charged.

The noted military hero Douglas MacArthur, while not from Norfolk, is closely associated with the city, and his burial spot attracts throngs of admirers to the city. On January 26, 1880, the Norfolk newspaper noted that "Douglas MacArthur was born. . .while his parents were away." This was not a medical first, just the first hometown report on a prominent local family. This was his mother's hometown, and though the general never lived here he did choose this as his final resting place. He declined the invitation to be buried in Washington saying he had never won a battle there. The MacArthur complex features a 22-minute film on his life plus 11 galleries filled with photographs and memorabilia including his corncob pipe and visored cap. There is no charge to visit. Hours are Monday–Saturday 10:00 A.M. to 5:00 P.M. and Sunday 11:00 A.M. to 5:00 P.M.

Norfolk has about 200 free festivals throughout the year. They normally take place in Town Park adjacent to Waterside. Call (800)368-3097 for details on these and other happenings in Norfolk.

Directions: From the Beltway I-495/95 take I-95 south to Richmond then take I-64 east to Norfolk.

Occoquan

Haunting Charm

The quaint artist community of **Occoquan,** less than an hour's drive from the Capitol, is eons away in tempo and lifestyle. Visualize roughly 100 craft shops, boutiques, galleries, gourmet food outlets and restaurants crowded within four square blocks and you get the idea.

Occoquan is listed on the National Register of Historic Places and designated a Virginia Historic District and, like the publicists of many old towns will tell you, it evokes "ghosts of the past." Many Occoquan shopkeepers, as you will learn, actually do claim spectral visitors from bygone days. The town's name means "the end of the waters" in the dialect of the Dogue Indians, the region's first inhabitants. Some people claim the expression "mean as an old dog" derives from the irascible temperament of the Dogue.

The early colonial settlers coexisted with the Dogue, but eventually the sheer number of Europeans drove out the Indians. At the Occoquan Inn, 301 Mill Street, where a series of establishments since colonial times have served the traveling public, the last Dogue Indian in Occoquan occasionally makes an appearance in an upstairs mirror.

In its early years the town was industrial; it was a milling community during the 18th century and was selected as the site of one of the colony's public tobacco warehouses in 1734. Today its commerce is fashion and the arts. Shopkeepers eagerly relate stories about the town's history, their craft (many artists teach classes in addition to selling their creations) and their ghosts.

It's a wonder the Frame Up, 307 Mill Street, hasn't gone up in flames. Even today the owner sometimes arrives at the shop to find a ghostly candle burning on the front counter. Just down the block at Miller's Lighthouse, the ghost-in-residence reputedly leaves sooty footprints near the spot where a coal bin was located in 1888.

Occoquan is habit forming. The endless variety of shops, the picturesque riverside location and the charming ambience will draw you back again and again. Even the ghosts keep coming. "Shopping Charlotte" regularly leaves traces of her visit by slightly disturbing or moving the merchandise at Waterfront Antiques, 206 Mill Street.

Visitors should savor the diverse craft shops slowly. You'll want to spend time appreciating the detail of the handmade quilts at the Country Shop and the intricately woven baskets at the Basket Case. The town also has some interesting eateries. At Sea, Sea & Co., 211 Mill Street, you can dine overlooking the Occoquan River; cover the length of Mill Street and make this your last stop. For hearty sandwiches and tempting homemade desserts stop at the Country Kitchen, where on pleasant days you can eat al fresco in the courtyard. A former school house is now the Maison Gateau. You can see reminders of the past if you look closely at the front sidewalk. The pavement is marked with an "L" and an "H" indicating which entrance was for the lower-school classes and which for the higher grades.

The emphasis in Occoquan is artsy-crafty, but if you want to delve into local history, stop at the **Miller's House,** circa 1750s, where a small museum provides more details. Hours are 11:00 A.M. to 4:00 P.M. daily. The majority of the shops are open 11:00 A.M. to 5:00 P.M. Monday through Saturday and NOON to 5:00 P.M. on Sunday. In most shops you can pick up a map of the historic district with a listing of all the businesses. For brochures on the county stop at the Prince William County Tourist Information Center at 200 Mill Street.

Directions: From I-495/95 take I-95 south to Exit 53; head north on Route 123 for ½ mile to the Occoquan turnoff.

Patuxent River Park

Trade Your Wheels for a Pontoon

An ideal way to explore at least part of Jug Bay's 2,000 acres of natural wilderness is to join a free marshlands ecology tour aboard one of **Patuxent River Park**'s pontoon boats. Trained naturalists discuss various aspects of the ecology on these 50-minute trips. Themes include bird-watching, aquatic study and nature photography.

Pontoons hold 20 passengers; all must be 13 years old or older. Advance reservations are necessary for these popular tours. Pontoon trips run from April through October. Call (301)627-6074. This is also the number to use to arrange special-use permits for hunting, fishing or camping in the primitive campgrounds. A photography blind is available for camera enthusiasts; this too must be arranged in advance.

If they prefer, nature lovers may explore the river on their own. Canoes can be rented, but you should call the above number to check availability. Mattaponi Creek and Jug Bay offer an abundance of wildlife. Canoeing is one of the best ways to spot some of the elusive residents. The park also schedules downriver canoe trips that give you a chance to see the river evolve from a woodland stream to a tidal wetland. Escorted canoe trips can be taken Tuesday through Saturday from mid-April to the end of October. Experienced canoeists can reserve a spot on the five-hour, eight-mile trip from Queen Anne Bridge to Jackson's Landing.

The river is just one attraction at Patuxent River Park. Park naturalists give guided nature walks through the **Black Walnut Creek Study Area**. Children six and up, accompanied by their parents, are allowed to join these free natures walks that introduce them to the plants and animals found in the marsh. These tours should be booked in advance.

The park does not neglect the historical significance of the region. The Patuxent River has influenced the social and economic history of the area for more than 300 years. To show what it was like for pioneers living along the river, park personnel demonstrate how settlers built a rough-hewn log cabin using a broad ax and adze. **Patuxent Village** also contains a smokehouse, tobacco stripping and packing barn, and a hunting and trapping shed.

More building tools can be seen in the **W. Henry Duvall Memorial Tool Collection.** Antique building tools surround a carpenter's workbench. Tools used by cobblers and wheelwrights share space with those used by country dentists. Another section of the exhibit showcases an old-fashioned kitchen. William Henry Duvall amassed more than 1,200 tools and farm implements that shed light on life in the 19th century. The collection exhibit is open Sunday 1:00–4:00 P.M.

Patuxent River Park opens at 8:00 A.M. and closes one hour before dark. The closing time is posted and strictly observed.

While in the area, be sure to include a stop at **Merkle Wildlife Refuge**, a short distance from Patuxent. The refuge has a Visitor Center and an observation platform. From here during the migratory season you will see enormous concentrations of Canada geese. You're also likely to spot a wide variety of ducks, and if you are lucky you might even see a bald eagle or a hawk. High-powered binoculars are helpful in identifying the birds feeding on the protected fields of this wildlife sanctuary.

Unlike the eastern shore wildlife refuges, Merkle is close to

Washington, convenient for visiting in the early morning before the birds leave for their day's foraging or at dusk when they return. The sanctuary hours are 8:00 A.M. to 5:00 P.M.

The Chesapeake Bay Critical Area Driving Tour links Patuxent River Park and Merkle Wildlife Sanctuary. This four-mile drive takes you through fields, forest and wetlands that border the Patuxent River in Prince George's County. You can pick up a brochure on this drive at Patuxent River Park.

Directions: From the Beltway I-495/95 take Exit 11, Pennsylvania Avenue for 7.9 miles. Then take the southern turn onto Route 301 and continue 3.8 miles to route 382, Croom Road. (Do not make the mistake of taking the earlier Croom Station Road.) Turn left onto Croom Road and continue 3.8 miles. Turn left at the sign for Patuxent River Park, Jug Bay Natural Area. For Merkle Wildlife Management Area continue on Croom Road for another mile. Turn left on St. Thomas Church Road for 2.8 miles, and you will see the sign for Merkle.

President's Park and White House Rose Garden

Rose Garden for the Nation

George Washington was the only president who did not reside in the White House. He did, however, select the site for the president's home in the newly designated capital city. Few visitors realize that the small granite shaft just south of the White House in **President's Park** memorializes the 18 landowners who settled the land on which the federal city was built. The four panels of the Settlers' Monument give the names and depict the corn, tobacco, fish and game that sustained them.

When John Adams moved his family into the barely completed White House, the grounds were still littered with kilns. It was in them that the bricks used in building the city were fired. At the time the elaborate President's House, as it was called then, was finished it stood alone. The only nearby buildings were a farmhouse and barn. Thomas Jefferson, the third President, put his aesthetic sense to use landscaping the White House grounds. Under his direction, sloping mounds were added on the south side of the house for privacy. It was the sixth president, John Quincy Adams, who began the practice of planting a tree on the 18 acres of the President's Park; most successive presidents followed his lead by planting a tree.

A map of the White House grounds includes a listing of commemorative plantings. Close to the White House visitors will see three southern magnolia, reminders of John F. Kennedy, and a willow oak planted during Lyndon B. Johnson's administration. As you look down towards Pennsylvania Avenue there are two white saucer magnolias from Ronald Reagan's administration, a red oak in honor of Dwight D. Eisenhower and a red maple from the Jimmy Carter years.

As the capital grew, additional plantings were added to maintain a green oasis amid the teeming city. Along the north side of the house there is a grove of trees that screens the White House from the traffic of Pennsylvania Avenue.

The Rose Garden is the scene of numerous parties and ceremonial appearances. The garden you see today was designed by Mrs. Paul Mellon at President Kennedy's request. But though the garden is fairly new, the design and plants are not. The garden is laid out in an 18th-century pattern, and includes some roses planted in 1913 by Mrs. Woodrow Wilson. This garden is quite close to the mansion, and French doors lead directly from the Oval Office into the Rose Garden.

A second garden, the **Jacqueline Kennedy Garden,** is to the east of the mansion. This intimate garden has frequently been used by the First Lady to receive and entertain guests. Finally, there is a Children's Garden that was added by the Lyndon B. Johnson family. This is the area opened to children on Easter Monday for the traditional Easter Egg Roll.

This is one of three occasions when the public is able to tour the grounds; there is a free tour given in the spring and author in the fall. For information on specific dates for these seasonal tours call the National Park Service at (202)619-7222.

Directions: The White House is at the center of the city at 1600 Pennsylvania Avenue.

Richmond

Virginia's Cosmopolitan Capital

You certainly can't take a one-day trip to Europe, but a visit to Virginia's cosmopolitan capital has an unexpectedly foreign flavor. In **Richmond** you can take in such diverse treasures as Zen-like sand pools, a 15th-century English country mansion and French Impressionist paintings by such masters as Renoir, Van Gogh and Monet.

Many famous Americans have left their mark on Richmond. Thomas Jefferson lived here when he served as Governor of Virginia from 1779 to 1781. John Marshall also made a home in Richmond, and his house is now preserved as a National Historic Landmark. The city served as the capital of the Confederacy and was so grand that it was called "a miniature Paris." The monuments and hand-paved boulevards still suggest Paris.

Like Paris, Richmond is particularly lovely in the spring. The city parks are abloom with dogwood and azalea, and none is more splendid than the extensive grounds of **Maymont**, one of only a few Victorian estates in Virginia that are open to the public. Maymont's enticements include a 33-room mansion furnished in a manner that explains why the 1880s and 1890s were called "The Gilded Age." Maymont's pleasures also include exotic gardens, old-fashioned surrey rides and a children's farm.

Maymont's Victorian mansion was built by James Henry Dooley in the late 1880s. The house is filled with art from around the world and furnished with flamboyant artifacts. Memorable items include 14-karat gold-plated chandeliers, a winged lion chair and an extravagant swan bed.

The grounds around the house are laid out in the English pastoral tradition that makes the landscape look surprisingly natural even though the plants are not indigenous. The Dooleys collected 185 varieties of trees from six continents, including many rare specimens. There is a self-guided walking tour that focuses on the trees of Maymont.

Even more appealing is the three-tiered Italian garden the Dooleys added between 1907 and 1910. The focal highlights of this garden are the cascading fountain and the "secret garden" visible from an overhanging promenade. It's worth a visit just to take in the heady aroma from the wisteria-covered pergola.

As the cascading fountain meanders downhill, it forms a more natural waterfall in the Japanese garden. Stone lanterns stand beside the stream and delicate bridges span the quietly moving water. In the springtime the delicate blossoms of the Kwanzan cherry trees add to the garden's appeal.

An alternative to exploring Maymont's extensive 105 acres on foot is to ride in a stylish old-fashioned carriage. On pleasant days from 1:00 to 5:00 P.M. these rides transport you back to the Dooley era. Preening peacocks flutter out of the surrey's path. At Maymont's **Children's Farm** young visitors can see and, in some instances, pet the farm animals. More exotic animals can be found in the wildlife habitats.

The grounds at Maymont are open daily 10:00 A.M. to 7:00 P.M. (winter closing is at 5:00 P.M.) The exhibit areas are open Tuesday through Sunday until 5:00 P.M. Donations are requested.

If Maymont reflects Italian and Japanese influences, **Agecroft** brings back Merrie Olde England. This is a genuine 15th-century English country house that was painstakingly dissembled, shipped across the Atlantic and carefully reconstructed beam by beam and pane by pane.

Agecroft was built in Lancashire a decade before Columbus sailed to America. It was shipped to Virginia in 1925. The story of Agecroft is told in a 12-minute slide presentation that precedes the house tours. As you explore, you will hear stories about life during the Tudor and early Stuart years from 1485 to 1650.

In the **Great Hall** the floor is covered with rushes. These were originally used to insulate the stone floor, moderate its irregularities and cover the accumulated debris. You'll also see a rush lamp, the source of the expression "burning the candle at both ends." Rushes were formed into wicks and then lit at top and bottom.

The derivation of the expression "born with a silver spoon in the mouth" becomes clear when you see the silver apostle spoons on display at Agecroft. These spoons were traditional christening gifts for the affluent. A more sinister custom of the era is revealed by the covered cups in Agecroft's dining room. In the 16th century the wary (and the paranoid) protected themselves from scheming poisoners with covered cups.

Agecroft's grounds also reflect the estate's English origins. The sunken garden is copied from Hampton Court. The Elizabethan knot garden is planted with herbs grown during the reign of Elizabeth I.

Agecroft is open 10:00 A.M. to 4:00 P.M. Tuesday to Saturday and from 2:00 to 5:00 P.M. on Sunday. Admission is charged.

Another exquisite garden can be found at the **Virginia Museum of Fine Arts**. The museum's sculpture garden is a delightful spot for an *al fresco* lunch. The cafeteria is open from 11:30 A.M. to 2:30 P.M. Tuesday through Saturday and from 1:00 to 4:00 P.M. on Sunday.

The museum's West Wing contains an impressive collection of French Impressionist paintings. There is also an extensive collection of decorative art including a massive "Sun" bed crafted of Macassar ebony and white oak in 1936. It rivals Maymont's swan bed in boudoir luxury.

The Virginia Museum of Fine Arts is open 11:00 A.M. to 5:00 P.M. daily except Thursday when hours are extended until 10:00 P.M. Sunday hours are 1:00 to 5:00 P.M. Donations are requested.

The museum is in **Richmond's Fan District**, a neighborhood of restored homes, picturesque cafes, and enticing boutiques and antique shops. A popular Richmond eatery is the district's Strawberry Street Cafe, 421 North Strawberry Street.

If you are heading downtown, another highly regarded restaurant is the Aviary in the James Center at 901 East Cary Street. Here the cuisine is American with a Californian flair. Just down East Cary is Shockoe Slip with its array of fascinating shops and the excellent Tobacco Company Restaurant. For an elegant meal consider Traveller's Restaurant in Robert E. Lee's Richmond home at 707 East Franklin Street. Reservations can be made by calling (804)644-3976.

Afternoon options include a stop at the Museum of the Confederacy, the Poe Museum, the Science Museum of Virginia, the Richmond's Children's Museum and The Valentine Museum (an urban history museum). Historic homes include the John Marshall House and Wilton House (Lafayette's Revolutionary War Headquarters). Civil War buffs will want to visit the Richmond National Battlefield Park.

Directions: From the Beltway I-495/95 take I-95 south approximately 100 miles to Richmond. From I-95 take the Boulevard Exit 14, Route 161. Travel south to Columbus Statue and turn left and follow Maymont signs through Byrd Park to Hampton Meadows parking area. If you want to head directly to Agecroft take Exit 15A and make an immediate left onto I-195 expressway. Take I-195 to Cary Street exit, and turn right on Cary Street. Continue to Malvern and follow signs. Bear left on Canterbury Road and continue to Sulgrave Road and make a left. To obtain a city map and literature call the Richmond Convention & Visitors Bureau at (804)782-2777 or (800)365-7272 or stop at the Richmond Visitor Center directly off I-95 at Exit 14.

Sotterley

Hollywood Matinee

Why not head for a real-life Hollywood matinee at **Sotterley**? All the ingredients of an exciting movie can be found at this picturesque working plantation in St. Mary's County, Maryland.

Even the story of Sotterley's restoration contains elements of drama. Like a Gothic novel it deals with two families—the Platers and the Satterlees. During the War of the Roses, the Satterlees lived at Sotterley Hall in Suffolk, England. They were Lancastrians, supporters of the Earl of Warwick and therefore enemies of Edward IV. Upon Edward's victory he dispossessed them of their family estate. The Platers were given Sotterley Hall in 1771 in return for their loyalty to Edward.

In 1910 when Herbert Satterlee purchased the gracious Georgian plantation in St. Mary's, which had been the home of four generations of Platers, the circle was complete. The Satterlees once again controlled Sotterley, albeit in Maryland not England.

There is another tale that stems from the residency of George Plater V. In what was called Madame Bowles's **drawing room,** which is painted a vibrant red, there is a card table. Gambling was to have a profound influence on Sotterley because, as the costumed docents explain, "George Plater V had a taste for gambling but not the skill." In 1822 this gentleman, already deeply in debt, lost his family home in a dice game with Colonel William Somerville. All George Plater took with him when he left was a table and a bed. Both are now back at Sotterley.

The drawing room is interesting for other reasons as well. If a movie were ever made, this would be a pivotal set for the room has both a secret compartment that was used to receive messages from Confederate sympathizers and a secret passage to an upstairs bedroom.

It is fun to speculate on why this hidden passage was built. One explanation offered is that with the danger of pirates anchoring at Sotterley's wharf and threatening the house, the passage offered a quick way to hide the family silver. There is a story that pirates did stop at Sotterley and that two were killed in a fight and are buried in the field between the house and the river. It is said that a pirate captain and two mates were seen from the window advancing on the house. Quick action by the Platers cost two of the pirates their lives and repulsed the foray.

The windows overlooking the flagstone veranda present yet another story opportunity. They are in the formal drawing room, or **Great Hall** (included in Helen Comstock's listing of the *Most Beautiful Rooms in America*). On one of these windows Governor Plater's daughter, Elizabeth, having received a beautiful diamond ring from her fianceé, Philip Barton Key (the uncle of Francis Scott Key), tested its quality by writing "Key" on the pane.

The drawing room is also architecturally interesting; all the wood was hand carved by Richard Bolton, an indentured servant. He also made the mahogany Chinese Chippendale trellis staircase. In the drawing room he raised the ceiling two and one-half feet, creating a bit of a problem for the upstairs bedroom, but providing a spacious drawing room. On each side of the fireplace he built carved shell alcoves.

Sotterley is exquisitely furnished. Particular pieces to notice are the partners' desk, the staircase clock so positioned that it could be read from the doorway of any of the upstairs bedrooms and the 11-piece toilet set—a more complete assortment than is usually seen. Be sure to see the picture of George Washington floating on a cloud and crowned with a halo. Don't miss the angels' faces; each has George Washington's countenance.

In addition to taking the 45- to 60-minute house tour, you are free to explore the grounds, several dependencies and a charming garden. The most interesting is the old **slave cabin,** one of nine that formerly stood along the "rolling road," down which hogsheads of tobacco were rolled to waiting ships. There is also a smokehouse where hams are still smoked for sale at the Sotterley

Gift Shop. Two gate houses flank the original entrance, and one is furnished to represent an old-fashioned schoolroom.

Sotterley is open June through September from 11:00 A.M. to 5:00 P.M. with the last tour at 4:00 P.M. Admission is charged. You can visit during April, May, October and November by appointment; call (301)373-2280. Groups of 15 or more can arrange a luncheon on the veranda or a picnic on the lawn. Like a good movie, Sotterley can be seen more than once.

Directions: From the Beltway, I-495/95 take Route 5 south about 20 miles to the fork of Route 5 and Route 235. Follow Route 235 about ten miles to Hollywood and make a left turn on Route 245. Sotterley is three miles down Route 245.

Susquehanna State Park

Well-Deserved Praise

From the country's earliest days, words of praise have been written about the Susquehanna River. Captain John Smith thought the river might lead to the fabled Northwest Passage, the long-hoped-for water route to the Asian continent. In writing about the river he said, "Heaven and earth seemed never to have agreed better to frame a place for man's commodious and delightful habitation."

Years later author Robert Louis Stevenson wrote "It was called the Susquehanna, the beauty of the name seemed to be part and parcel of the beauty of the land, that shining river and desirable valley."

Stevenson's description of the countryside where the Susquehanna meets the Chesapeake Bay is still apt. **Susquehanna State Park** encompasses 2,200 acres of this scenic landscape. The heart of the park is the Rock Run area. The land remains as it was in the 1800s, and there are three historic points of interest.

In 1794 a stone four-story, water-powered **gristmill** was built by John Stump. The mill has been completely restored and the 12-ton wheel, essential gears and pulleys are again functional. Volunteers grind cornmeal between 2:00 and 4:00 P.M. on the weekends. You can explore the mill 10:00 A.M. to 6:00 P.M. on weekends and holidays from Memorial Day through September.

Just upriver from the picturesque riverside mill is the **Jersey Toll House** where the Rock Run tollkeeper once lived. It is no longer furnished but instead has exhibits on reforestation and the bay. Also nearby you will see the 13-room Carter Mansion. It is furnished with 19th-century antiques. Both houses are open at no charge during the same hours as the mill.

Perhaps the most popular park attraction is the **Steppingstone Museum**, which is a short distance from the Rock Run area. You can get a picture of rural life around 1900 at this outdoor living-history agricultural museum. When you tour this modest stone farmhouse you can watch costumed workers busy with their chores. It's easy to imagine the family gathered around the piano in the Victorian parlor for a sing-along. In the well-stocked kitchen meals are still prepared using old-fashioned utensils.

A volunteer is usually on hand in the adjacent barn to demonstrate the old tools displayed in J. Edmund Bull Antique Tool Collection. The tools are arranged by use in categories like layout tools, smoothing planes, shaping tools, finishing saws and others.

More skills are demonstrated in a nearby shed that showcases skilled craftsmen who provided the necessary equipment to support this agricultural life. On any given weekend you're apt to see a blacksmith practicing his craft, a cooper making barrels, a woodworker or tinsmith.

Those items not made by craftsmen were purchased at the Country Store, and the museum has another large barn filled with items found in these all-purpose stores. The Old Country Store sells handcrafted items and hard candy, but additional items are exhibited. The store has a collection of old carriages, unusual kitchen gadgets and old-fashioned nostrums.

The Steppingstone Museum is open weekends May through the first Sunday in October. Admission is charged.

These reminders of the past are not the only attractions at Susquehanna State Park. During April, shad run the river and fishermen line the banks. At other times the pike, perch and bass make this one of the best fishing spots on the East Coast.

Directions: From the Beltway I-495/95 take I-95 north to the Havre de Grace exit. Do not head into Havre de Grace on Route 155, instead head west towards Bel Air. After roughly ¼ mile make a right turn onto Earlton Road and proceed for ½ mile. Turn left on Quaker Bottom Road and follow for one mile to Steppingstone Museum entrance on your right. For the Rock Run area stay on Quaker Bottom until you come to Rock Run Road and make a right. The Carter Museum is on the right. Along the river you'll see the Jersey Toll House and Rock Run Mill. (You may want to combine this foray with a stop at Havre de Grace; see selection.)

U.S. Agricultural Research Center

Uncle Sam Has a Green Thumb

If you don't have time for an all-day foray, consider spending a few hours at the 7,250-acre **U.S. Agricultural Research Center** in Beltsville, Maryland. It's the world's largest and most complex agricultural research center. After even a brief visit you'll be a walking compendium of little-known facts.

Spring is the best time to visit Beltsville because piglets, lambs and calves are in the fields and paddocks. Remember, this is not a petting farm. These animals are under preventive quarantine not because they are sick but because they are healthy, and the research staff wants to keep them uncontaminated by human illnesses.

Be sure to stop at the feed lot to observe the beef cattle. You will discover that their diet can be made up, in part, of newsprint or phone directories, excluding the comic sections or yellow pages (because of their toxic dyes). This information derives from studies on developing feed that does not compete with human diets. Sixty-five percent of beef cattle in the U.S. are fed partially by paper. The cramped, concrete feed lots do not permit cattle to exercise, which means the beef has a higher percentage of fat and tastes better.

The oldest part of the research center is the dairy barn where the herd was established in 1918. You'll need to get to the center before 9:00 A.M. to watch the cows milked, but children raised in the city and suburbs find this procedure fascinating—well worth an early arrival. Urban visitors are surprised to learn that the pig is the smartest animal on the farm. Pigs are often used for medical research because they metabolize food like humans.

Animals are only one aspect of the research conducted at Beltsville; the second major thrust is plant research. Here is a rare chance to observe a field that is monitored by the Landsat satellite. The satellite can photograph and determine from space what crop is growing and whether it is healthy. This information provides a basis for important crop reports. Fertilization and irrigation projects also can be monitored by satellite. During the spring and summer months you can see the plots where researchers are cloning apple trees and developing machine-harvestable fruits. At other times you can see the greenhouses where extensive research is conducted.

There are four greenhouse areas: the fruits and vegetables, the ornamental flowers and shrubs, the economic crops and a problem center handling national concerns like pesticide degradation. Those interested in plants may want to check out the National Agricultural Library, which has 1.7 million volumes.

You can take a free 1½-hour tour of Beltsville from 8:00 A.M. to 4:00 P.M. Monday through Friday. The Visitor Center is open during the week from 8:00 A.M. to 4:30 P.M. Tours are by appointment only; call (301)344-2483. You can drive around the facility on your own, but you will miss the background given on the escorted tours.

Directions: From the Beltway I-495/95 take Exit 25, U.S. 1 to Powder Mill Road, Route 212. Turn right and proceed to the Visitor Center on your left where you can pick up a map of the facility.

Winterthur Museum and Gardens

Ignore the Name and Visit Year-Round

Despite its name, Winterthur is a tempting destination in all seasons. Garden paths wind for 2½ miles through meadows and forest, past creeks and ponds in a delightful wooded wonderland. Winterthur Museum and Gardens in Delaware is only two hours from the Washington Beltway.

Winterthur, an 1839 country home, reveals the vision of Henry Francis du Pont. In 1927 when du Pont inherited the property, he began purchasing woodwork from houses along the eastern seaboard for his Delaware estate. His outstanding collection of American decorative arts from the 17th to 19th century fill the rooms of this house. As he added to his collection, he also added to his house until he had 196 period room settings containing over 89,000 objects made or used in America between 1640 and 1860. It is hard to choose which pieces best reflect the scope of this collection. Special items include six silver tankards made by Paul Revere; a pair of sofas owned by John Dickinson, known as the "penman of the American Revolution"; a secretary re- markably similar to one by Nicholas Brown that sold at auction for over $12 million; and John Trumball's portrait of George Washington at Verplanck's Point. There are also excellent ex- amples of domestic architecture, furniture, silver, pewter, paint- ings, textiles and ceramics.

A walk through the 200-acre garden, set in a 980-acre estate, is a delight at any time of the year. The spring months present the most glorious show of floral color, while the autumn land- scape features the brilliant hues of foliage. In creating the garden, du Pont took full advantage of the estate's natural topography and the native vegetation of the Brandywine Valley. His skillful addition of exotic plants created a setting that features such points of interest as the 8-acre Azalea Woods; the Quarry Garden, an unusual naturalistic garden of bog and rock plants where colorful wildflowers and primroses bloom each spring; and the Sundial Garden, formerly the site of the family's croquet and tennis courts.

A wide variety of birds make their home at Winterthur, and during the fall migratory waterfowl stop to rest on the ponds. Benches are placed at several scenic spots throughout the garden so that you can sit quietly and admire both the birds and the view. Admission to the garden is included with tour tickets. A garden map is available for self-guided tours. Guided tram tours are offered mid-April through October, weather permitting. The garden is open until dusk.

Winterthur offers a variety of tours throughout the year, including two-hour specialty tours of the Period Rooms. The one-hour "American Interiors" tour changes seasonally and features Yuletide decorations in November and December and spring plant materials in April and May.

In October 1992, Winterthur opens the Galleries, a new exhibition building offering self-guided tours. The first floor will contain *Perspectives on the Decorative Arts in Early America,* six installations designed to introduce visitors to the collection. *Perspectives. . .*can be toured in any order, allowing visitors the flexibility to explore the displays based on their own interests. The gallery also features interactive video screens and five stations where visitors can touch reproduction objects.

The second floor will feature two galleries scheduled to open at later dates. One gallery will house Winterthur's renowned furniture study collection, while the second will display changing exhibitions. The building's design also includes a small theater on the first floor that will be used for lectures and slide presentations.

Winterthur makes every effort to accommodate visitors with disabilities. Museum and garden tours, including the Garden Tram Tour, are available to visitors in wheelchairs. Sign language tours as well as tours for the visually impaired are available by advance request, TTY-428-1411.

For more information, call or write the Winterthur Information and Museum Tour Office, Winterthur, DE 19735, (302)888-4600 or (800)448-3883.

Spring Calendar of Events

MARCH

Early:

Needlework Exhibit—Woodlawn Plantation, VA (703)780-4000. More than 1,500 pieces of embroidery, canvas work, pillows, coverlets, quilts, wall hangings, counted thread work and crewel work are displayed at this event that continues for several weeks. This is America's oldest and largest needlework exhibition.

Festival of St. Patrick—St. Patrick's Church, Washington, D.C. (202)347-1450. This church at 924 G Street, NW, annually sponsors an Irish cultural festival featuring Irish craftspeople, musicians and dancers.

Mid:

Maple Syrup Demonstration—Cunningham Falls State Park, Thurmont, MD (301)271-7574. Each year for several weekends in mid-March maple syrup demonstrations acquaint visitors with this traditional spring ritual. Park rangers start boiling the sap in the morning, and it takes about five hours before they can scoop out the syrup and give visitors samples. You can see trees that are being tapped and watch a video presentation on syrup making.

Mid-Atlantic Wildfowl Festival—Virginia Beach, VA (804)464-1484. Each year there is an exhibit, show, and sale of art that features wildfowl including antique decoy and photographic work.

Tavern Days–London Town Publik House & Gardens, Edgewater, MD (410)956-4900. In the 18th century the tavern was the social center of community life. Itinerant craftsmen plied their trade during their tavern stay. Craftsmen will be on hand at this colonial ferry tavern during this festival.

Kite Festival—Gunston Hall Plantation, Lorton, VA (703)550-9220. Each year a 200-year-old Mason family kite-flying tradition is recreated at Gunston Hall. Children under 16 are admitted free for this festival featuring kites, puppets and pony cart rides.

Late:

Easter Conservatory Display—Longwood Gardens, Kennett Square, PA (215)388-6741. Delphiniums, daffodils, tulips, azaleas and a splendid array of flowering plants make a yearly visit to this annual show a popular outing. Extensive conservatories and beautifully landscaped grounds with striking fountains make this a garden to see in every season.

Spring Flower Display—Brookside Gardens, Wheaton, MD (301)949-8230. Fuchsias, hydrangeas, azaleas, lilies, and spring-flowering bulbs provide color at this spring flower showcase.

Maryland Day—St. Mary's City, MD (301)862-0990. This annual birthday party features craft demonstrations, country cooking,

music and dance. A Symbolic Session of the General Assembly is
held in the Reconstructed State House.

Easter Flower Show—U.S. Botanic Gardens, Washington D.C.
(202)225-8333. Each year this flower show adopts a different flower
theme.

Smithsonian Kite Festival—Washington Monument Grounds, D.C.
(202)357-3244. Kite makers and flyers of all ages compete for prizes
at this yearly festival.

APRIL

Early:

Easter Sunrise Service—Arlington National Cemetery, Washington,
D.C. (202)475-0856. The date of this Sunday morning service
changes each year, depending on when Easter falls. Service is held
in the Memorial Amphitheater.

White House Easter Egg Roll—Washington, D.C. (202)456-2200. The
place for children to go on Easter Monday is the White House
where a wide variety of entertainment, games and special events
lend an air of excitement to this normally formal presidential
residence. Visits by both the President and the Easter Bunny please
young and old. If you time your arrival for an hour after the event
begins you can avoid a lot of the early crowd. You may, however,
also miss the First Family, because when they are in residence,
they tend to put in an early appearance.

National Cherry Blossom Festival—Tidal Basin, Washington, D.C.
(202)737-2599. When nature and the calendar are in harmony and
the roughly 6,000 Japanese cherry trees along the Tidal Basin
bloom during the festival, it is a glorious sight. A parade with
bands and princesses from the 50 states mark this yearly
celebration. There are also free concerts, an annual marathon and
the ceremonial lighting of the Japanese Lantern.

Spring Garden Tours—White House, Washington, D.C. (202)456-2200.
You can tour the Jacqueline Kennedy Rose Gardens and the West
Lawn gardens.

Daffodil Festival—Gloucester, VA (804)693-2355. The Daffodil Mart
has over 4,000 varieties of daffodils. This annual carnival features
these lovely flowers plus arts and crafts, a parade and games.

Mid:

Daffodil Show—London Town Publik House & Gardens, Edgewater,
MD (410)956-4900. London Town's garden is always delightful in
the spring when the daffodils bloom, but for this event the show
also moves inside where they have a juried Daffodil Show. Exotic
varieties are exhibited and there are exquisite flower arrangements.
This show may start the second week of April.

International Azalea Festival—Norfolk Botanical Garden, VA
(804)622-2312. Each year since 1954 during the third week in

April, Norfolk has hosted the International Azalea Festival to salute the North Atlantic Treaty Organization. There are two acres of azaleas at the garden, and this special event features a parade and the coronation of the Azalea Queen.

John Wilkes Booth Escape Tour—Surratt House, MD (301)868-1121. The Surratt Society sponsors a trip each spring and fall along the route that John Wilkes Booth took after he assassinated Lincoln at Ford's Theater. Historical footnotes fill in the details of this dramatic escape attempt that ended with Booth's death in a barn on what is now Fort A.P. Hill military base. Reservations are a must for this all-day event.

Trolley Car Spectacular—National Capital Trolley Museum, Wheaton, MD (301)384-6088. All of the museum's operable cars are in action or on display. This is a great time to photograph the collection of vintage American and European trolley cars.

Late:

Historic Garden Week—Virginia, (804)644-7776 or (804)643-7141. Over 35 areas throughout the state open more than 250 historic gardens, estates and private homes in the largest and one of the oldest Garden Weeks in the country. Lunch, candlelight tours, musical programs, teas and tours are part of this annual event.

Spring Farm Festival—National Colonial Farm, Accokeek, MD (301)283-2113. Farm fun includes corn-husk doll making, spinning and dyeing wool, sheepshearing, butter churning, basket weaving, straw hat making and an annual colonial militia muster.

Pennsylvania Crafts Fair Day—Brandywine River Museum, Chadds Ford, PA (215)459-1900. An annual fair in the museum courtyard which features pottery, weaving, basket making, scissor cutting and much more. Most items are for sale.

Civil War Encampment—Surratt House, MD (301)868-1121. Civil War units set up camp, provide demonstrations of black powder firings, exhibit military equipment and uniforms as well as answer visitors questions. Costumed docents give tours of the house.

Old Town Alexandria Homes and Garden Tour—Alexandria, VA (703)838-4200. Step back in time as you tour the historic houses of this Virginia community. Refreshments are served at several of the houses and visitors get a real feel for this city's renowned hospitality.

Wings & Things–Paul Garber Facility, Suitland, MD (301)357-2700. Open house at this facility that restores historic aircraft and spacecraft. The day includes a variety of aerospace-related activities.

Tulip Display—Sherwood Gardens, Baltimore, MD (410)366-1630. Over 80,000 tulips are planted in a community garden between Stratford Road and Greenway.

Potomac International Regatta—Potomac River, Washington, D.C.

(202)333-3838. U.S. teams compete with English college rowing teams during this annual event. The best viewpoint is from Washington Harbour in Georgetown.

Early:

Mother's Day Tribute–Mary Washington House, Fredericksburg, VA (703)373-1569. The last time George Washington saw his mother was on March 12, 1789, as he headed for New York to be inaugurated as America's first president. Each year on Mother's Day weekend this farewell visit is re-created.

Patuxent River Discovery Day–Patuxent River Park, Upper Marlboro, MD (301)627-6074. At this park and in the seven counties through which the Patuxent River flows, discover the unique resources of the river through a series of educational, interpretive and historical programs.

Gross National Parade—M Street, Washington, D.C. (202)683-3215. An unorthodox parade with humorous floats and groups travels from M & 18th Street to M St. and Wisconsin Avenue. WMAL sponsors this event which benefits the Police Boys and Girls Clubs of D.C.

Spring Festival–Ellicott City, MD (410)992-2463. Juried and non-juried exhibit of handmade arts and crafts. Often the festival includes an old-fashioned Maypole.

Old Dover Days—The Green, Dover, DE (302)734-2655. Crafts, historic tours, entertainment, homemade food, garden tours and more are part of this annual event.

Chesapeake Bay Bridge Walk—MD, (410)563-7104. Each year they close a span of the Bay Bridge to let people walk across the 4.3-mile bridge. Buses take walkers from parking areas and then transport them back across the bridge.

Apple Blossom Festival—Adams County, PA (717)677-7444. The first weekend in May, when the apple blossoms are at their peak, the area holds an old-fashioned country festival in Gettysburg amid the county's 20,000 acres of orchards.

Reenactment of the Battle of New Market—New Market Battlefield Park, VA (703)740-3101. Booming cannons, cracking muskets and rebel yells add to the color and excitement when uniformed members of reactivated Civil War units stage this 1864 battle. Young boys will find this particularly interesting as cadets from nearby Virginia Military Institute, many barely 15, had been called out to fight in this battle which gave the Confederacy its last victory in the Shenandoah Valley.

Spring Festival—Montpelier Mansion, Laurel, MD (301)776-2805. Cultural and artistic events are part of this day-long festival.

Jamestown Day—Jamestown Colonial Historical Park, VA (804)229-1607. This event commemorates the landing of the colonists at

Jamestown and the establishment of the first permanent English-speaking settlement in the New World.

Folk Fest—Mercer Museum, Doylestown, PA (215)345-0210. The Bucks County Historical Society sponsors this festival featuring town and country crafts of the 18th and 19th centuries. You can see pioneer crafts like baking in a squirrel tail oven, boiling soap or stringing a rope bed. There is folk music and dancing, a quilting bee, military encampment and a medicine show.

Azalea Show—London Town Publik House & Gardens, Edgewater, MD (410)222-1919. The grounds are abloom with brilliant azaleas and they also have plant.sales and plant identification.

Mid:

Market Square Fair—Fredericksburg, VA (703)0371-4504. Following a tradition that began in 1738, each spring the square in Fredericksburg is decorated with flags and colorful canopies for a combination country fair and bazaar. Artisans demonstrate their wares and costumed hostesses sell homemade baked goods.

Heritage Day—Belair Stables, Bowie, MD (301)262-6200. Colonial craft demonstrations, music, Civil War encampment, refreshments and the chance to tour this historic stable.

Roses and Mayflowers Garden Tour—William Paca Garden, Annapolis, MD (410)267-6656. A self-guided walking tour of the private and public gardens of this 18th-century community. Strawberries, cream and tea are served in the William Paca Garden.

Late:

Fort Frederick Rendezvous—Fort Frederick State Park, MD (301)842-2155. The Maryland Forces, which were active during the French and Indian War, demonstrate frontier skills and ranger tactics.

Virginia Hunt Country Stable Tour—Upperville, VA (703)592-3711. Once a year Virginia's elegant thoroughbred horse farms open their stables and grounds to the public.

Strawberry Festival—Sotterley, Hollywood, MD (301)373-2280. Shortcake, jam, jelly, tarts and ice cream are some of the tasty strawberry treats. House tours and children's games add to the fun.

Chestertown Tea Party Festival—Chestertown, MD (410)778-0416. On May 23, 1774, in sympathy with their compatriots in Boston, a group of Chestertown, Maryland protestors boarded the brigantine *Geddes* and dumped the dutiable tea into the Chester River. This escapade is re-created each year as part of this festival. Streets are closed to traffic, and craftsmen demonstrate and sell their wares. Militia demonstrations, music, dancing and a wide variety of refreshments round out this event.

Kemper Open—Potomac Tournament Players Club, Avenel, MD (301)469-3737. Golfers rarely miss this annual sports event.

This handsome Sumatran tiger belongs to a species that is endangered in the wild. Courtesy National Zoological Park, Smithsonian Institution.

Summer

Albert Powell Trout Hatchery and Antietam National Battlefield

See the Small Fry

If you want to plan a foray to please the guys, young and old, combine fishing and Civil War history. Fishermen, children and nature lovers enjoy the **Albert Powell Trout Hatchery** outside of Hagerstown, and history buffs find Antietam National Battlefield the most interesting Civil War site in Maryland.

Each year commercial hatcheries in Washington State ship roughly 500,000 eggs to the Albert Powell Trout Hatchery. When the eggs arrive, they are placed in trays in a flow-through incubator. In two to three weeks, the eggs begin to hatch, and the trout fry are moved to indoor tanks where they stay for two to three months until reaching fingerling size.

The young fish are moved outside in the spring as space becomes available in the raceways. The trout are taken from the hatchery to stock streams throughout Maryland. The goal of the hatchery is to raise 150,000 adult rainbow trout, averaging 10 to 11 inches, within 15 months after hatching. The hatchery holds 25,000 for an additional year; these become prize catches at between 15 and 18 inches in length. Some of these large specimens are included in every spring shipment. The Albert Powell Trout Hatchery stocks Maryland streams from Washington County eastward while the Bear Creek Rearing Station in Garrett County stocks the western portion of the state.

There is no formal exhibit area or visitor center at the hatchery. Visitors are welcome to wander along the walkways between the series of raceways filled with trout of all sizes. If you have questions stop at the hatchery office, which is open daily at no charge from 9:00 A.M. to 4:00 P.M.

Heading south of Hagerstown on Route 66/34 you come to **Antietam National Battlefield**. On September 17, 1862, the armies of the North and South fought one of the bloodiest battles of the war across these Maryland fields. By the end of the day there were more than 23,000 casualties.

Stop first at the Visitor Center where you will learn about the three phases of this day-long battle. Letters from soldiers on both sides give a personal perspective on this ghastly encounter. As

69

Lieutenant Graham of the 9th Regiment, New York Volunteers wrote: "I was lying on my back. . .watching the shells explode overhead and speculating as to how long I could hold up my finger before it would be shot off, for the air seemed full of bullets. When the order to get up was given I turned over quickly to look at Col. Kimball, who had given the order, thinking he had become suddenly insane." Despite what another called a "fiend-like" frenzy of bullets, Captain James Horn managed to sketch the chaos on the battlefield and after the war did a large painting that hangs in the Visitor Center.

If you have time, watch the 26-minute film, *Antietam Visit*, shown every hour. The movie tells the story of President Lincoln's visit to Antietam shortly after the battle. Lincoln used the South's failure to carry the war into the North as a timely opportunity to issue the Emancipation Proclamation. He had hoped to issue it in the wake of a decisive Northern victory, but Antietam was not a victory for either side.

The lack of a decisive victory is remarkable because McClellan obtained a copy of Lee's orders to his generals just before this encounter. The Northern army knew how thinly the Confederates were spread over the Maryland countryside, but McClellan did not act on his information. In fact, he waited until the Southern troops were reinforced before beginning the confrontation—two days late for his appointment with destiny.

General Hooker said of the morning's first encounter in the cornfield, "It was never my fortune to witness a more bloody, dismal battlefield." The line of battle crossed the cornfield 15 times, and by the end of the engagement every stalk of corn was cut and the dead lay strewn across the field.

Hooker's Northern troops gained only half a mile in this bloody prelude. Later in the morning the opposing troops met along a sunken country lane, ever after called the Bloody Lane. Four thousand casualties resulted from this four-hour encounter that ended from sheer exhaustion with neither side gaining ground or winning the confrontation.

The last stage of the battle took place around the Lower Bridge, now called Burnside Bridge. More than a four-hour impasse at this bridge kept the Union troops from being effectively used elsewhere. Four divisions were held in position by 450 George riflemen.

The battle ended where the Hawkins Souave Monument now stands. A footpath leads to this monument that overlooks the entire battlefield. The Antietam National Cemetery is the final resting place for Union soldiers killed in battle. According to official reports compiled by Marcus J. Wright for the U.S. War Department, the Union army had 2,108 men killed, 9,549 wounded, 753 missing for a total of 12,390. Confederate losses were 2,700 killed, 9,024 wounded, 1,800 missing for a total of 13,524.

Antietam National Battlefield Visitor Center is open daily, except major holidays, from 8:30 A.M. to 5:00 P.M. September through May and 8:00 A.M. to 6:00 P.M. in the summer months. A nominal fee is charged, and you can rent cassette tapes that give details on the battlefield. With the tapes it takes roughly 1½ hours to drive through the battlefield.

Directions: From the Beltway I-495/95 take I-270/70 west to Hagerstown, Maryland, exit on Route 66 and travel north 100 yards to the hatchery entrance on the left. For Antietam continue south on Route 66 to Boonsboro. Then take Route 34 south to Sharpsburg. The Visitor Center is north of Sharpsburg on Route 65.

Assateague Island National Seashore and Virginia Barrier Islands

Sand, Surf and Stallions

If the commercial development along the Atlantic Coast from Rehoboth Beach, Delaware, to Ocean City, Maryland, makes you yearn for an unspoiled beach, try visiting Assateague Island only six miles from Ocean City. Its 37-mile beach is a lure to swimmers, beach-combers, bird-watchers, naturalists and fishermen.

Assateague Island has a two-mile state park, but most of the island is managed by the National Park Service as a natural environment. If you are observant and lucky, as you explore the island you may catch a glimpse of a Sika deer, fox, raccoon, varied waterfowl or one of the famous wild ponies. Reputedly these horses are survivors from a wrecked Spanish galleon, but a more likely explanation is that they are descendants of stock grazed by settlers. Throngs of spectators visit **Chincoteague,** the smaller Virginia island sheltered by Assateague, to watch the ponies swim the channel (see Chincoteague Island selection) as part of the popular pony penning held the last Wednesday in July.

Going to Assateague Island from the Maryland side (two-thirds of the island is in Maryland and the rest in Virginia, but there are no roads linking the two sections), you'll see the Barrier Island Visitor Center on the mainland side of the Sinepuxent Bay Bridge. Here you can pick up printed information on both the ecological and anthropological history of Assateague.

It's said that the pirate Edward Teach, also known as Blackbeard, once kept a wife hidden in one of the island's pine groves. Optimists still like to believe that ten of the pirate's ironbound chests are buried somewhere on the island. The chests were valued at more than 200,000 pounds sterling in 1750; their worth today would be staggering.

The Visitor Center puts on daily interpretive programs. It houses an aquarium and exhibits and provides information on swimming, fishing, clamming, crabbing, hiking and boating. You can explore Assateague by canoe or other shallow-draft boats. Hike-in and canoe-in camping sites are available by reservation. The island is open during daylight hours year-round; a nominal entrance fee is charged.

If your outing to Assateague inspires you to look for a spot even more unspoiled and remote, then consider a day trip along the Atlantic's last frontier—**Virginia Barrier Islands**.

Sponsored by the Nature Conservancy, 25 to 30 boat tours are scheduled each season along the 18 islands that stretch below the Maryland/Virginia border to the mouth of the Chesapeake Bay. The Virginia Coast Reserve encompasses 35,000 acres of sandy islands and salt marshes. One of the principal pleasures of these cruises is the variety of waterfowl and migratory birds to be seen. The islands provide breeding grounds for numerous species of nesting birds: geese, loons, ibises, egrets, hawks and the rare peregrine falcons. Keen-eyed passengers may also spot some of the islands' abundant wildlife.

These trips, lasting from 8:00 A.M. until 3:30 P.M., are for the hardy. There are no facilities on board nor are there any on the unpopulated islands. The open boat meandering through the tidal marshes provides maximum visibility but also maximum exposure to the elements. It leaves from Oyster, Willis Wharf or Cape Charles, VA. Reservations must be made well in advance; for details on the spring and fall trips call (804)442-3049 or write Virginia Coast Reserve, Brownsville, Nassawadox, VA 23413.

If you want additional information on camping details about Assateague write or call: Assateague State Park, Route 611, 7307 Stephen Decatur Highway, Berlin, MD 21811, (410)641-2120 or Assateague Island National Seashore, Route 611, 7206 Seashore Lane, Berlin, MD 21811, (410)641-3030 or the Visitor Center at (410)641-1441.

Directions: Take I-95/495 Exit 19 to Route 50 all the way to the outskirts of Ocean City. Take a left on Route 611 to the Visitor Center and Assateague. For the Virginia Barrier Islands take Route 50 to Salisbury; then take Route 13 south to Nassawadox and over to the Virginia Coast Reserve headquarters.

Battle Creek Cypress Swamp Sanctuary, Flag Ponds Nature Park and Calvert Marine Museum

At the Water's Edge

The names **Battle Creek and Marine Museum** suggest a military or historical foray, but actually these two offbeat destinations concern themselves with the ecology and natural history of southern Maryland.

Even many longtime explorers of this area are not aware that the northernmost stands of bald cypress (so called because they shed their leaves each fall) in North America are right here in Calvert County. These 50- to 125-foot giants amaze first-time visitors. The swampy terrain hasn't changed much from the time 70,000 to 120,000 years ago when the bald cypress looked down not on tourists but on prehistoric mammoths and scaly crocodiles. Today the animals you may spot are considerably less exotic but still interesting to urban adventurers—white-tailed deer, muskrats, opossums, frogs and turtles.

A quarter-mile platform trail takes you into the swamp and brings you close to the bald cypress. You can get a good look at the cypress "knees." Some scientists think these ungainly root-like protuberances stabilize the cypress tree in the mud. Another theory claims that they furnish oxygen to the tree.

In the summer the **Battle Creek Nature Center** has a full program of guided walks, lectures, nature films and field trips. A reduced schedule of programs is offered year-round. The center also has displays on the mammals, birds and reptiles that make their home in this sanctuary. Young visitors like to watch the bees in the glass-enclosed hive make honey from the nectar of a tulip poplar.

You can visit the sanctuary from 10:00 A.M. to 5:00 P.M. Tuesday through Saturday and 1:00 to 5:00 P.M. on Sunday. From October through March it closes at 4:30 P.M. Battle Creek is not open on Mondays or on Thanksgiving, Christmas or New Year's Day.

A very different natural world awaits just down the road at the 327-acre **Flag Ponds Nature Park**. Within this park are three miles of hiking trails that cover a diverse terrain including two freshwater ponds, the forested heights of Calvert Cliffs and a sandy Chesapeake Bay beach. There are observation platforms, a fishing pier and a visitors center with wildlife exhibits. From the early 1900s until 1955 this sheltered bay harbor was a major "pound net" fishery that supplied croaker, trout and herring to the Baltimore markets. One building, Buoy Hotel Number Two, survives and serves as an exhibit center on the Flag Ponds fishing industry. The park's name is derived from the native blue flag iris.

A park entrance fee of $3 per vehicle is charged from April through October. Hours are 10:00 A.M. to 6:00 P.M. daily from Memorial Day through Labor Day, and on weekends only the rest of the year.

If you continue as far down as you can go on this peninsula, you'll reach the **Calvert Marine Museum** at Solomons. This quaint fishing town is built around one of the world's deepest natural harbors. The museum shows visitors the local maritime history, the paleontology of Calverts Cliffs and the biology of the Patuxent River and Chesapeake Bay.

The museum has a discovery room that encourages visitors to search for fossil sharks' teeth in a salted sandbox. You can take your find home as a souvenir of your experience. Other hands-on activities include raising and lowering a ship's sail and handling aquarium specimens under the watchful eyes of museum guides.

For those interested in fossils there are reminders of some of the prehistoric beasts that may well have roamed the Battle Creek Cypress Swamp. Young visitors may handle the fossils and imprinted remains that date back to the Miocene Epoch, 12 to 19 million years ago.

Historical displays start from the colonial period and continue to the present. Economic as well as political history is covered, and there is a shipbuilder's lean-to with tools from the three shipyards that prospered in this area more than 50 years ago. Blacksmith and sailmakers' shops add another dimension to the story. Frequent demonstrations of ship carving are given on the weekends, and there is a collection of wooden models representing the various boats that plied these waters: bugeye, dory, sloop, schooner, skipjack, skiff and even a log canoe.

Outdoors you'll see full-size examples of many of these small craft and work boats plus the **Drum Point Lighthouse.** Drum Point was built in 1883 to signal the entrance to the Patuxent River. It was one of 45 screw pile cottage-style lighthouses that guarded the bay. Today only three remain.

The best way to experience the waterman's life is to get out on the water, and you can book a ride on an 1899 oyster bugeye, the *Wm. B. Tennison*, docked at the museum's wharf. The *Tennison* sails Wednesday through Sunday on a first-come, first-serve basis. The boat does not sail with fewer than ten passengers.

One of the museum's exhibits, the oyster house, is located a half-mile farther south. The old oyster-packing house, now on the National Register of Historic Places, contains an exhibit that covers commercial fishing, not only of oysters but of eels, clams and crabs.

The Calvert Marine Museum is open 10:00 A.M. to 5:00 P.M. daily. The main exhibit area is open without charge, but there is a nominal fee to explore the Drum Point Lighthouse and the oyster-packing house.

If time remains, swing by to see the **Cove Point Lighthouse**. This tower lighthouse, also on the National Register, is one of the few survivors of the once popular bay lighthouse. Although you can't climb the tower, the vantage point is an excellent spot from which to survey the bay and Calvert Cliffs.

To see the cliffs close up take the trail at Calvert Cliffs State Park. The cliffs were first described by John Smith in 1608. If you attempt this walk in mid- to late summer be sure to be well covered because ticks abound. Although digging at the cliffs is not allowed, you can scavenge for shells or fossils. The park also has picnic tables and playground equipment.

One last stop you may want to make is the **Calvert Cliffs Nuclear Power Plant Museum**. A converted tobacco barn, it has dioramas and automated exhibits about the cliffs. You can also observe the nuclear power plant from an overlook; taped messages explain the installation and operation of this facility. The museum is open at no charge daily from 9:00 A.M. to 5:00 P.M. except Christmas.

Directions: From the Beltway I-495/95 take Route 4 south past Prince Frederick; turn right on Sixes Road and watch for signs. At Gray's Road, turn left and proceed for ¼ of a mile to the Battle Creek Cypress Sanctuary. Return to Route 4/2 and continue south; a short distance past Port Republic you will see a sign indicating a left turn into Flag Ponds Nature Center. For Solomons and the Calvert Marine Museum continue south on Route 4/2. When you are 200 yards from the Thomas Johnson Memorial Bridge turn left for the museum. Access to Cove Point Lighthouse is off Route 4/2 on Route 497, and the entrances to Calvert Cliffs and the nuclear power plant are clearly marked on Route 4/2.

If you plan to visit Calvert Marine Museum by boat, you must enter the mouth of the Patuxent River from the Chesapeake Bay. Then stay to the right and enter Solomons Harbor. The museum is on the west shore of Back Creek.

Bucks County

Old Look to New Hope

You can raft or tube the Delaware River, ride a steam train or mule barge, explore a wildflower preserve or tour a significant Revolutionary War site—the options are many in scenic **Bucks County,** Pennsylvania, about 3½ hours north of Washington.

New Hope is one of the best places to start exploring Bucks County. This famed artists' community abounds with interesting shops and galleries. Some of the more unusual ones are on side streets such as Ney Alley and Mechanic Street.

To get a look at a charming old home, visit the **Parry Mansion**, circa 1784, at 45 South Main Street. It is open courtesy of the New Hope Historical Society and now serves as a museum of decorative arts from 1775 to 1900. You can tour the mansion from May through October on Friday, Saturday and Sunday from 1:00 to 5:00 P.M. A nominal admission is charged.

Experience history in a unique way at New Hope by riding on the **New Hope & Ivyland Rail Road** or on a mule barge along the Delaware Canal. The railroad once again runs steam trains along its tracks. For years this popular tourist attraction used diesel locomotives, but recent restoration has put a 1925 Baldwin coal-fired steam locomotive back into operation. The New Hope & Ivyland Rail Road celebrated its 100th anniversary in June 1991, and its vintage 1920s Reading Railroad passenger cars again chug behind an authentic puffing steam locomotive. Passengers board at New Hope's 100-year-old depot, with its quaint witch's peak roof.

The nine-mile train ride, starting at the depot alongside the Delaware Canal, takes 50 minutes for the round trip between New Hope and Lahaska. The picturesque route takes you over Pauline's Trestle where, in 1914, actress Pearl White was filmed in the *Perils of Pauline* and past a farmhouse that was part of the Underground Railroad that helped slaves escape from the South in the years before the Civil War. Train buffs like to stop at the Freight House Gift Shop to check out the collectibles and souvenirs. The train runs weekends in March, April and December and daily from May through November. For additional schedule information call (215)862-2332.

History books describe the race to the West between the railroad and the canal. In New Hope you can compare the different modes of transportation by first taking the steam train excursion then boarding the **New Hope Mule Barge** Company's barge for a leisurely two-mile ride along the Delaware Canal, both a state park and a National Historic Landmark. You'll pass the Canal House Gardens Restaurant and Bar where patrons sit canal-side and watch the passing scene. Crossing an aqueduct the barge heads out into the surrounding countryside, past cottages dating from the Revolutionary War and lovely stone workshops and studios. The Delaware Canal Garden is an oasis of color at the mule-barge landing. Barges run from April through mid-November. In April and from mid-October on it runs Wednesday, Saturday and Sunday at 1:00, 2:00, 3:00 and 4:30 P.M. From May into October it runs daily adding an 11:30 A.M. (which also runs in fall) and 6:00 P.M. ride. For additional information call (215)862-2842.

If you want to travel under your own power, then head for **Point Pleasant** for canoeing, rafting or tubing on the Delaware River. All the trips are down river, so you don't have to work too hard. The river has a series of small rapids, not enough to worry the faint of heart but just enough to provide an element of excitement. Young and old can tube this shallow river. The two- and four-hour outings are great fun; you'll even float past Treasure Island. If you plan to include this option on your outing it's a good idea to make advance reservations; call (215)297-TUBE.

The Point Pleasant Canoe & Tube outfit also schedules hayrides through the countryside. One-hour hayrides are given from NOON to 4:00 P.M. from May through November. The area around Point Pleasant is quite scenic; you should save time to drive through the charming community of Lumberville. There are quite a few bed-and-breakfast inns along the river including the Black Bass Hotel (215/297-5815), the Golden Pheasant Inn (215/294-9595), the 1740 House (215/297-5661), and the Isaac Stover House, owned by Sally Jessy Raphael (215/294-8044). All but the last inn serve meals. Another pretty spot to dine is the Cuttalossa Inn on River Road in Lumberville (215)297-5082.

Confirmed shoppers may want to browse through **Peddler's Village** while the rest of the family explores other options. There are more than 70 shops set in a country village arrangement. Five restaurants and the 18th-century Golden Plough Inn make this an attractive setting year-round. There are tours of the inn on Sunday afternoons from 12:30 to 2:00 P.M.

History buffs should not miss nearby **Washington Crossing Historic Park** where on Christmas night 1776 George Washington crossed the icy Delaware River. Two old homes, the ferry inn, a gristmill, blacksmith shop, Durham boat house and country store make up the main section of the park. Be sure to stop at the Visitor Center and see a copy of Emanuel Leutze's famous painting *Washington Crossing the Delaware*. Nearby, and part of the park, is Bowman's Hill Tower. From the top of this 10-foot-high observation tower you get a bird's-eye view of Buck's County. In this section of the park you can explore the 100-acre wildflower preserve, home to a great variety of native plants found in Pennsylvania. It is best visited in the spring and early fall when the wildflowers peak.

Families with young children may want to spend all day at **Sesame Place in Langhorne**. This Bucks County attraction is geared for kids from three to thirteen, but even adults who have enjoyed the show over the years will have a fondness for this family-oriented theme park with its computer gallery, science exhibits and Sesame Street locations. It's special fun on a hot summer day as there are numerous water activities including a 1,000-foot man-made river. Tubing here is safe for even young children. If you are contemplating a visit on a summer weekend, call to make sure the park is not filled to capacity, (215)757-1100. The park is open daily from early May to mid-September and then weekends only until early October.

If you know ahead of time that you are going to be visiting in this area call the Bucks County Tourism Commission and obtain a travel guide and map of the region, (215)345-4552. Another closeby spot is the Mercer Museum (see selection).

Directions: From the Washington Beltway I-495/95 take I-95 north into the southeastern corner of the county. Take the Newtown exit off I-95, make a left on Route 332 west and continue into Newtown. Then follow Route 413 out of Newtown to Buckingham. Turn right at Route 263 (which merges into Route 202 north) and continue into Lahaska where you will find Peddler's Village. If you continue on Route 202 you will arrive in New Hope. For Point Pleasant take Route 32, River Road, north along the Delaware River. For Washington Crossing State Park take Route 32 south. If you want to head directly to Sesame Place from I-95 take Exit 29A, Morrisville, and follow Route 1 north to the Oxford Valley Exit. Turn right on Oxford Valley Road and continue to second traffic light and turn right.

Chesapeake Bay Maritime Museum

St. Michaels Magic

The streets of St. Michaels are quiet during the week, but on weekends the boutiques and antique shops lure day-trippers to this picture-perfect Eastern Shore community. The harbor area boasts three popular restaurants—the Crab Claw, Longfellows and the Town Dock—plus the fascinating **Chesapeake Bay Maritime Museum**.

If the word museum conjures an image of a dark, cluttered building, you will be pleasantly surprised by this one right on the water. There are indoor and outdoor exhibits, including boats both launched and dry docked. Enjoy this 16-acre complex at a leisurely pace. You'll want to explore the 1879 lighthouse, the small boat exhibit, aquarium and museum outbuildings.

The museum's focal point is the stilt-legged **Hooper Strait Lighthouse**, one of three hexagonal cottage-style lighthouses to have survived. Once lighthouses like those could be seen firmly anchored in the Chesapeake Bay, screwed into the muddy bottom by giant steel piles shaped like screws.

If you've ever romanticized the life of a lighthouse keeper, a visit here will destroy your illusions. The quarters were spartan, and the lighthouse keeper's family could join him only two weeks out of the year. Although he received periodic leave, tending the light was a lonely and rugged life.

Although this is not as tall as a traditional stone lighthouse, it gives you from the top a commanding vista of the bay and harbor. Working fishermen still ply the waters of St. Michaels. One skipjack now retired is the *Rosie Parks*. Until 1974 this vessel was part of the oyster-dredging fleet.

Museum staff restore and repair the old workboats in the boat shop. The skill and expertise of St. Michaels' builders are renowned. They crafted the first Baltimore clipper and the first racing log canoe. You can see the tools of the trade, learn the techniques of craft and see finished results in the small boat shed. The display includes yachts, workboats and hunting skiffs.

The bay traditions of boat building, commercial fishing, yachting, waterfowl hunting and navigation are all part of the story told at this museum. One exhibit building has a collection of guns and handcrafted decoys, both working decoys and exquisite, decorative ones. The realistic details of these decoys create the illusion that the birds are stuffed and not carved out of wood.

From hunting to fishing, if you want to see examples of the catch from the Chesapeake Bay waters check the museum's aquarium. The museum staff caught these specimens.

Economic history is only one thrust of the museum. The events that took place in and around St. Michaels are also covered. You'll discover why St. Michaels is called "the town that fooled the British" from an incident in the War of 1812. The perhaps apocryphal story reveals that canny residents hung lanterns high in the trees to trick the British anchored off shore into firing high, thus sparing the town any damage. The Chesapeake Bay Building covers the history of this area from prehistory to current times. A Waterman's Village re-creating everyday life on the bay is under construction.

The Chesapeake Bay Maritime Museum is open daily from 10:00 A.M. to 5:00 P.M. during daylight savings. On summer Saturdays it stays open until 7:00 P.M. Late fall through December and in early spring it is open daily 10:00 A.M. to 4:00 P.M. From January to mid-March the museum is open only on weekends 10:00 A.M. to 4:00 P.M. Closed on major holidays. Admission is charged.

Directions: From the Beltway I-495/95 take Route 50 to Easton. From Easton take Route 33 to St. Michaels. In St. Michaels turn right on Mill Street for the museum located at the end of the street at Navy Point.

Chesapeake & Ohio National Historical Park at Great Falls

Locks Offer Key to Past

On July 4, 1828, two events occurred that irrevocably changed transportation in America. In Washington, President John Quincy Adams turned the first shovel of dirt for the Chesapeake and Ohio Canal. In Baltimore, the sole surviving signer of the Declaration of Independence, Charles Carroll, laid the first stone for the Baltimore and Ohio Railroad. The race to the West commenced.

Builders anticipated that the canal would link Washington and Pittsburgh. But the railroad provided an easier connection, and the canal never extended as far west as intended. It ended 185 miles from the capital in Cumberland, Maryland. The completed section is an engineering marvel that raised the water level 605 feet by a series of 74 locks.

To understand how the locks worked take a ride on the *Canal Clipper* that plies the narrow waterway at the **Chesapeake & Ohio National Historical Park in Great Falls**, Maryland. Passengers board outside the Great Falls Tavern Visitor Center. When all are aboard, the captain blows the giant lock horn and a bygone era comes to life.

The trip gets off to a fascinating start as passengers experience the "locking through" maneuver. When the boat enters the lock, a valve is opened and the water level rises eight feet to bring the boat even with the next level of the canal. Once the boat is raised, operators open the "upstream" lock and hitch the boat to a mule team for the rest of the 90-minute trip.

Even during the canal's heyday, the boats covered only four miles an hour. It took roughly ten minutes to negotiate each lock. Boats traveled the length of the canal in six days. The canal's route spanned 11 tributaries of the Potomac River. In order to deal with them, the engineers borrowed from the Romans and built a system of aqueducts that allowed the canal boats to float over the tributaries. Some of these aqueducts rose 25 feet above the river.

Another challenge for the engineers were the steep stone mountains of Western Maryland. Rather than building the canals around the mountains, the engineers went through them. The best example is the 3,100-foot **Paw Paw Tunnel**, about 28 miles southwest of Cumberland, Maryland. This tunnel is also part of the C&O National Historical Park, and there is still a towpath inside the tunnel. If you decide to visit here be sure to bring along a flashlight as it is dark in the tunnel.

The canal boats no longer make the long journey to Cumberland; the Canal Clipper actually travels little more than a mile, still far enough to give you a glimpse of what traveling on the canal was like. Passengers and crew join in a sing-along, like those held on quiet evenings when earlier canal boats made their slow way up the canal. The captain frequently traveled with his wife and children, and these sing-alongs provided relaxation for all. The young sons of canal captains earned four cents a day walking the mule team along the towpath.

The canal boat trips are fun and informative. Crew members regale passengers with stories about life along the canal in 1876. One thing you'll learn is that it costs more for your one-mile ride than it did for the 185-mile trip. The round-trip voyage cost 37½ cents. At the time just after the Civil War when canal traffic peaked, as many as 700 boats made the trip each day. The canal operated until 1924, slightly less than 100 years after it opened.

There are no reservations for canal trips, which run during the summer months from Wednesday through Sunday. Tickets go on sale two hours before each departure and on weekends they sell out fast. Call (301)299-2026 for a recorded message on the Canal Clipper or (301)299-3613 if you need additional information.

While you wait for your scheduled departure, be sure to see the exhibits at the Visitor Center. The large white building, built in 1830, was once a canal tavern. Now it houses exhibits that provide background. A sign above the mule bells explains that they "satisfy the mules' sense of style." The center also shows an audio-visual presentation on the history of canals.

It's fun to walk the path to the rocky promontories of Great Falls. The direct overlook of the falls has been closed since 1972 when Hurricane Agnes washed out the trail. However, you can still get good views of the dramatic churning waters of the Potomac River. On sunny days the rocky shore looks like a rookery for sunbathers. The rocks are very treacherous, and park signs warn visitors of the dangers.

After your trip into the past, you may enjoy an alternative ride along the canal in Georgetown. Tickets are available at the C&O Canal Historical Park Visitor Center at the Foundry Mall, located between 30th and Thomas Jefferson Streets in Washington, D.C. The trip, except the passing scenery, is the same as at Great Falls. For more information call (202)472-4376.

During winter months the canal beckons skaters. It freezes over in extreme cold spells, but the Park Service Rangers open it only when it is safe. You can check to see if the ice is right by calling (301)299-2026. If you do not get an answer to your call, there is no skating that day.

Directions: From the Beltway, take Exit 40, Cabin John Parkway to Great Falls, Maryland, or take River Road, Route 190, out to Potomac and turn left on Falls Road, Route 189.

College Park Airport Museum

Air Fare

The birthplace of aviation in this country, as we all know, is Kitty Hawk, North Carolina. But few know that **College Park Airport** is viewed as "the cradle of American aviation." The story behind this title can be explored at the College Park Airport Museum.

In 1908, the Wright brothers wanted to sell their idea for a flying machine to the Army and demonstrated their craft to Army brass at Fort Myer, Virginia. The Army wanted a flying machine that could carry two people aloft for at least an hour, travel at least 40 miles an hour and land undamaged. The Wright plane met these standards. On August 2, 1909, the Army Signal Corps accepted the aircraft as Signal Corps Airplane No. 1.

The next step was to train two military officers to fly the plane. An aerial balloon was sent aloft to find a location for the flying school. A field near the Maryland Agricultural College in College Park was chosen and became College Park Airport. During the trials at Fort Myer, Orville Wright was injured in the first air casualty, so only Wilbur came to College Park in October 1909 to train the officers.

From the beginning, College Park was the scene of a succession of aviation firsts, dramatic events that are captured in photographs displayed at the museum. At College Park on October 26, 1909, Lt. Humphreys became the first U.S. military officer to fly. The next day a friend of Katherine Wright's went up with Wilbur to become the first woman passenger.

In November of 1909, the first U.S. Naval Officer to fly in a U.S. owned plane, Lt. George C. Sweet, took off from College Park. Later that month, the plane was severely damaged. After the mishap, it was crated and sent to Fort Sam Houston in Texas, ending, for a time, Army use of the College Park field. But civilian use kept the airport in service; thus it is considered the world's oldest continually operated airport.

In 1910, Rexford Smith worked here, perfecting a biplane he had designed. The following year the National Aviation Company began providing flight instruction on Wright, Curtis and Bleriot airplanes. The government appropriated money for aviation in 1911, and work began at the new Signal Corps Aviation School at College Park in June of that year.

This led to another flurry of firsts. The first bomb-dropping device was tested by Riley Scott, its inventor, who went on to win acclaim at the Paris Exposition of 1912. There was an amusing footnote to the first "long cross-country flight" on August 21, 1911. Returning after their flight from College Park to Frederick, Maryland, the pilots became "disoriented" or, more accurately, lost. They had to land to ask directions to College Park. In their takeoff the plane stalled and the craft was damaged. The chagrined pilots ended up taking the train home.

Despite the successful firing of an airplane-mounted machine gun in June 1912, the War Department insisted that the airplane would be useful to the military only for reconnaissance missions. Later in 1912, the College Park Signal Corps operation ended, but again civilian operations continued.

The government resumed activities there in 1918, when the Post Office began the first regularly scheduled airmail service in the United States. The museum displays one of the early flying suits and goggles used on these flights as well as a collection of the first airmail stamps.

There is an embarrassing story connected with the inauguration of airmail service. The first flight left, not from the airport, but from Potomac Park in Washington. Dignitaries, including President Woodrow Wilson, were on hand on May 15, 1918, to witness this historic occasion. The pilot attempted takeoff, but the plane wouldn't budge. A crew ran out and spent 30 minutes checking out every conceivable malfunction, until someone finally thought to check the gas tanks—only to discover there was no fuel. This was not the end of the story; the pilot, perhaps rattled by the delay, took off in the wrong direction, following the railroad tracks south instead of north. Realizing he was not heading toward Philadelphia, he landed in Waldorf to get directions. The landing was bad and the plane's propeller broke. Consequently, the 140 pounds of mail had to be delivered by truck.

During the years 1927 through 1935, the U.S. Bureau of Standards used College Park Airport as the site of their experiments with "blind" or instrument landing systems. On September 5, 1931, the first blind landing in the history of aviation was made at College Park.

In 1973, the Maryland National Capital Park and Planning Commission purchased College Park Airport. It has been preserved both as an historic landmark and as an operating airfield. The museum's extensive collection of photographs and aviation memorabilia provides visual reminders of the important series of firsts that occurred here. There are also films that bring to life the Wright brothers work at Ft. Myer and College Park Airport as well as the pioneering efforts of other innovative aviators who flew here. Plans are underway to have an ongoing film series on

Hollywood's version of aviation. On pleasant weekends visitors can watch volunteers restoring a Boyd aircraft just outside the museum.

The **College Park Airport Museum** is open at no charge Wednesday, Thursday and Friday from 11:00 A.M. to 3:00 P.M. and weekends from 11:00 A.M. to 5:00 P.M. Depending on the time of your visit you can stop for lunch or early dinner at the 94th Aero Squadron Restaurant adjacent to the airfield. The restaurant suggests a French farm during the turbulent days of WWI. Its bunkered corridors and military memorabilia create the illusion the farm is occupied by Allied troops. Many of the tables overlook the still-active runways of College Park Airport. A few tables have hook-ups so diners can listen in on the conversations between cockpit and tower. You can also picnic at Calvert Road Community Park, located between Kenilworth Avenue and the museum on Calvert Road. The park has an interesting 18-hole frisbee golf course.

Directions: The College Park Airport Museum is inside the Beltway, off Kenilworth Avenue at Beltway Exit 23. Turn right onto Calvert Road and proceed to the street immediately before the railroad tracks. As the sign indicates, the museum is on the right on Corporal Frank Scott Drive.

Dupont-Kalorama Houses

Be an Insider

The Dupont-Kalorama Consortium unites seven mansions into an easily combined walking tour of close-in northwest Washington. Among its members are four impressive house museums. In descending order of opulence they are Anderson House, the Heurich Mansion, Meridian House and the Woodrow Wilson House. The other three former houses, now given over to museums—the Phillips Collection, Textile Museum and Fondo del Sol Visual Arts and Media Center—are described in the Dupont-Kalorama Museums selection.

Since so many of the grand old private homes in this neighborhood are now either embassies, headquarters for national organizations or offices, touring these house museums is one of the few ways to get a glimpse of the lifestyle of the American rich in the 19th and early 20th century.

Most Washingtonians have noticed the impressive exterior of **Anderson House**, one of the last of the turn-of-the-century Beaux Arts mansions built in Washington. At 2118 Massachusetts Avenue, it is a landmark on one of the main arteries into downtown Washington. The walled entryway, with its massive columns and arched openings, appears daunting even to longtime residents, but don't be put off. This lavish palace was built for career diplomat Larz Anderson and his wife in 1905 for something like $800,000. Its design includes a grand hall, ballroom, magnificent staircase and 18 kinds of marble. Anderson was the American Ambassador to Belgium and Japan, and he returned to Washington with an outstanding collection of European and Oriental antiques and works of art. Downstairs there is a 16th-century Italian-style ballroom. Concerts are given here on the second Saturday of each month at 2:30 P.M., except in May and November when they are on the first Saturday. Also, the Air Force Chamber Orchestra entertains on the 2nd and 4th Wednesday of each month from October through May.

Visitors take the flying staircase (so called because of its cantilevered appearance) to the second floor, where in the European tradition the major living space is found. As you climb the stairs you see a striking wall-size painting done by Jose Villegas around 1880. Anderson bought the painting in 1905 for 80,000 gold dollars. Upstairs in the Key Room where the Andersons customarily received their guests there is a priceless collection of Japanese lacquer and lovely wall murals. The French Drawing Room has silk tapestries from the Gambara Palace in Venice, and its ceiling is covered with 23-carat gold leaf. The English Drawing Room holds, unsurprisingly, some English old master paintings and several Ming vases dating back to about 1600 to 1620. In the Dining Room are two large Imari porcelain bowls given to Mr. Anderson by the Emperor of Japan. You'll also see a portrait of Mrs. Anderson and tapestries from the Barberini Palace in Rome. Although the Andersons had no children, Mrs. Anderson wrote children's books, and her husband had bronze sculptures made of some of her whimsical characters.

At Mr. Anderson's death in 1937 the house and its contents were given to the Society of Cincinnati, a group of lineal male descendants of commissioned officers who served in the American Revolution. Mr. Anderson was a descendant of a wealthy Continental Army officer. The Society is the oldest patriotic organization in the country, founded in 1783. You see exhibits on the Society and on the American Revolution in the ground floor rooms including a fascinating collection of military miniatures, weapons, portraits and other memorabilia from Continental Army officers. The Society's library contains an extensive collection of books dealing with the Revolutionary War, including biographies of the officers. There are excellent genealogical references for families descended from the original colonists.

The Anderson House is open Tuesday through Saturdays from 1:00 to 4:00 P.M. The library is open Monday through Friday from 10:00 A.M. to 4:00 P.M. If you are traveling from out of town call ahead to make sure the library will be open (202)785-2040. There is no admission fee, and you do not need to be a member of the Society to use it.

The **Christian Heurich Mansion** is now the headquarters of the Historical Society of Washington, D.C. This 31-room late Victorian home reflects America's Gilded Age. It was built for Christian Heurich in 1894, at a cost of roughly $60,000. Heurich was an upper-middle-class businessman. The Christian Heurich Brewery, which produced Senate beer, was located on the site of the Kennedy Center. The Old Vat Room in the original Arena Theater was part of his brewery. Heurich was 102 when he died in 1945.

Since the family lived here until 1955 it has been retained, not restored. Over the years it has been described as "late-Victorian Richardson Romanesque" and also as "Rathskeller Bizarre"—plenty to see, in other words. Although the house has 17 fireplaces, Heurich would never permit a fire to be lit. His was also the first fireproof house in Washington; the walls were 18 inches thick. Throughout the house there is exquisite wood paneling and hand-carved furniture, the work of seven carvers. The ceilings are decorated with gamboling nymphs, and wood carvings adorn the fireplace. The minstrels's gallery and suit of armor look very English. In later years an art deco garden room was added. During the work week, picnickers are welcome to eat lunch on the shaded benches in this charming garden.

The Historical Society of Washington, D.C., in the Heurich Mansion opens its library to the public. It is one of the best repositories of books, papers and photo sources on the nation's capital (another excellent source is the Martin Luther King Public Library) and an excellent resource for genealogical researchers.

The Heurich Mansion, at 1307 New Hampshire Avenue, N.W., is open Wednesday through Saturday, NOON to 4:00 P.M. Guided tours are given throughout the day, the last at 3:15 P.M. There is a nominal admission. There is, however, no charge to use the library. Hours are Wednesday, Friday and Saturday from 10:00 A.M. to 4:00 P.M. A Washingtoniana Bookstore is located on the first floor.

Meridian House International is actually two mansions designed by John Russell Pope. Meridian House is one of the country's outstanding examples of 18th-century French urban architecture. Pope designed this stately mansion in 1921 for American diplomat Irwin Boyle Laughlin. The Georgian mansion next door was built by Pope in 1911 for diplomat Henry White. Later the house was purchased by Eugene and Agnes Meyer, owners of the *Washington Post*. Neither house is fully furnished. There is a Reception Gallery, Library and Drawing Room in the Meridian House. Both estates are now used for changing exhibits, concerts, special programs and private parties. The garden at the back with its pebbled courtyard planted with 41 linden trees and garden statuary is very European-looking. The garden itself is open to the public.

Meridian House International is an educational and cultural organization that encourages inter-cultural understanding through exchanges of people, ideas and the arts. The house is used extensively as an orientation center for foreign visitors. Meridian House is open Tuesdays through Fridays and on Sundays from 2:00 to 5:00 P.M. There is no admission fee. To find out about special exhibits and programs, many of them children-oriented, call (202)667-6800.

The last of the house museums—the **Woodrow Wilson House**—is perhaps the most historic of the quartet if not the most elaborate. The house at 2340 S Street was the first house Woodrow Wilson ever owned. He retired to this red brick Georgian Revival townhouse when he left the White House on March 4, 1921, and it was here he died on February 3, 1924.

Surprisingly, this is Washington's only presidential museum, and it looks remarkably the same as it did when the Wilsons lived here surrounded by reminders of his career as a scholar, politician and world leader. Within this time capsule visitors get a tantalizing glimpse of the home life of the Wilsons. Though Mrs. Wilson furnished their bedroom exactly as it had been in the Executive Mansion, it is the library that gives you the most intimate perspective on the 28th president. Surrounded by the 8,000 books in his personal collection (including nine he had authored), Wilson listened to the Victrola Talking Machine that played records with a wooden needle. There was also a graphoscope so that Wilson could watch movies at home. He liked the silent westerns and the comedies of Charlie Chaplin. In the closet, that is still filled with Wilson's clothes and belongings, you see reminders of other recreational interests like his golf clubs.

Among the decorative items that fill the house are gifts from foreign governments (the Gobelin tapestry in the drawing room was a wedding gift to the Wilsons from the people of France) and autographed portraits of many world leaders. There is even a baseball signed by King George of Great Britain, the only baseball ever signed by a British monarch.

Another fascinating window to a bygone age is the tour of the staff and work areas such as the butler's pantry, the back staircase and the well-stocked kitchen. As in the popular PBS series, you see both Upstairs and Downstairs.

The Woodrow Wilson House is open Tuesday through Sunday from 10:00 A.M. to 4:00 P.M. Admission is charged.

Directions: The Dupont-Kalorama district is in the Dupont Circle area. The Consortium's walking tour map and guide is available at each of the seven members and from the Consortium at (202)387-2151. There is on-street parking throughout the area or you can park in one of several parking garages on Connecticut Avenue.

The Flying Circus

The Red Baron Flies Again

Barnstorming once brought thrills and adventure to small towns across the country. The **Flying Circus** near Bealeton, Virginia, is one of the few remaining spots in America where you can relive the halcyon days of aviation. It boasts that it offers "the authenticity of a museum with amusement park thrills."

The old-fashioned shows are performed on Sunday afternoons at 2:30 starting in May and continuing through October. The Circus is run by a group of aviation enthusiasts: airline pilots and military personnel. One airline pilot describes his job with the Circus as a hobby: "The Circus gives you freedom to enjoy what you're doing. At 200 feet, you can feel your speed, see the ground go rushing by under you. At 35,000 you feel like you're standing still."

Those who spend their Sundays performing at the Flying Circus have frequently spent many additional leisure hours rebuilding their old biplanes. The double-wing aircraft you'll see flying in this barnstorming show are normally found only in museums, but here they take to the sky once more. Flying Circus performances usually include a 1940 De Haviland Tiger Moth, Stearman, Waco and two 1929 Fleets.

If you remember the movie, *The Great Waldo Pepper*, or *Those Magnificent Men in Their Flying Machines*, you'll realize that these daredevils not only take old planes up, they put them through their paces. Audiences come to the edge of their seats watching these seemingly fragile aircraft made of cloth, wood and wire turn somersaults, fly upside down and dive towards the ground only to pull out at what appears to be the last possible moment.

Stunts include breaking a series of balloons with a propeller blade, slicing a falling ribbon three times before it reaches the ground, parachuting and wing walking. Some things never change, and just like audiences in the 30s and 40s, the crowd saves its biggest applause for the wing walker. The entire throng seems to hold their breaths as the wing walker hangs on by his heels while the plane makes a slow pass across the field. Fortunately there are clowns and tethered hot-air balloons to relieve the crowd's tension.

When the show ends, the planes are left on the field for the audience to inspect, but the announcer does request, "Don't touch the planes, though you can occasionally fondle the pilots." Kidding aside, you can talk to the enthusiastic pilots many of whom have spent their Sundays at the Flying Circus for years. You can even book a short ride, with or without aerobatics, in one of the vintage planes. Riding in the front cockpit, you feel like you are alone in the sky. After donning the necessary helmet and goggles, it is easy to feel like a flying ace. Don't forget the camera; the entire day is one you'll want to capture on film.

The field opens at 11:00 A.M., and you can picnic or purchase food and drink at the snack stand. Admission is charged for the barnstorming show. A small museum sells souvenirs and plane models. Special events include a model airplane competition, antique car meet and the mid-August hot-air balloon festival; for details call (703)439-8661.

Directions: From the Beltway I-495/95 take I-95 south to the Fredericksburg area where you will take Route 17 northwest for roughly 21 miles. The Flying Circus, which is well marked, is just off Route 17 on Route 644 near Bealeton.

Franciscan Monastery

A One-Stop Trip to the Holy Land

If you can't get to Rome and would like to come close to experiencing one of the most offbeat tours in the Eternal City, then visit the **Franciscan Monastery** in northeast Washington. This unusual mission church has re-created the subterranean passages known as the catacombs of Rome.

During the long years of religious persecution, Christians gathered for prayer and funeral rites in the narrow underground walkways of the catacombs, which extended 600 to 900 miles underneath Rome and the surrounding countryside. The walls of the catacombs were niched to serve as graves for Christian martyrs.

In Washington's Franciscan Monastery the catacombs contain chapels with murals and religious sculpture. As you make your way through this abbreviated underground passage you will see the Grotto of Bethlehem, a copy of the Grotto of the Nativity in Bethlehem as well as a copy of Mary's home in Nazareth.

The monastery itself is of considerable interest. Its exterior resembles the early Franciscan missions in California. Built in 1898 and redecorated in 1949, the monastery houses reproductions of a number of the sacred shrines in the Holy Land, such as the Holy Sepulchre and Calvary.

Surrounding the monastery are rose gardens and re-creations of shrines in Europe and the Holy Lands. You are transported to the Middle East by the replica of Jerusalem's Grotto of Gethsemane and to France by the Grotto of Lourdes. In the garden itself colorful spring bulbs and flowering trees yield to brilliant azaleas. Late May and June are the best times to see the roses, though they do bloom throughout the summer ending with a final fall burst.

The Franciscan Monastery is a fascinating spot regardless of your religious affiliation. It is open daily with guided tours of the church and catacombs on the hour from 9:00 A.M. through 4:00 P.M. excepting the NOON hour. Sunday tours are from 1:00 to 4:00 P.M. Admission is free but donations are gratefully accepted. Vespers and Benediction are offered at 3:30 P.M. on Sunday except June, July and August. Masses are said throughout the week; call (202)526-6800 for times.

Directions: From the Beltway, I-495/95, take Route 50 into the city. Turn right on South Dakota Avenue. Make a left turn on Taylor Street, N.E., and another left on 14th Street NE. Turn left on Quincy Street for the Monastery at 1400 Quincy Street.

Glen Echo Park and Clara Barton National Historic Site

A Modern Chautauqua

To those who remember **Glen Echo**'s days of garish glory—the brilliantly lit midway and the plummeting roller coasters—the old amusement park looks as exciting today as a faded scrapbook. There is, nonetheless, a cultural revival taking place here.

In the 1890s, an enthusiasm for the idea of democratic education swept the country. This Chautauqua Movement sought to provide religious and educational programs for everyone. Grandiose plans anticipated that Glen Echo would be America's greatest center of culture. A malarial epidemic doomed the project. The only thing that remains from that optimistic era is the old Chautauqua Tower where bells once summoned students to classes.

The spirit of Chautauqua lives on at Glen Echo through workshops and classes for children and adults in a wide range of disciplines. Artists create, teach, demonstrate and sell their work at Glen Echo. During the summer there are free informal workshops as well as theater performances geared for children. From

90

1911 until 1968, Glen Echo was a popular amusement park. Several of the rides remain but only one, the hand-carved Dentzel Carousel, built in 1922, is still operational. Folk art specialists consider it one of the finest carousels in America. You can take a ride on weekends from May through September. For information on activities at Glen Echo call (301)492-6266.

The parking lot that serves Glen Echo also serves the **Clara Barton National Historic Site**. The National Park Service administers both, but the sites are totally separate and quite different in scope and intent. Ms. Barton chose this location overlooking the C&O Canal and the Potomac River for her home because she was interested in the Chautauqua Movement.

Clara Barton gained a well-deserved reputation as the "Angel of the Battlefield" for her nursing of injured soldiers during the Civil War. She worked with field surgeons at Second Manassas, Antietam, Fredericksburg, the Wilderness and Spotsylvania. After the war she attempted to locate missing soldiers. She published lists of names of soldiers missing in action, trying to gain information on their whereabouts for their families at home. Clara Barton located more than 22,000 soldiers in four years of grueling effort after the war.

She went to Europe to recover from the emotional toll of her work. Instead of finding rest, Clara Barton discovered the great cause of her life—the International Red Cross. She worked with the Red Cross in the Franco-Prussian War, then returned home to help create the American Red Cross. She served as president of this organization from 1882 to 1904. Under her auspices the American Red Cross provided relief to victims of the Johnstown Flood of 1889 and the Galveston Hurricane of 1901.

For many years people thought that Clara Barton built her home in Glen Echo out of wood from the hotel built in Johnstown to aid flood victims. Later research suggests that very little of that wood was in good enough condition to use, most of it being rotten and wormy. The design of the Glen Echo house, however, is similar to that of the relief hotels at Johnstown. Some of the wood to build the Barton house may have been part of President McKinley's inaugural platform. In March 1867, the financial officer of the American Red Cross, George Pullman, purchased 3,200 linear feet of the platform.

Clara Barton's home is a 35-room, three-story Victorian house, which she used as headquarters for the Red Cross. The 36 cabinets, or closets, were filled with disaster supplies. The house has many architecturally intriguing features. For example, from the main hallway you can look up to the railed galleries on the second and the third floors. Ms. Barton called the third floor the Topmost Room.

Clara Barton spent the last 15 years of her long life in this

91

house. She died at Glen Echo on April 12, 1912, at the age of 90. After resigning as president of the Red Cross at the age of 82, she went on to establish the National First Aid Association.

The Clara Barton National Historic Site is open daily at no charge from 10:00 A.M. to 5:00 P.M., closed on federal holidays. There are special events scheduled at the house throughout the year; for information call (301)492-6246. Be sure to see the 20-minute film about Clara Barton's life before you tour the house.

Directions: From the Beltway I-495/95 take Exit 40, Cabin John Parkway, Glen Echo and the Clara Barton Parkway. Follow the signs to the Clara Barton NHS and Glen Echo. At MacArthur Boulevard, turn left. The house is ½ mile on the left. While you are on the Cabin John Parkway you will pass the parking lot for Lock 7 of the C&O Canal—an excellent place to start a hike along the canal.

Gunston Hall and Mason Neck National Wildlife Refuge

Home for the Legal Eagle and Bald Eagle

George Mason left an enduring legacy; both his words and his home are still well known. When fellow Virginian Thomas Jefferson penned the Declaration of Independence he borrowed from George Mason who, in his 1776 Virginia Declaration of Rights, wrote: "That all men are by nature equally free and independent and have certain inherent rights. . .namely, the enjoyment of life and liberty, with the means of acquiring and possessing property, and pursuing and obtaining happiness and safety." Mason's words also inspired the United Nation's Declaration of Human Rights and provided a framework of freedom for numerous countries around the world.

Mason's concern for detail is evident in his well-chosen words and in his carefully planned plantation home, **Gunston Hall**, a few miles south of Alexandria, Virginia. But sometimes the affairs of state and his plantation responsibilities made him a little careless on the home front. His son, John, wrote, "I have frequently known his mind, tho' always kind and affectionate to his children, so diverted from the objects around him that he would not for days together miss one of the family who may have been absent. . ." Perhaps George Mason's childhood had not provided a satisfactory role model; his own father drowned in the Potomac River when George was only ten, thus he spent his life after that without paternal guidance.

Distracted Mason might have been, but he did spend more time at home than other leading figures of the Revolutionary period. This did not reflect lack of ardor, just poor health; Mason suffered from gout and had to serve the cause through his writings. Despite his ailment, Mason attended every session of the Constitutional Convention in Philadelphia during the sweltering summer of 1787. He was one of the principal architects of the Constitution, but when, despite all his lobbying, he was unable to include a Bill of Rights or a ban on slavery in the final version, he refused to sign.

In the study at Gunston Hall you'll see the walnut writing table where Mason drafted his patriotic polemics. Mason traveled primarily in his mind, keeping track of the progress of the Revolutionary cause and doing his best to contribute to the emerging nation. His son John noted, "The small dining room was devoted to (my Father's) service when he used to write, and he absented himself as it were from his family sometimes for weeks together and often until very late at night during the Revolutionary war. . ."

Gunston Hall's exterior is somewhat modest, but the interior is unrivaled in its exquisitely carved woodwork. The mansion was designed by William Buckland, a 21-year-old indentured carpenter whom Mason's brother hired and sent from England. He incorporated the styles popular in London: Palladian, Classical, Gothic and Chinese. Research during the 1980s revealed evidence of far more elaborate wood trims than had survived the intervening centuries. Much of it has now been reconstructed. For the chinoiserie dining room Buckland used scalloped frames with intricate fretwork over the windows and doors, with similarly designed mantel, over-mantel and over-door ornaments. The Palladian drawing room was done in the style derived from the works of the 16th-century Italian architect, Andrea Palladio. The center passage has been restored to its original Classical Revival grandeur, its walls covered with brilliant blue-painted paper and lined with fluted white pilasters support a complete Doric entablature. The stairwell has been papered with a yellow "pillar and arch" design. In the rooms are portraits of several family members including George Mason's first wife, Ann Eilbeck Mason, of whom George, said, "She never met me without a smile."

Gunston Hall is also noted for its formal boxwood garden. Perhaps the best vantage point is from the main house. You can clearly see the 280-foot boxwood allee, which was planted by George Mason. This allee, a long avenue bordered by trees or shrubs, leads to the Potomac River overlook, flanked by matching gazebos. On either side of the allee on both upper and lower terraces are geometrically designed beds of flowers.

A two-mile Barn Wharf Nature Trail begins at the front of the house and covers a part of the 849-acre plantation grounds. During the spring, wildflowers bloom alongside the trail, and blue-birds nest in hollow trees nearby.

Gunston Hall is open daily 9:30 A.M. to 5:00 P.M. It is closed Thanksgiving, Christmas and New Year's Day. The Visitor Center has exhibits and a movie on the highlights of George Mason's illustrious career.

On land near Gunston Hall you'll discover the first **national wildlife refuge** established specifically for the protection of our national bird, the bald eagle. This 2,300-acre federal refuge serves as a resting place for the bald eagle and also as a home to a wide variety of wildlife. The terrain includes uplands forest, wooded swamps and riverfront marshland. Autumn foliage makes the forested area a radiant treat in late September and October. Since Mason Neck is located on the Atlantic Flyway, migratory birds such as canvasback, black ducks, mallards and teal come here in the fall by the thousands. The Great Marsh, a 285-acre portion of the sanctuary, attracts migratory birds to rest.

The refuge differs from a park, being designed and managed for wildlife rather than for people. Although there are hiking trails of various lengths through certain sections of the refuge, some areas are closed to public access. These portions, containing untamed dense forest and inaccessible swamp and marshland as well as managed forests and grassland, are set aside to provide needed habitat and protection to the bald eagle and other species. The refuge has over 600 blue heron nests, making this colony or "heronry" one of the largest in the state. Although visitors to the refuge don't see the nests, they are quite likely to see great blue herons flying over or feeding in the adjacent marshes and water-ways. The trails are open free of charge during daylight hours year-round.

Between Gunston Hall and the refuge is **Mason Neck State Park**, a 1,804-acre tract of land also set aside to protect the bald eagle habitat and to provide recreational opportunities. Visitors can enjoy hiking, picnicking, wildlife observation and park pro-grams focusing on the environment and local flora and fauna. For park maps drop by the Visitor Center.

Directions: From the Beltway I-495/95 take Virginia Exit 1, U.S. 1 south to State Route 242. Turn right on Route 242 for both Gunston Hall and Mason Neck National Wildlife Refuge and State Park.

Harpers Ferry National Historical Park

Civil War Hot Spot

The Civil War is rife with ironies, but events associated with **Harpers Ferry** rank high on any list of these contrary, or unexpected, episodes. Seventeen months before the war began, John Brown raided the town's Federal arsenal, and all hope of reconciliation between the abolitionists in the North and slave-owners in the South was shattered.

Each summer that turbulent era comes alive at Harpers Ferry. The streets of the West Virginia town at the confluence of the Potomac and Shenandoah rivers fill with costumed shopkeepers and soldiers who bring back the Civil War years. Escorted walking tours include fascinating tales about historical events.

One of the most popular tours covers the raid that made Harpers Ferry famous around the world. On October 16, 1859, John Brown, a violence-prone Freesoiler from Kansas, led 18 followers (he had three more supporters who waited with the group's supplies across the river in Maryland) in a raid. Their objective, the guns in the Federal arsenal.

Brown was gambling that if he obtained weapons, blacks in the South would rally to his banner. He believed this would force the South to renounce slavery. One of his inspirations was Nat Turner's 1831 slave revolt that forced a vote on slavery in the Virginia Legislature; the measure to abolish slavery lost by only one vote.

Be sure to stop at the **John Brown Story Building** (listed as stop #7 on the park's self-guided walking tour map). Brown was a fiery and complex leader. It's fascinating to gaze at six pictures taken of him, each seems to have captured a different man.

Brown and his band entered the town quietly, but the townsfolk became alarmed at the sight of blacks carrying guns. When the alarm sounded, the raiders barricaded themselves in the firehouse, ever after called John Brown's Fort. (Promoters took the fort to the Chicago World's Fair in 1932-33 but it attracted only eleven tourists.)

It is ironic that the Federal force against Brown was led by Lieutenant Colonel Robert E. Lee and Lieutenant J.E.B. Stuart. Both resigned their commissions when war became certain and later became famous Southern generals.

There never was any question of the outcome of Brown's raid. Federal troops stormed the firehouse. They killed ten of Brown's men and captured Brown and four others; four managed to escape. In less than two months the captives were tried, convicted and sentenced. On December 2, 1859, John Brown was hanged. In the crowd that watched were John Wilkes Booth and Stonewall Jackson, two men who would play pivotal roles in the years to come.

As John Brown prepared for the gallows he wrote a message that predicted the Civil War. You can take a walking tour that focuses on the military confrontations fought in and around Harpers Ferry during the war. The arsenal was a magnet for the

North and South. Both armies wanted to acquire additional munitions, and neither wanted their enemy to rearm.

There is a walking tour at the park that focuses on the guns of Harpers Ferry, and on weekend afternoons volunteers demonstrate how the early flintlock rifles and muskets worked. Visitors appreciate why these guns had to be replaced when they watch volunteers try many times before successfully firing one. While this may be embarrassing for the volunteers, for the army it was often lethal. You'll discover that the expression "going off half-cocked" originated from the unhealthy habit the guns had of doing just that. You'll also discover that many of the early guns were made by several craftsmen. One artisan would do the stock, another the lock and perhaps yet a third the barrel. When they combined the process into the hands of one craftsman, he made the gun "lock, stock and barrel."

The National Park Service tours are well worth your time, so do try to join at least one. A well-annotated map makes it easy to explore on your own, plus there is a short background slide program given on the hour at the John Brown Museum. Every half hour a 26-minute film on John Brown is shown.

It's fun to wander in and out of the restored shops along the historic town's main street. In the Dry Goods Shop an authentic looking ad encourages patrons to purchase pieces of the rope used to hang John Brown. Another sign suggests that the men of the town should buy a Colt pistol to protect their loved ones.

If you want to take a short hike, explore the trails on Virginius Island, the site of the old John Hall Rifle Works. Another option is the path behind St. Peter's Catholic Church to Jefferson Rock, a scenic overlook. When Thomas Jefferson saw the view he claimed that it was "worth a voyage across the Atlantic." This endorsement may be true, but it is worth mentioning that at the time Jefferson supposedly made the remark he had yet to make the crossing.

Harpers Ferry National Historical Park is open daily 8:00 A.M. to 5:00 P.M. During the summer the park remains open until 6:00 P.M. The admission fee is per vehicle.

Directions: From the Beltway take I-495/95, then take Exit 35, I-270 west to the Frederick area. Pick up Route 340, which will take you to Harpers Ferry.

Hershey

How Sweet It Is

When you arrive in **Hershey,** Pennsylvania, a sign welcomes you with the message "Come for the Chocolate—Stay for the Fun." There is a wide variety of attractions in Chocolate Town, U.S.A.

Even the road sign at the junction of Chocolate Avenue and Cocoa Street, the "Chocolate Crossroads of the World," is a popular photo opportunity for visitors. Other Disneyesque touches include the streetlights shaped like candy kisses—some are chocolate and some foil-wrapped.

For a one-day outing it's best to head directly for the main parking lot at Hersheypark. Free buses and trams take you to all the major points of interest. Start your foray at **Chocolate World** where an amusement-like ride takes you through an exhibit that entertainingly tells the story of chocolate from the planting of cocoa on tropical plantations to the processing at the Hershey plant. This replaces the plant tour Hershey once offered. After your ride, explore extensive chocolate outlet shops.

When you leave Chocolate World catch the free bus to **Hershey Gardens**, which is laid out on 23 acres below the Hotel Hershey. The gardens were begun in 1936 when Milton Hershey, founder of the company, was asked to contribute one million dollars to establish a National Rosarium in Washington. He decided instead to invest in a garden in his own community. His instructions were to establish "a very nice garden of roses."

The garden today is far more ambitious than his original modest request. In addition to more than 30,000 rose bushes of every type and hue, there is a profusion of spring bulbs and autumn chrysanthemums plus the standard summer annuals. The garden is arranged in 16 sections including the Italian, English, Japanese, Colonial and Herb gardens. It's also worthwhile to walk up to the Hotel Hershey and stroll around the formal gazebo-bedecked gardens.

Once you're back on the bus you can opt for a stop at the **Hershey Museum of American Life**. There you'll find exhibits covering man's earliest explorations on this continent. A collection of antique weapons reveals the skillful dexterity of early dwellers on this continent. Moving through the Woodland Period of prehistory to the Indians of colonial time, the display highlights the dress and artifacts of the American Indians. Many household items including dishes, furnishings, glassware and ornaments reflect the changing patterns of American life. Military displays cover early encounters including the War of 1812, the war against Mexico from 1846 to 1848, the Spanish-American War and World War I. The Hershey Museum of American Life is open 10:00 A.M. to 5:00 P.M.; during the summer it remains open until 6:00 P.M. An admission is charged.

Then of course, there is **Hersheypark**—the oldest of the theme parks—that dates back to 1906. A major revamping in the early 1970s made it more competitive with new rivals. There is a variety of thrill rides, children's rides and an animal area called ZooAmerica.

Directions: From the Beltway I-495/95 continue north on I-95 to the Baltimore Beltway I-695. Take that west and pick up Route 83 north to Harrisburg and then follow Route 322 east to Hershey.

Historic St. Mary's City

The Past is Present

In the reconstructed **State House** of 1676 various costumed townsfolk and randomly selected visitors testify in court proceedings before Lord Philip Calvert, governor of the colony.

A bailiff dressed in 17th-century garb asks the witness, "Do you swear to tell the truth. . .?" The witness may not answer with the proper courtroom demeanor, but then these reenacted trials combine history with entertainment. It's all part of the Publick Times Weekends at Historic St. Mary's City, and the testimony is taken from long-ago cases ranging from pig theft to treason.

For the settlers at St. Mary's, Maryland's first capital, these trials were the equivalent of today's television mini-series. The colonists, both male and female, attended the court sessions and felt free to express their views on the proceedings. Today visiting participants are quick to pick up the colonial jargon, joining in with a "heaven forfend" or "fie on it."

The courtroom dramas are but one of several ways the staff at St. Mary's brings the past to life at this 800-acre outdoor living history museum. You're apt to find some action at the wharf where the *Maryland Dove* rides at anchor. Men in the crowd are invited to "buy a wench" as part of the reenactment of indentured servant auctions. Settlers who could not afford passage worked off their fares once they arrived.

Costumed guides are also on hand to acquaint you with the **Maryland Dove**, a replica of the 40-ton square-rigged pinnace that carried the colonists' supplies. Most of the settlers traveled aboard the larger, 300-ton *Ark*. When you board the *Dove*, reflect on what it would have been like sailing toward an uncertain future on a ship this size. The *Dove* was large enough to cross the Atlantic but small enough to serve as a trading ship up the coastal rivers and bays of the New World.

The *Ark* and the *Dove* carried 18 British gentlemen, the Catholic priest Father Andrew White and 140 indentured servants. Leonard and George Calvert, brothers of Cecilius Calvert, the second Lord Baltimore and Royal Proprietor, led the group. This courageous band left England on November 22, 1633, and made landfall at Point Comfort, Virginia, on February 26, 1634. In early March they reached St. Clement's Island, Maryland. Leonard Calvert, the governor of the new colony, met with the local Yeocomico Indians and purchased one of their villages where his group established the St. Mary's settlement.

They could not rest after their stormy four-month crossing but had to plunge immediately into the struggle to wrest an existence in this totally alien environment. For a look at what the settlers encountered when they came ashore take the five-mile trail to the **Chesapeake Indian Lifeways Center**, a re-created Woodland Indian longhouse. You also can drive the short distance to this site.

The Indian center is part of a 66-acre Chancellor's Point Natural History Area. Exhibits at the center illustrate how man has interacted with the surrounding land and water since prehistoric times. A self-guided trail through the wooded preserve takes you past spots where Indian camps once stood. Fossils have been found here dating from 12 million years ago when a shallow sea extended all the way to Washington.

If this area concentrates on how the Indians lived off the land, the **Godiah Spray Plantation** site portrays the day-to-day life of a colonial planter. This reconstructed settler's house and barn offer an interesting contrast between the rural English style of architecture and its subsequent adaptation by colonial builders. The plantation house and the old barn were built by the English method and the new barn and the freedman's cottage by the New World technique.

As part of the Publick Times Weekend, living history interpretations at the plantation site give a glimpse of daily life in the 17th century. A diary kept during the 1600s by Robert Cole, a planter who lived 20 miles from St. Mary's, provides many of the details for the living history.

Picnic tables overlook the St. Mary's River, but it's fun to remain in the 17th-century framework and enjoy lunch at **Farthing's Ordinary**, where costumed indentured servants serve colonial (and modern) fare. Lunch is served from 11:00 A.M. to 3:00 P.M.

Historic St. Mary's exhibits are open from 10:00 A.M. to 5:00 P.M. Wednesday through Sunday during the summer months; weekends only in April, May and September through November. Admission is charged. The **Brentland Farm Visitors Center** is open daily except on major holidays. The center shows an introductory video and has an archaeology exhibit hall and the Maryland Merchant Museum Shop. Visitors can watch continuing archaeological work Wednesday through Sunday from 10:00 A.M. to 4:00 P.M. from mid-June through mid-August. Three rare and significant lead coffins have been uncovered at the Chapel Field site. This project is investigating the founding of the Catholic Church in America, attempting to glean insights into life in one of the earliest Catholic colonies in the United States. Historic

St. Mary's City has special events throughout the year; call (301)862-0990 for details.

While in Historic St. Mary's City you can see the campus of St. Mary's College of Maryland that was established in 1839, the Trinity Episcopal Churchyard where the original State House once stood, the Leonard Calvert Monument and the Margaret Brent Memorial Garden and Gazebo. Margaret Brent is noteworthy because in 1648 she petitioned the colonial legislature for the right to vote. She was a landowner, lawyer and the sole executor of Governor Leonard Calvert's estate. Her request was denied.

Directions: Take the Beltway I-495/95 to Pennsylvania Avenue Exit, Route 4. Continue on Route 4/2 (the roads merge below Sunderland) over the Gov. Thomas Johnson Bridge at Solomons and continue to light at Route 235. Take Route 235 south through Lexington Park to Mattapany Road where you will see a large brown historic site sign for Historic St. Mary's City. Turn right onto Mattapany Road and continue for 2 miles to Route 5. Turn left onto Route 5 and then make the next right onto Rosecroft Road and follow signs to the Visitor Center.

Kenilworth Aquatic Garden

Watery Wonderland

The sonorous croak of a bullfrog, the buzz of dragonflies and the whispery swish of marsh grass responding to even the slightest breeze make **Kenilworth Aquatic Garden** a sensory treat. This cool watery wonderland offers a world far removed from the nearby blistering sidewalks of downtown Washington. The 12-acre oasis on the city's northeast fringe is virtually unknown yet it combines accessibility with exotic appeal.

Wandering along the narrow footpaths that weave in and out among the ponds gives you a feeling of being in some foreign land. You'll see aquatic plants that have been gathered from Manchuria and Egypt as well as from the Amazon and other far-flung spots. More than 100,000 aquatic plants delight the eye. In late July and early August the basketball-size lotus blooms amaze first-time visitors. Thousands of the giant blossoms rise from stalks five to six feet high, so you actually get an eye-level perspective on these ancient flowers. One venerable Manchurian lotus was germinated from seed that dates back over 1,000 years.

The Egyptian lotus, a white water lily, is considered a sacred flower by the Hindus. In Hinduism as well as other Eastern religions the lotus represents fertility; in ancient Egypt it was identified with the sun. It is no wonder its ethereal blooms have a timeless appeal.

Mid-June is the peak season for approximately 70 varieties of day-blooming lilies. But the night-blooming varieties are even more vibrant. If you visit in the early morning you can still catch these nocturnal beauties. Their brilliant colors glitter in the sun like iridescent jewels—amethysts, rubies, sapphires. One Amazon lily has giant green pads that measure six feet across and can support a small child—not that this should ever be tested. If you walk quietly you can find frogs and turtles sunning themselves on the lily pads. You might glimpse an occasional harmless water snake.

What's nice about this aquatic garden is its series of ponds that offer diversity, abundance and robust growth. In addition to the lilies and lotus, you see water hyacinths, water poppies, rose mallow, water primroses, wild irises, bamboo, elephant ears, cattails, umbrella ears and more.

More visitors find themselves wondering how all this came to be. It's a surprise to learn that this was not a government project but the work of one dedicated hobbyist, Walter B. Shaw. In 1882, Shaw, a Civil War veteran, began planting water lilies in an unused ice pond beside his home on the Anacostia River. The lilies thrived and Shaw dredged new ponds and planted more lilies. He eventually added lotus and other aquatic plants, and the gardens were underway.

By 1912, Shaw was no longer able to maintain his collection, and his daughter, Helen Fowler, began managing the garden. As early as the 1920s, the garden was a Washington curiosity with sufficient appeal to entice President Calvin Coolidge and his wife to stroll the cool paths. In 1938, the Department of the Interior acquired the garden, and it became a national park site, the only park devoted exclusively to aquatic plants.

Kenilworth Aquatic Gardens is open at no charge during daylight hours, but park staff are only on hand from 7:00 A.M. to 3:30 P.M. The parking lot gates close at sunset. Keep in mind that many of the lilies close during the heat of the day. If you visit at dusk be sure to apply insect repellent; during the middle of the summer this precaution is advisable at all times.

Directions: Kenilworth Aquatic Gardens is located inside the Beltway in northeast Washington. Take Kenilworth Avenue, southbound to Quarles Street. Bear right and across the Eastern Avenue overpass, then turn left onto Douglas Street and turn right for the gardens.

Lititz

Pretzels, Chocolates, Moravian Music

If you are invited to do the twist in Lititz, it's not an invitation to dance," it's a chance to twist your own pretzel at the **Sturgis Pretzel House**, where this salty snack was introduced to America.

When you reach Lititz, Pennsylvania, it's easy to spot the pretzel bakery; it is the Main Street shop with the oversize pretzel above the door. Even your ticket of admission is a pretzel, but you are advised to refrain from eating it until the tour starts.

Pretzel making is a hands-on exercise for workers and visitors. The latter are often surprised to discover that the soft pretzels are indeed still made by hand and baked in 200-year-old ovens. Sturgis provides a brief apprenticeship for more than 150,000 visitors a year, who try their hand at rolling, crossing and shaping these tasty treats. Even quick studies can't match the speed of longtime workers who turn out 20 soft pretzels a minute. No matter what their speed, all novice bakers are rewarded with an official pretzel-twister certificate. There is no substitute for mechanization if you want speedy production; machines that are used to make pretzels produce over 200 per minute.

The tour ends in the bakery shop where freshly baked pretzels are sold. This may be one of the few places you will find the uniquely shaped horse-and-buggy pretzels that always attract comments at parties and school cafeterias. Sturgis Pretzel House, 219 E. Main Street, is open 9:00 A.M. to 5:00 P.M. Monday through Saturday. There is a nominal admission.

Sturgis is but one of two producers of tasty treats in Lititz; the second is **Wilbur Chocolate Co.** You can almost follow your nose the few blocks to the company's factory at 46 N. Broad Street. The company's free Candy Americana Museum tells the story of chocolate from the cocoa bean to the finished product, from china chocolate pots to old-fashioned metal and wooden candy containers.

Although insurance concerns prohibit visitors from touring the factory, you learn how candy was originally made at Wilbur's in the re-created early 19th-century kitchen. Many factory visitors are understandably more interested in content than containers and methods; they can't resist the temptations at the outlet store. In addition to hand-dipped chocolate and other candy, the shop sells candy-making supplies. Wilbur's is open 10:00 A.M. to 5:00 P.M. Monday through Saturday.

After picking up both salty and sweet snacks you are ready for a picnic at **Lititz Springs Park**, noted as the site of the nation's first community-wide Fourth of July celebration in 1818. Twenty-five years after the festival began, floating candles were added to the ceremony. Nowadays more than 5,000 candles line and float in the stream that flows through the park. The Fairyland of Candles Festival includes an outdoor concert, the Queen of Candles Pageant and traditional fireworks.

There are still other interesting eateries to visit. Across the street from Wilbur's is Sundae Best, which offers sandwiches and delicious desserts. Another spot noted for its chocolate desserts is the **Wells Warwick House** on N. Broad Street. If you like dining in historic settings, you must try lunch or dinner at the General Sutter Inn, a former stagecoach stop on the town square.

The best place to learn about the history of this quaint town is the Moravian Church, circa 1786. Lititz was established in 1756 as one of the country's first Moravian communities. Its name commemorates the barony of Lititz in Bohemia where persecuted Moravians were given sanctuary. In accord with their religion the Moravian settlers built separate housing for men and women. The Brethrens' House and the Sisters' House stand on opposite sides of the church. George Washington used the Brethrens' House as a military hospital during the Revolution.

While touring the Moravian Church you become aware of the significance the Moravians attached to music. Members of this religious sect were among the first musical educators in America; they produced a considerable portion of the religious music composed in the U.S. during the 18th century. They also crafted musical instruments, as you will see if you visit the musical instrument museum associated with the church. The museum is open Saturday NOON to 4:00 P.M. for a nominal fee.

Across Main Street form the church is the **Johannes Mueller House** where you get an idea of the lifestyle of the early German settlers. Mueller, a Lititz printer and dyer of linen, built this seven-room house in 1792. The house has been furnished with period pieces collected from the families of early residents. It is open from Memorial Day through October on Monday through Saturday 10:00 A.M. to 4:00 P.M. During May the house is open Friday, Saturday and Monday. There is a small charge.

Directions: From I-495/95 take I-95 to the Baltimore Beltway (I-695) and head west to I-83. Follow I-83 to York, Pennsylvania. In York take Route 30 east to Lancaster, where you will pick up Route 501 north to Lititz.

The Mariners' Museum

Miniature Marvels Plus World-Famous Full-Size Ships

For centuries men have sailed the seas seeking treasure, but August F. Crabtree created treasures, inspired by the very ships that once embarked on these quests. His miniature ships, mounted

like precious gemstones in the darkened room at **The Mariners'
Museum** in Newport News, are works of art.

The 16 intricately crafted models are the labor of a lifetime.
Mr. Crabtree started out building full-scale boats at a shipyard
in Vancouver, British Columbia. His imagination and skill led
him to Hollywood, where he turned a hobby into a livelihood
by building ship models for the movies. One of his projects was
the model of Lord Nelson's ship in *That Hamilton Woman*.

When The Mariners' Museum acquired its Crabtree collection
in 1934, the museum, then 20 years old, took on new life. The
accuracy of his models brings to life historic vessels like the
Mora, William the Conqueror's flagship for his 1066 invasion of
England. For American history buffs there are the *Santa Maria*
and the *Pinta*, two of Columbus's ships.

The attention given to the tiniest detail on these ships, already
reduced to miniature proportions, is mind-boggling. Magnifying
glasses are attached to several cases because the details are too
fine to be appreciated by the naked eye. A 1687, 50-gun English
ship is populated by roughly 270 figures—men, women, animals
and mythological creatures. To fashion crude fur garments for
the miniature prehistoric men aboard a raft and a dugout canoe,
Crabtree trapped and skinned mice.

One of Crabtree's last models was Cunard's first red-and-black
funneled passenger steamer, the *Britannia*. Sailing on the premier voyage, Charles Dickens remarked that his cabin was "an
utterly impracticable, thoroughly impossible and profoundly
preposterous box." His description of the dining room as "a
gigantic hearse with windows in the sides" was no less harsh.

It's worth the drive to see the Crabtree gallery, but this is just
one of 14 galleries in the museum. There is another outstanding
collection composed of boardroom models done on a scale of ¼
inch to a foot. Models of such well-known vessels as the *Queen
Elizabeth I* and the *Rotterdam* that once graced the meeting
rooms of ship owners are displayed here.

Though all of these models have been crafted long ago, you
can observe modeling in progress several days a week in the
carving gallery. Here, too, you'll find an outstanding array of
figureheads. The more than 20 lifelike figures, mostly female,
adorned the bow of tall ships. The most striking, a 1½-ton golden
eagle, now spreads its wings 18½ feet over the museum entrance.
The eagle once rode the waves on the *Lancaster*, a U.S. Navy
frigate.

One prized figure nearly got a museum staffer in trouble. The
museum purchased a carved likeness of St. Paul from a collector
in Providence, Rhode Island. When the staff member came to
collect it, he wrapped the figure in a blanket to protect it, then

placed it in an open rumble seat. A passing motorist mistook it for a corpse and called the police.

Considered one of America's premier nautical museums, it has 50 full-size vessels collected from around the world, the most complete international exhibit in the Western Hemisphere. The vessels range from primitive to modern, commercial to recreational, spanning the globe and the centuries. The oldest examples are crude dugout canoes and vessels shaped from skin. Regional varieties include a Venetian gondola, Portuguese kelp boat, Spanish sardine boat, Dutch jotter, Brazilian raft and Chinese sampan. A sleek experimental yacht from today looks like it could win any race it entered.

These selections are only the high points of the museum's 26,000-item collection. Staffordshire figures, Sevres and Derby ceramics, Liverpool creamware and delicate scrimshaw pieces share a nautical motif. Paintings, photographs and exhibits tell us of confrontations at sea. The Chesapeake Bay gallery centers on the regional story, tracing boating and fishing on the bay since Europeans first arrived in the New World. Providing the proper ambience in this gallery is the still-operational beacon from the Cape Charles lighthouse.

Either before or after you explore the galleries take the time to see *Mariners*, the outstanding film about modern seafarers shot on such exotic locations as Tutucorn, India, and Sri Lanka.

The Mariners' Museum is set amid a 550-acre park and wildlife sanctuary. If you want to spend the day you can enjoy a picnic, rent a boat, or hike one of the nature trails that wind through the woods and around the 165-acre lake.

The Museum is open from 9:00 A.M. to 5:00 P.M. Monday to Saturday and NOON to 5:00 P.M. on Sunday. Admission is charged.

Directions: From I-495/95 take I-95 south towards Richmond; take the I-64 east exit, and at Newport News get off on Exit 62-A and follow Route 17 to the museum entrance.

National Colonial Farm and Oxon Hill Farm

Sowing Seeds of the Past

Workers at the National Colonial Farm and Oxon Hill Farm take their field work literally, bringing to life the 18th and 19th centuries. These two farms are only a few short minutes from Washington, yet they transport visitors back centuries and give them a chance to learn history from dusty fields instead of dusty books.

At the **National Colonial Farm** in Accokeek, archaeological evidence suggests that five prehistoric groups inhabited this land. This was also the site of an important town of the Piscataway Indian empire. Captain John Smith stopped here in 1608 and called the town he encountered Moyaone. Research suggests that the Piscataway town had been standing on this location over 300 years before Smith's visit. Unfortunately there are no reminders of this fascinating period of pre-European habitation.

It is the 18th century that is re-created at the National Colonial Farm, on the banks of the Potomac River across from George Washington's Mount Vernon. At this colonial freeholder's plantation, authentically clad workers till the fields, perform household chores and prepare food. The staff make many of the kitchen tools from gourds grown on the farm.

There is both a kitchen garden and an herb garden. Be sure to have someone on staff show you the **Rosamonde Bierne Memorial Herb Garden** because under their careful supervision you can touch, smell and taste the herbs, many of which have medicinal properties and should not be touched without guidance. Herbs also served cosmetic and culinary purposes. The farm's Herb Shop sells dried herbs and herbal products.

Tobacco, the colonial cash crop, still grows in the fields as well as corn and wheat. Since the colonists didn't drink water, fruit from the orchard was necessary to make juice and wine. The farm buildings include an out-kitchen and an authentic tobacco barn. A nature trail winds along the river bank.

At the hands-on **Oxon Hill Farm**, staff dressed in bib overalls and long cotton work dresses establish the time period as the late 19th century as do the farming methods they demonstrate. Visitors get the chance to milk a cow or collect eggs.

The farm's livestock includes cows, sheep, goats and donkeys that graze in a large fenced pasture. Children enjoy petting these well-behaved farm animals. During weekends youngsters ride in the hay wagon or even on one of the farm's good-natured horses.

City dwellers may have difficulty recognizing some of their favorite vegetables growing here, but unobtrusive signs provide the names. In neat rows you'll see green beans, corn, peas, beets, tomatoes, squash, onions, lettuce and tomatoes among others.

On weekend afternoons demonstrations show current farm activities such as planting the field, feeding the animals, sheering the sheep, threshing the crop or making syrup at the farm's sorghum mill. The Oxon Hill Farm is open at no charge from 9:00 A.M. to 5:00 P.M. daily. For information on special events call (301)839-1176.

The National Colonial Farm is open Tuesday through Sunday from 10:00 A.M. to 5:00 P.M. The farm has special events on the weekends throughout the spring, summer and fall. A nominal admission is charged. There is a picnic area, the Saylor Memorial Grove and a pier adjacent to the parking lot.

Directions: From the Beltway I-495/95 take Exit 3, Route 210, Indian Head Highway south. For Oxon Hill Farm make an immediate right at the first light once you cross back over the Beltway. Then turn right again onto the entrance road for the farm. For the National Colonial Farm continue down Indian Head Highway roughly 10 miles to the traffic light at Bryan Point Road and make a right. Take Bryan Point Road for four miles to the National Colonial Park.

National Zoological Park

Not Quite Born Free

It's a paradox—animal lovers enjoy visiting zoos, yet feel uncomfortable seeing proud beasts confined. The new approach to zoos minimizes this discomfort by giving animals far more liberty in the large free spaces now provided. There is at least an illusion of freedom.

The frisky pandas, stars of the **National Zoo** since their arrival in 1972, frolic in an enclosure large enough to include trees and play equipment. Their confinement seems more protective than restrictive, as does the newly refurbished outdoor enclosure for gorillas.

The National Zoo has come a long way since it was established by Congress in 1889, just a little more than 30 years after the country's first zoos opened in Cincinnati and Philadelphia. When the Washington collection began, the animals were kept in a pen near the White House. A herd of buffalo represented the country's western plains while other animals, gifts from foreign lands, represented far-flung habitats. As the collection grew it was moved to a 175-acre site along Rock Creek. Today the National Zoo contains more than 3,500 animals representing roughly 480 species.

You can spend all day or enjoy a very brief visit as the various trails that wind through the zoo are color-coded and range from the ten-minute Lion Trail with orange directionals to the 45-minute green Crowned Crane Trail. The main walkway is a red-paved route. You will best appreciate the zoo if you allow time to watch the antics of the animals. The prairie dogs are neither exotic nor imposing, but they are a delight to watch dart about, pausing in alert attention before going to ground. Another spot worth lingering by is the seal pool. These sleek swimmers are constantly entertaining. Good weather or bad you can always find activity in the aviary where colorful tree-flying birds dazzle the eye.

When you arrive at the zoo check on the feeding schedule for the pandas, an event all visitors should observe. Also note the

Photo: Jessie Cohen

Baby Kejana was the first gorilla born at the National Zoo in nineteen years (May 1991). Courtesy National Zoological Park, Smithsonian Institution.

times for the seal and sea lion training sessions. Elephants too are put through their paces at regularly scheduled times. Educational programs and exhibits are offered at the ZOOlab, BIRDlab and HERBlab on Fridays from 10:00 A.M. to 1:00 P.M. and on weekends from 10:00 A.M. to 2:00 P.M. If you are traveling to the zoo specifically for these programs, be sure to call ahead because schedules occasionally change; call (202)673-4821.

The National Zoological Park is open daily. From May through mid-September hours are 8:00 A.M. to 8:00 P.M. with the buildings opening from 9:00 A.M. to 6:00 P.M. During the winter the grounds close at 6:00 P.M. and the buildings close at 4:30 P.M. There is a parking fee but no admission. You can picnic at the zoo or purchase light refreshments on site.

Directions: From the Beltway I-495/95 take Exit 33, Connecticut Avenue, in towards Washington. The zoo is in northwest Washington in the 3000 block of Connecticut Avenue. The zoo is also accessible off Rock Creek Parkway, via Beach Drive and at the junction of Harvard Street and Adams Mill Road.

Northern Neck

Explore George's Neck of the Woods

Virginia's **Northern Neck** abounds with natural charm. This narrow peninsula lies between the Potomac and Rappahannock rivers. At almost every turn of the road, you come upon an inlet, creek or river.

At the upper end of the Neck you can visit the **George Washington Birthplace National Monument**, a place of bucolic tranquility. The view from the Visitor Center of the quiet waters of Pope's Creek is worth the drive, and the meandering trail up to the plantation house offers numerous scenic vistas as does the second walking trail in this park.

Both the 14-minute film *A Childhood Place* and the colonial living farm re-create 18th-century life at Pope's Creek. They also both emphasize the natural beauty to be found on the Northern Neck. Changing seasons, the cycle of the crops and the transitory pleasure of migratory birds are all beautifully portrayed in the film. Visitors sense that so much of what they see around them was here when George Washington was a boy at **Pope's Creek Plantation.**

George Washington was born here on February 22, 1732, but when he was three years old the family moved to what later became known as Mount Vernon. After his father died, George returned to Pope's Creek to spend some of his adolescent summers with his half-brother Augustine.

The location of the original house, destroyed by fire on Christmas Day 1779, is carefully marked and a Memorial House stands nearby. George's father acquired the land when he married the daughter of a Virginia gentleman, Colonel Nathaniel Pope. The newlyweds were given 700-acres along Pope's Creek, and George's father built an eight-room house. Only a small tea table and an excavated wine bottle are original, but period pieces give visitors a glimpse of the lifestyle enjoyed by the Washington family. So do the artifacts recovered during the archaeological excavations of the site that are on display in the Visitor Center.

The fully operational kitchen is filled with old utensils, and there is a weaving room and farm workshop. The fields are planted and the colonial herb and flower garden carefully tended. During the summer months there are special weekend demonstrations of crafts and farm chores like sheep shearing, tobacco planting, harvesting and curing.

A picnic area overlooks the water. This park is also completely accessible to disabled visitors. Transportation is available from the Visitor Center to the historic area for those who can't manage the walk. The George Washington Birthplace National Monument is open daily, except Christmas and New Year's Day, from 9:00 A.M. to 5:00 P.M.

You can also picnic at the nearby **Westmoreland State Park** where there is both an Olympic-size swimming pool and a beach on the Potomac River. Here, too, you will be able to glimpse the river as you explore the scenic woodland hiking trails.

Just past this state park and not more than 15 minutes from the Washington plantation is **Stratford Hall**, the Lee family home. It is amazing to find the ancestral homes of these two important American families practically side by side. Stratford Hall's elegant manor house incorporates the Italian style of placing the major living areas on the second floor, rather than the first-floor arrangement common to most plantation homes. This 1,580-acre (once it was 4,100 acres) plantation also has dependencies, a garden, stable and working gristmill.

Stratford Hall is open daily, except Christmas, from 9:00 A.M. to 4:30 P.M. If you decide not to picnic, you can lunch in the estate log cabin dining room open 11:30 A.M. to 4:30 P.M. from April through October.

Directions: From the Beltway, I-495/95, exit on Route 5 south, then pick up Route 301 south to Route 3. All of these attractions are located off of Route 3. George Washington Birthplace National Monument is on Route 204 off Route 3 and Stratford Hall is off Route 214. Westmoreland State Park's entrance is on Route 3.

Ocean City Life Saving Station Museum and Furnace Town

Bathing Suits and Rescue Pursuits

If a gray drizzle or a sunburn interferes with your day at the beach, head down to the very end of the boardwalk in Ocean City, Maryland. Whether you are a first-time Ocean City visitor or a regular, you'll find something to interest you in the **Ocean City Life Saving Station Museum**.

The first Ocean City Life Saving Station, part of a network along the country's 10,000-mile coastline, opened on December 25, 1878. The station that now serves as a museum was built 13 years later when a larger, more modern facility was required. The museum's collection is ranked as one of the largest of its kind in the country.

The first exhibit room gives you an overview of the Life Saving Service from its beginning in 1848 to 1915 when it merged with the Revenue Cutter Service to form the U.S. Coast Guard. In the boat room, where rescue equipment was kept when the station was operational, you can still see the apparatus used in early sea rescues. The restored 26-foot, double-ended, self-bailing rescue surf boat is the largest exhibit. This surfboat, one of the few remaining examples, was originally used at Caffey's Inlet in North Carolina.

The surfcar, or lifecar as it is also called, is more unusual. The metal, barrel-like rescue boat that many think resembles a tiny submarine measures 11 feet by 4 feet and weighs 225 pounds. The surfcar was needed to save lives on immigrant-laden ships that were frequently beached along the Atlantic Coast. The watertight surfcar held two to four passengers; the more traditional breeches buoy could take only one person.

If you want to see how the breeches buoy works watch the short movie showing the rescue of the *Olaf Bergh*. In 1946 this Norwegian freighter mistook the Fenwick Light for the entrance to the Delaware Bay. She ran aground off 94th Street in Ocean City. The *Olaf Bergh*, like so many ships in those turbulent years, was hugging the shore too closely in fear of German U-boats. There is also a photograph showing the Norwegian consul watching the removal of the crew by breeches buoy.

Another museum exhibit should discourage divers in search of treasure in the waters around Ocean City; the displayed items found by wreck divers would not send treasure hunters into the deep as they are mostly old bottles and shells. Most visitors find more beauty in the shells collected from area waters. Nostalgia buffs will be interested in comparing the oversize aerial photograph of the beach resort in the mid-1940s with the 1981 shot. Another enlargement shows the damage Ocean City suffered after the severe March storm of 1962.

The museum elicits its most heartfelt response when visitors reach the second-floor exhibits and hear Laughing Sal. For many who remember her from the old days the oversized lady, who stood bowing, waving her arms and laughing uproariously at the crowds entering Jester's Funhouse on the boardwalk, is an old acquaintance. Laughing Sal was memorialized by John Barth in his *Lost in the Funhouse* stories. He wrote, "You couldn't hear it without laughing yourself." Now her laughter bellows out at a push of a button, for which visitors line up to activate.

You're likely to have the last laugh when you see the collection of old-fashioned bathing suits dating back to the turn of the century. Visits to the beach were once so rare that bathers actually rented swimming attire. You'll see examples of these far-from-dapper rentals. There is also a daring number from the early 1900s made of ten yards of heavy wool. The bathing suit display shows progress from bloomers to bikinis.

In the museum's upper reaches are the popular models of eight well-known boardwalk hotels. These miniature buildings were re-created in every detail, even down to corner hinges and tiny tourists strolling the boardwalk, none, however wearing slogan-covered T-shirts.

Another interesting attraction not far from the Ocean City area is **Furnace Town**, a restored Nassawango Iron Furnace community. It is easy to imagine the miners, sawyers, colliers, molders, firemen, carters, draymen and bargemen who worked and lived here between 1832 and 1847. The furnace is one of the finest specimens still standing, and diagrams in the museum explain how the iron-making process worked. After seeing the furnace you can tour the double-forge blacksmith shop, smokehouse, broom house, 19th-century print shop, 1874 Old Nazareth Church and the country store where handcrafted items are still sold. During the summer months 19th-century crafts, like broom making, printing, weaving and gardening, are demonstrated from NOON to 4:00 P.M., although not all volunteers are on hand every day. There is even a living-history presentation on early Methodism and church lore. For those with more time there is a woodland nature trail with five boardwalk sections that cross a cypress swamp. If you plan to hike the trail take mosquito repellent.

The Ocean City Life Saving Station Museum is at the south end of the boardwalk in Ocean City, Maryland. The museum is open daily June through September from 11:00 A.M. to 10:00 P.M. In May and October the museum is open Thursday through Saturday from 11:00 A.M. to 4:00 P.M. During the rest of the year it is open on weekends from NOON to 4:00 P.M. A nominal admission is charged.

Furnace Town is open daily April through October from 11:00 A.M. to 5:00 P.M. A nominal admission is charged.

Directions: From the Beltway I-495/95 take Route 50 east across the Chesapeake Bay Bridge and through Salisbury to Ocean City. For Furnace Town turn off Route 50 at Salisbury on Route 12 south and travel 16 miles to Old Furnace Road. Turn right and travel ¾ of a mile; entrance is on the left.

The People's Place and Amish Farms

Question Quencher

From the air the area around Lancaster, Pennsylvania, looks like a patchwork quilt. The meticulously laid-out farmlands are carefully tended. Up close, as you drive along the rural roadways, you sense a simple way of life that harkens back to the early days of the American farmer. This impression of an uncomplicated lifestyle stems from the fact that farmers still practice the old methods, particularly the several thousand Old Order Amish who use no electricity or new-fangled farm machines.

Visitors are curious about the very different way of life here, but the Amish are anxious to protect their privacy. This conflict becomes evident if tourists try to take photographs of them. The Amish believe that picture taking violates Biblical teachings against graven images.

To learn about the lifestyle and beliefs of the Amish and Mennonites, visit The **People's Place** museum in Intercourse, Pennsylvania. The 28-minute documentary, *Who Are the Amish?* shown here captures the spirit and feelings of the "plain people." Viewers laugh, half in embarrassment, as a voice asks the questions tourists ask themselves but don't verbalize, such as why the Amish don't own or use automobiles or why they wear their unusual garb. If some of your questions aren't answered the staff will discuss the movie and clear up any lingering confusion.

People's Place offers "an adventure into another world," handling nine dimensions of Amish life and how they contrast with the mainstream or "English" lifestyle. As part of the transportation dimension visitors are invited to sit in the front seat of a buggy and operate the turn signals. You get to try on Amish bonnets, aprons or men's winter and summer hats. In a children's classroom you see pages of work from grade one through eight. Other subjects considered are the community spirit evident in such Amish practices as barnraising and quilting bees. There is also a collection of folk art.

People's Place is open Monday through Saturday 9:30 A.M. to 9:30 P.M. From November through March it closes at 5:00 P.M. Admission is charged. You will find additional information at the Book and Craft Shoppe. You can purchase beautiful handwork at the Old Country Store, which specializes in quilts. Thirty more food and craft shops called the Kitchen Kettle Village are located behind People's Place.

If you want to explore the Amish world beyond a museum, arrangements can be made at the Kitchen Kettle Village to take a 2½-mile buggy ride through the countryside. You'll experience what it's like to move slowly while cars race past. There is also the option of a short ten-minute ride around Intercourse.

Whether you pass slowly in an Amish buggy or drive along Route 772, see if you can spot the **Amish farms**. One sure clue is the lack of wires leading to a house. Many of the Amish farms have small produce and craft stands along the road.

If you want a closer look at an Amish farm there are three choices: The Amish Homestead, The Amish Farm and House, and The Amish Village. Although none of these is actually owned by an Amish family, the 71-acre **Amish Homestead** does have an Amish family in residence, although not in the farmhouse tourists explore. The Homestead provides a look at a grossdawdy, or grandfather, house. These extended farmhouses are popular with the Amish because they provide living quarters for family members of several generations. Here too you can take a buggy ride around the field after you tour the farm. The Amish Homestead opens daily 9:00 A.M. In winter, spring and fall it closes at 5:00 P.M. and in summer at 7:00 P.M. It is located at 2034 Lincoln Highway East, Route 30, in Lancaster.

The second option, the **Amish Farm and House,** gives you a look at a ten-room typical Pennsylvania-German stone farmhouse. After touring the house you can stroll around the farm buildings. Hours are daily 8:30 A.M. to 5:00 P.M. in spring and fall; winter closing is at 4:00 P.M. and summer 6:00 P.M. The farm is located not far from the Amish Homestead at 2395 Lincoln Highway East.

The **Amish Village** is in Strasburg on Route 896. Here you'll be given a tour of a typical Old Order Amish farmhouse. You can also visit a one-room schoolhouse and an operational blacksmith shop. Hours are daily 9:00 A.M. to 5:00 P.M. in spring and fall and until 6:00 P.M. in the summer. It is closed during the winter.

While in the area, don't miss the treat of eating in a family-style Pennsylvania Dutch restaurant. Regional specialties include "sweets and sours" as appetizers and a tempting array of desserts like shoofly pie and fruit cobblers. You have a choice of three or four main dishes and a variety of fresh vegetables.

For a list and map of these restaurants stop at the Pennsylvania Dutch Convention and Visitors Bureau at 501 Greenfield Road in Lancaster.

Directions: From the Beltway I-495/95 take I-95 north to the Baltimore Beltway I-695 and head west to Exit 24, I-83. Continue on I-83 to York, then pick up Route 30 east to Lancaster. The trip takes about two hours one way.

Wheaton Village

People Who Live in Glass Houses

Wheaton Village is an 88-acre reconstructed glassmaking town that evokes the Victorian era when the flames never died in the furnaces of south Jersey. The gingerbread architecture, village green, quaint one-room 1876 Central Grove Schoolhouse and the General Store replicate the turn of the century. You'll see thousands of examples of glassmakers' skills in the village museum, which boasts one of the world's largest glass collections, then watch skilled workers create glass objects in the still-operational 1888 factory.

The **Museum of American Glass** reveals the scope, complexity and artistry of glassmaking. Exhibits trace the development of glassmaking and give examples and a brief history for each pivotal era. The foyer itself re-creates a Victorian Cape May, New Jersey, hotel lobby. The chandelier once hung in Atlantic City's Traymore Hotel; the brass wall sconces decorated the walls of the Waldorf Astoria in New York. A series of period rooms include numerous decorative and utilitarian glass items. Particularly interesting are the elegant dining room and well-stocked kitchen.

In all, the museum has more than 7,500 pieces of American glass dating from 1609, when glassmaking began in the New World at Jamestown, Virginia. The first glass factory in the country was established in New Jersey as early as 1739.

The earliest pieces were functional and were used to store medicine and preserve food. The museum dispels the myth that the term "booze" is dervied from the E.G. Booz Bottle in which Old Cabin Whiskey was sold. The expression derives from the 16th-century English slang word "boozy," meaning drunk.

By the middle of the 19th century, craftsmen were creating decorative glass. One outlet for creativity was the crafting of paperweights, and the museum has many imaginative examples. To start your own collection stop at the village's Arthur Gorman Paperweight Shop. The selection here spans a wide price range from reasonable to extravagant (such as Tiffany glass and art nouveau pieces).

After the museum you'll be ready to see glass made at the 1888 **Glass Factory.** Carl Sandburg described this Millville factory as follows: "Down in southern New Jersey, they make glass. By day and by night, the fires burn on in Millville and bid the sand let in the light." They did indeed burn the factory fires seven days a week, 24 hours a day.

The fires still burn, but not as intensely. Three times a day (11:00 A.M., 1:30 and 3:30 P.M.) glassmaking demonstrations are given in the factory. A skilled craftsman explains the process and shows how a paperweight is made. If you want a hands-on experience, call ahead (609)825-6800 and make reservations to make your own paperweight. Only visitors 21 and older may register, and the fee in 1991 was $40. Both spectators and participants find it fascinating to watch as the glass takes shape and the flowers, leaves and bubbles are added.

Glassmaking is only one of the crafts demonstrated at Wheaton Village. In the **Crafts and Trades Row** you get to watch potters, weavers, tinsmiths, woodcarvers and lampworkers at work. Picturesque Victorian shops along Main Street include Dr. T.C. Wheaton Pharmacy (where you can sample homemade ice cream, sundaes and sodas from May through October), the Village Bookstore, the West Jersey Crafts Co., the Brownstone Emporium and the General Store.

Children appreciate the playground and miniature steam train, the C.P. Huntington, that leaves from the 1880 Palermo Train Station. The open-sided cars wind around the perimeter of the village; the ride is particularly scenic in the spring when the azaleas bloom and in the fall when the leaves are colored.

It is a mere 40 minutes from Wheaton Village to Atlantic City, and the contrast between the wooded paths at the glassmaking village and the glitzy boardwalk at the gambling Mecca is profound. Just 11 miles north of Atlantic City is the 20,000-acre Brigantine National Wildlife Refuge with an eight-mile, self-guided route leading past waterfowl impoundments.

Wheaton Village is open daily 10:00 A.M. to 5:00 P.M. April through December. Hours during the winter months depend on the weather; call for details. The village is closed on major holidays. Admission is charged.

Directions: From the Beltway I-495/95 take I-95 north to Wilmington, Delaware, where you will cross into New Jersey and take Route 40 east to Route 55. Continue on Route 55 south to Millville exit; signs mark the Wheaton Village entrance.

Zwaanendael Museum and Lewes
Delaware Dutch Treat

It sounds like a mythical kingdom—the land of the whale, the swan and the unicorn—but this symbolic trinity figured prominently in the tales of the founding of **Lewes** (pronounced Loo-is), Delaware.

Henry Hudson discovered the Delaware Bay in 1609, but the first Dutch settlers didn't arrive until 1631. They sailed on their ship *De Walvis* (the whale) into the quiet inlet where the Delaware Bay meets the Atlantic Ocean, and because the marshy region was abundantly populated by wild swans, the 33 newcomers called their settlement Zwaanendael, the valley of the swans.

The figurehead on their ship was not, as you might expect, a whale but a unicorn, part of the heraldic coat of arms of Hoorn, their hometown in Holland. The curious Delaware Indians were fascinated by this single-horned beast and wanted the Dutch to give them the large wooden talisman. When the Indians were denied it, they burned the stockade and massacred the settlers.

To see a model of the early settlement visit the **Zwaanendael Museum**. Despite their inauspicious beginning, this was not the end of Dutch efforts to establish an outpost in the area. Their second settlement suffered the same fate as the first, but from a new foe. On Christmas Eve 1673 the second enclave was burned by Calvert supporters from the neighboring Maryland colony who did not want the Dutch infringing on their territory. By 1682, the English had wrested control of the area and renamed the settlement Lewes.

Later on two occasions pirates attacked the town, and ultimately on April 6 and 7, 1813, during the War of 1812, the townspeople had to defend themselves against the British. This tumultuous history is covered in the museum.

The museum's collection includes a wide variety of domestic articles, handmade coverlets, quilts and samplers speak for the skills of yesteryear. China and silverware indicate changing tastes. There are also a few pieces of 17th-century pewter.

Another display is devoted to antique toys. An 1860s stagecoach is driven by a team of miniature horses. A later form of transportation is the 1922 Toonerville Trolley, with driver. There are also dolls, dishes, puzzles, cradles and carriages.

The medicinal display has a number of interesting features. Do you know the derivation of sugar coating? You'll find out when you read about the pill roller recovered from a drug store in Milton, Delaware. The paste, or main component of the pill, was placed on an iron cutter and sliced to size. Then the segments were put in a round box with sugar and shaken until they were properly shaped and coated.

The museum, built in 1931 to commemorate the 1631 settlement, replicates the Town Hall in Hoorn, Holland. The brick building with its colorful blue trim and red and white shutters has a statue of founder David Pietersen de Vries atop its peaked facade.

The Zwaanendael Museum, at Savannah Road and King's Highway, is one of 23 points of interest on the town's walking tour. A Lewes guide can be picked up at the Lewes Chamber of Commerce office in the Fisher-Martin House at 102 Kings Highway. If you prefer escorted tours, then join walks offered Tuesday, Thursday and Fridays at 10:00 A.M. by the Lewes Historical Society. They begin at the Thompson Country Store at 119 Third Street, part of a complex of restored 18th-century buildings.

You don't have to join the tour to explore this complex. Pick up penny candy at the old store, then check out the gift shop in a former blacksmith shop. You'll be able to tour a one-room "plank house," furnished as it would have been by settlers in the 1700s. The straw-filled mattresses in the sleeping loft and crude wooden kitchen furniture bespeak a spartan existence.

In contrast, the 18th-century Burton-Ingram House represents a much more elegant lifestyle. Lovely Chippendale and Empire furnishings from old Lewes families fill the rooms. The lower level of the house was constructed using ballast from the cargo holds of one of the first ships to dock at Lewes.

Also in the complex are the Hiram Burton House, which was furnished by a local antique dealer, and the Rabbit's Ferry House now used as an artist studio. This ferry house was built using a technique called brick-nogging. Bricks were laid between wooden beams and then white washed. Lastly, there is an 1850s Doctor's Office outfitted with old medical equipment.

The walking tour includes many more historic structures including the Maull House where in 1803 Jerome Bonaparte, the brother of Napoleon, reputedly brought his wife when stormy seas forced them ashore. Legend has it that Betsy Bonaparte would not take her seat at an elaborate dinner until the silver candlesticks from the ship were brought to the table.

A house that survived a barrage during the War of 1812 is known today as the Cannonball House and Marine Museum. The exterior still has a cannonball embedded in the wall, and inside you'll see nautical exhibits. Opposite the town post office is the 1812 Memorial Park where a defense battery stood. You'll see four large guns and a smaller one that were supposedly seized from a pirate ship. On the lower terrace of the park is a World War I naval gun.

After a morning's historical tour you can spend the afternoon at the beach. Lewes offers a choice of the Delaware Bay at the public beach or the Atlantic Ocean at **Cape Henlopen State Park.** This 1,200-acre park is located at the edge of Lewes where the bay meets the ocean. If you have the energy, you should climb Hamburger Hill on the Seaside Nature Trail. You'll be rewarded with a splendid view of the two lighthouses on the Delaware capes. The sand dunes at Henlopen were called a "miniature Sahara" by the *National Geographic*. It is the closest to Washington of any unspoiled ocean beach.

The Zwaanendael Museum is open at no charge Tuesday through Saturday from 10:00 A.M. to 4:30 P.M. The Lewes Historic Society Complex is open Tuesday through Friday 10:00 A.M. to 3:00 P.M. and Saturday 10:30 A.M. to 3:30 P.M. A fee is charged to tour these buildings. Cape Henlopen State Park is open daily during daylight hours.

Directions: Take the Beltway I-495-95 to Route 50 exit and proceed on Route 50 across the Bay Bridge. At Route 404 turn right and continue east past Bridgeville to the merge with Route 18 to Georgetown. At Georgetown continue east on Route 9 into Lewes.

Washington's Military Bands Summer Series

Free military concerts are presented from Memorial Day through Labor Day beginning at 8:00 P.M.

Mondays:	U.S. Navy Band–U.S. Capitol/west side
Tuesdays:	U.S. Army Band–Sylvan Theater on the Washington Monument Grounds
	U.S. Air Force Band–U.S. Capitol
Wednesdays:	U.S. Marine Band–U.S. Capitol
Thursdays:	U.S. Navy Band–Navy Memorial Plaza
Fridays:	U.S. Army Band–U.S. Capitol
	U.S. Air Force Band–Sylvan Theater
Saturdays:	Rotating branches–Navy Memorial Plaza
Sundays:	U.S. Marine Band–Sylvan Theater

Army Band:	(703)696-3399
Marine Band:	(202)433-4011
Navy Band:	(202)433-2525
Air Force Band:	(202)767-5658

Additional Programs:

The American Sailor. Presented every Wednesday at 9:00 P.M. from late May to September at the Washington Navy Yard waterfront. This is a multi-media presentation focusing on the history and character of the U.S. Navy. Reservations required to assure free seating. (202)433-2218

Concerts on the Avenue. From Memorial Day through Labor Day at the U.S. Navy Memorial on Thursday and Saturdays at 8:00 P.M. The Navy Band plays on Thursdays and other service bands rotate on Saturday evenings. (202)433-2525

Twilight Tattoo Series. From mid-July to late August on the Ellipse grounds between the White House and the Washington Monument at 7:00 P.M. There is a free pageant that combines the patriotic spirit and music of a traditional military parade with the history of the U.S. Army. (202)696-3570

Marine Corps Sunset Parades. Tuesday at 7:00 P.M. at the Iwo Jima Memorial featuring the U.S. Marine Drum and Bugle Corps and Silent Drill team. Free shuttle service from Arlington Cemetery Visitor Center.

Marine Corps Evening Parades. On Friday evenings at 8:45 P.M. from early May through August at the Marine Barracks, 8th and Eye Streets, SE. Reservations necessary to secure free seats. (202)433-6060

Summary Calendar of Events

Early:

Dupont-Kalorama Museum Walk—Dupont Circle & Kalorama Road Neighborhood, Washington, D.C. (202)387-2151. Eight galleries, museums and historic homes host a festive day of interactive tours, textile demonstrations and hands-on art programs.

Occoquan Days Craft Show—Occoquan, VA (703)494-7959. Several hundred craftspeople and artists from across the country take part in this annual event.

Strawberry Wine Festival at the Vineyard—Linganore Winecellars, Mt. Airy, MD (301)795-6432. Local arts and crafts are demonstrated and sold, music is provided and you can tour the winery and taste the new strawberry wine plus seven other grape and fruit wines.

Red Cross Waterfront Festival—Alexandria, VA (703)549-8300. A family-oriented festival featuring ship tours, boat races, nautical exhibits, water safety demonstrations, boat rides, an art show, music and numerous food booths. It's held along the picturesque Alexandria waterfront.

Antique Car Show—Sully Plantation, Chantilly, VA (703)759-5241. More than 350 antique, specialty and vintage vehicles, a craft fair and flea market, fashion show, entertainment, plus the chance to tour this 1794 historic house.

Deer Creek Fiddlers' Convention—Carroll County Farm Museum, Westminster, MD (410)848-7775. An old-fashioned musical competition; adding to the fun are craft demonstrations, country cooking and a chance to tour this historic farm house.

Harborfest—Town Point Park, Norfolk, VA (804)627-5329. Weekend-long festival featuring tall ships, boat races, nautical exhibits, ethnic food, boat parade, musical entertainment and fireworks. Considered by many the East Coast's premier waterfront festival.

Mid:

Militia Weekend—St. Mary's City, MD (301)862-0990. See a 17th-century militia encampment, observe camp life and weapons drills. The fun includes craft demonstrations.

Flag Day Celebration—Fort McHenry, MD (410)962-4299. At Fort McHenry where the sight of the flag still flying after the Battle of Baltimore inspired Francis Scott Key to write the national anthem, it is particularly appropriate to celebrate Flag Day. Band concerts, military drill teams and a "Pause for the Pledge" are part of the day's events.

Carroll County Arts Day–Carroll County Farm Museum, MD (410)848-7775. You can observe old-time crafts at this festival. Blacksmithing, quilting, spinning, weaving and pottery are

demonstrated. You can also enjoy an art show, musical
entertainment, country food and a tour of the 19th-century farmhouse.

Lily Pons Days—Lilypons Water Gardens, Buckeystown, MD
(301)874-5133. Water gardening techniques explained,
entertainment, art exhibits and refreshments plus the chance to see
the aquatic blossoms at this extensive commercial garden.

Children's Chautauqua Day—Glen Echo Park, Glen Echo, MD
(301)492-6229. Entertainment and art workshops for young visitors.

Late:

Festival of American Folklife—National Mall, Smithsonian,
Washington D.C. (202)357-2700. Music, crafts, ethnic foods and the
folk heritage of people from all across the country come together
each summer at this outdoor melting pot.

Gettysburg Civil War Heritage Days—Gettysburg, PA (717)334-6274.
A living history encampment, band concerts, Civil War lectures, a
reenactment of the Battle of Gettysburg and fireworks on July 4th
mark this annual commemoration.

Maryland Forces in Garrison–Fort Frederick State Park, MD (301)842-
2155. Reactivated Maryland Forces garrison the fort and bring to
life the days when this was a frontier outpost during the French
and Indian War (1755-1763). You can see marching, drilling and
training in the ranger tactics the Maryland Forces once used.

Zwaanendael Heritage Garden Tour—Lewes, DE (302)645-8073.
Walking tour of the historic area including the lovely gardens adds
a bonus to a day at nearby Rehoboth Beach.

JULY

Early:

National Independence Day Celebration—Washington Monument,
D.C. (202)619-7222. The finale of fireworks on the Monument
grounds caps off a day-long celebration that includes a dramatic
reading of the Declaration of Independence, a parade and a variety
of free entertainment.

July 4th Celebration—Harbor Waterfront, Annapolis, MD (410)263-
7940. Watch fireworks over the water after listening to a concert by
the Naval Academy Band.

Baltimore's Independence Day Celebration—Inner Harbor, MD
(410)332-4191. All-day fun with music, celebrities, jugglers and
plenty of available food capped off with fireworks over the harbor.

Old Time 4th of July—Maymont Park, Richmond (804)358-7166.
Croquet games, relay races and carriage rides provide family fun.
You can also enjoy the attractive gardens, tour the Dooley Mansion
and explore the animal habitats and children's farm. Lots of music
and plenty of food precede the fireworks.

4th of July Celebration—Colvin Run Mill, Great Falls, VA (703)759-5241. Children's contests, parade, brass band, mill tour and a reading of the Declaration of Independence.

Great Brunswick River Race—C&O Canal Historical Park, Lock 30, Brunswick, MD (301)694-6040. Homemade rafts and boats race on the Potomac River in this fun-filled community event.

Children's Colonial Days Fair—Yorktown Victory Center, Yorktown, VA (804)887-1776. Young visitors can play 18th-century games and participate in craft activities.

Mid:

Lotus Blossom Festival—Lilypons Water Gardens, MD (301)874-5133. Mix lotus blossoms, wine tasting and musical programs plus rides on a horse-drawn surrey. Crafts and country food also featured.

Civil War Life—Sully Plantation, Chantilly, VA (703)759-5241. Soldiers from units on both side camp, drill and skirmish. There is music and dancing of the period, a court martial is reenacted and there is storytelling.

Old Fashioned Games Day—Steppingstone Museum, Havre de Grace, MD (410)939-2299. Turtle races, frog jumping contests, children's games, puppet show, storytelling, clowns plus pony and hayrides make for a fun day.

18th-Century Market Fair—Claude Moore Colonial Farm at Turkey Run, McLean, VA (703)442-7557. A living history re-creation of a market fair in the early 1770s with merchants and craftsmen plying their trades.

Civil War Reenactment—Surratt House, MD (301)868-1121. Costumed volunteers re-create Civil War units. They set up camp and give rifle demonstrations.

Pork, Peanut & Pine Festival—Chippokes Plantation State Park, Surry, VA (804)294-3625. More than 200 craftspeople, entertainment and country cooking are part of this festival that celebrates the region's three main industries.

Late:

Virginia Scottish Games—Alexandria Episcopal High School, VA (703)860-5227. The two-day Celtic festival features pipers, highland dancers, drummers, fencers and fiddlers from 26 clans across the U.S., Canada and Europe. You can purchase Scottish food and wares in colorfully decorated tents. This is a rare opportunity to watch such ancient games as the caber toss, stone put, sheaf toss and haggis hurl.

Mountain Heritage Festival—Shenandoah National Park, Skyline Drive, VA (703)743-5108. Mountain crafts and music highlight this two-day event. There is clogging and square dancing.

Military Field Days—Fort Frederick State Park, MD (301)842-2155. The three major confrontations fought on American soil are represented. Hundreds of uniformed men set up camps, engage in tactical demonstrations and fight mock battles from the French and Indian War, the American Revolution and the Civil War.

Pony Round-Up and Penning—Chincoteague, VA (804)336-6161. Each year the wild ponies of Assateague Island are rounded up and they swim to Chincoteague where they are auctioned off. Those that are unsold are returned to Assateague. A Fireman's Carnival on Chincoteague coincides with this event.

AUGUST

Early:

Old Fashioned Corn Roast—Union Mills Homestead, MD (410)848-2288. This old-time festival is part of a tradition that goes back to 1797 when the Shriver family started their convivial corn roast. You can watch the corn being roasted on iron stoves and then partake of a barbecued chicken lunch. A span of 185 years of American rural life can be observed at the Union Mills Homestead.

Folk Arts Festival—Virginia Beach, VA (804)471-5884. Arts and crafts, entertainment, hands-on craft workshops for children and plenty of food highlight this popular annual event.

Old Fiddlers' Convention—Galax, VA (703)236-2184. For over 55 years this convention has met in Virginia. It's one of the oldest and largest fiddlers' conventions in the world.

Jonathan Hager Frontier Crafts Day—City Park, Hagerstown, MD (301)739-8393. Picnic along Hagerstown's Lake, enjoy a wide variety of frontier crafts and tour the historic Hager House and the Washington County Museum of Fine Arts.

Mid:

August Court Days—Leesburg, VA (703)752-6118. In colonial times the circuit court opening was an occasion for dancing, feasting and obtaining community news. You can relive an 18th-century court opening at this annual fair. There are craft demonstrations, over 100 craft booths, live music, a children's fair, pony rides, dancing in the street and reenactments of actual court cases. Vignettes illustrate various forms of colonial punishment.

Havre de Grace Art Show—Tydings Memorial Park, Havre de Grace, MD (410)879-4404. Over 300 artists and craftspeople exhibit and sell their work. Walking tours of this picturesque community add to the fun.

Balloon Festival—Flying Circus, Bealeton, VA (703)439-8661. Watch while operators inflate a number of hot-air balloons which float in colorful profusion over the air field. This is in addition to the regularly scheduled air show.

Late:

Civil War Reenactment—James Long Park, Manassas, VA (703)335-7060. Relive the battle that started the Civil War.

Jamestown Children's Festival—Jamestown Settlement, VA (804)229-1607. English games of the 17th century can be enjoyed by young visitors. Indian arts and crafts, nautical demonstrations and militia drills are also part of this event.

Draft Horse and Mule Day—Oatlands, Leesburg, VA (703)777-3174. See how draft horses worked during the South's plantation era. Food, music and crafts add to this day on the farm.

Maryland Renaissance Festival—Crownsville, MD (410)266-7304. Beginning in late August and continuing until mid-October this 16th-century English fair features games of chance, crafts and period entertainment.

International Children's Festival—Wolf Trap Farm Park, Vienna, VA (703)642-0862. This three-day event features performances on five stages plus hands-on workshops. Groups from around the world perform.

Photo: Richard Frear

Autumn leaves frame beautiful Dark Hollow Falls in the Shenandoah National Park, Virginia. Courtesy National Park Service.

Arlington National Cemetery

Honor Guard

Arlington National Cemetery is one of the area's most poignant reminders of our country's past. The land itself is linked to two of America's most revered families: the Washingtons and the Lees. George Washington Parke Custis, the foster son of our Founding Father, built a home here designed to be a treasury of Washington heirlooms. In 1804 Custis married Mary Lee Fitzhugh and years later their daughter, Mary Anna Randolph Custis, married Robert E. Lee in the family parlor. After the Civil War, the house, because it was owned by Robert E. Lee, was confiscated by the Federal government.

The Arlington grounds were used to bury slain Civil War soldiers, not by plan but by happenstance. In May 1864, President Lincoln and General Meigs visited the wounded tended in tents on the grounds of Arlington House. The fatalities were increasing and a burial site was essential; thus it was decided to use the estate's land for the dead. By the end of the conflict, thousands were buried at Arlington. Many of these soldiers were unidentified; there are 2,111 Civil War unknowns buried beneath a massive sarcophagus south of Arlington House. Later, veterans of earlier conflicts were interred here, many unidentified.

The most famous memorial in the U.S. is the **Tomb of the Unknowns.** An honor guard parades before this special monument where on Armistice Day 1921 an unknown soldier from World War I was entombed. On Memorial Day 1958, during the Eisenhower administration, unknown American soldiers from World War II and the Korean conflict were interred. Today an impressive ceremony takes place daily when the 3rd U.S. Infantry guards change duty here—every 30 minutes during the summer and every hour the rest of the year. At night the guard changes every two hours.

You can pick up a map of the cemetery and find the tombs of men who made American history—Philip H. Sheridan, William Jennings Bryan, John J. Pershing, George C. Marshall, Walter Reed, Robert E. Peary, Richard E. Byrd, James V. Forrestal, John Foster Dulles, Audie Murphy, Omar Bradley, Virgil Grissom, Roger B. Chaffe and two presidents of the United States—William

Howard Taft, the 27th president, and John Fitzgerald Kennedy. An enternal flame marks the grave of the assassinated president. His two children who predeceased him are buried there as is his brother Robert Kennedy. Many who remember the days of Camelot make a pilgrimage here.

Another oft-visited site is the **Iwo Jima Memorial** north of the cemetery. This 78-foot sculpture is carved after a stirring photograph taken of the Marines raising the U.S. flag during World War II. During the summer you can see the impressive Sunset Review every Tuesday evening. This formal Marine pass-in-review military exercise includes trooping the colors and marching the troops (all in their formal dress uniforms) past the commanding officer for an exchange of salutes. The Marine Band plays for the sunset program.

Arlington National Cemetery is open April through September from 8:00 A.M. to 7:00 P.M. From October through March it closes at 5:00 P.M. Cars may not be driven through the cemetery, but there is a tourmobile, which allows a glimpse of the major areas. Frequent stops permit you to get on and off the open-sided buses.

Directions: Arlington National Cemetery is directly across the Potomac River from Washington via the Arlington Memorial Bridge.

Blackwater National Wildlife Refuge and the Ward Museum of Wildfowl Art

Duck, Duck, Drake

Blackwater is a wildlife refuge located on the Atlantic Flyway, the migratory path for millions of birds. The flyway extends from Canada to Florida with Blackwater near the center. This Maryland refuge established in 1932 encompasses 16,667 acres of tidal marshland, freshwater ponds and woodland areas. It has become one of the chief wintering areas for Canada geese as well as a haven for the endangered southern bald eagle and the Delmarva Peninsula fox squirrel.

In peak migratory periods you may see as many as 40,000 Canada geese and close to 20,000 ducks. More than 250 species of birds have been spotted at the refuge including snow geese, mallards, black ducks, pintail, widgeon, teal, whistling swans and shovelers.

The best way to see Blackwater is to take the five-mile **Wildlife Drive,** which winds along a canal and through the marshland. Often you come close enough to the ten-pound geese that you feel you could touch them. An observation tower enables you to get a panoramic view of the unspoiled landscape. Be sure to bring binoculars. It is exhilarating to see thousands of honking geese flying in V-formations. Canada geese are social birds; they form close-knit family groups. When flying in formation the older birds will alternate in the lead position.

Blackwater National Wildlife Refuge and the Wildlife Drive are open daily during daylight hours. The Visitor Center is open 8:00 A.M. to 4:00 P.M., closed on major holidays. There is a nominal entrance fee for the Wildlife Drive; there is no charge for the Visitor Center. If you have time, there are two trails within the refuge, the ½-mile Woods Trail and the ⅓-mile Marsh Edge Trail. These give you a chance to spot a wide variety of birds.

While in the area you can extend your day by driving farther into southern Dorchester County and heading across the scenic Narrow Ferry Bridge, connecting Hoopers Island with the mainland. The picturesque fishing villages on Hoopers Island are fun to explore.

Another option to include on your excursion is a stop at the **Ward Museum of Wildfowl Art** whose new quarters opened in 1992. Formerly on the campus of Salisbury State University, the museum is now in a wooded waterfront setting along Shumaker Pond. If you visit this museum after Blackwater you will appreciate the accuracy and realism of the finely crafted decoys on display; they seem ready to take wing.

Operated by the Ward Foundation, the museum traces the development of decoy carving from its early days when carvings were first made to aid hunters. The oldest decoy is an Indian reed-and-feather decoy that dates from 1000 A.D. Decoy carving remained primarily functional until 1918 when the passage of the Migratory Bird Act prohibited market hunting of wildfowl to supply restaurants. It was then that decoy carving became an art or craft form.

Decorative decoys varied with geographic regions. At the museum you see examples from 14 areas including two from Maryland, Crisfield and Susquehanna Flats, and two from Virginia, the Back Bay and the Eastern Shore. Seeing the annual winners in the World Championship Wildfowl Carving Competition (sponsored by the Ward Foundation) are worth any extra time and mileage it may take you to get here. They are exquisite! It is worth noting that one of the pioneer decoy carvers, Lem Ward, started selling his decoys at 50 cents and eventually earned around $2,000 a piece.

The museum's move to greatly expanded quarters broadened the scope of their exhibits. New areas include a habitat theater with a program focusing on the impact of man on the ecosystem that sustains wildfowl and a carver's workshop where visitors watch the resident carver.

The Ward Museum of Wildfowl Art is open Tuesday through Saturday 9:00 A.M. to 5:00 P.M. and Sundays 11:00 A.M. to 5:00 P.M. Admission is charged. There is an orientation film in the Welcome Theater. The Ward Museum Gift Shop and Signature Gallery has a fine collection of artistic collectibles.

Directions: From the Beltway I-495/95 take Exit 19, Route 50, to Cambridge, then go right on Route 16 to Church Creek. From there take Route 335 for four miles and turn left on Key Wallace for the Visitor Center. For the Ward Museum of Wildfowl Art continue on Route 50 to Salisbury, then turn right on Beaglin Park Drive. The Museum is on your left at the corner of Beaglin and Shumaker Road.

Blue Ridge Parkway

Peaks Your Interest

Some part of the spectacular 470-mile **Blue Ridge Parkway** lies within a one-day drive of half the population of the United States. On peak autumn weekends they all seem to visit at once.

Proper timing of your trip is crucial if you want to catch the autumn foliage at its peak. It's worth the effort to see the glorious hues from the mountain overlooks. A mid-week trip is best for avoiding the worst of the crowds. Traditionally the fall color starts in early September and often extends into November with the peaks occurring around mid-October. The timing and intensity of the foliage depend on such variables as the amount of rainfall, the temperature and sunlight and the elevation of the terrain.

The Blue Ridge Parkway begins in Waynesboro, Virginia, where the 105-mile Skyline Drive (see selection) through Shenandoah National Park ends. The parkway extends to Cherokee, North Carolina, where the Great Smoky National Park begins. It was Virginia Senator Harry F. Byrd who suggested a scenic parkway connecting the two national parks. Byrd obtained President Franklin Roosevelt's support for the project, and construction began on September 11, 1933. It wasn't until September 11, 1987, that the last segment of the parkway around Grandfather Mountain in North Carolina was dedicated.

The splendid Blue Ridge Parkway is scenic in any season. The first 356 miles follow the eastern edge of the Appalachians. The last 114 miles travel through the southern end of the massive Black Mountains and through the Craggies, the Pisgahs and the Balsams before reaching the Great Smoky Mountains.

The parkway designers wanted motorists to savor the scenery, not rapidly pass it by. There are ten visitor centers and 275 turnouts that give travelers a chance to get out and enjoy the overlooks, trails and areas of special interest.

Rockfish Gap, Virginia, is milepost zero on the Blue Ridge Parkway. The lowest elevation on the parkway is at milepost 63.6 where the elevation is 649 feet. At this spot there is a footbridge over the James River that leads to a restored canal lock. You can continue on the trail to a scenic river bluff. To reach the highest elevation on the parkway, 6,053 feet, travel into North Carolina to milepost 431 at Richland Balsam. The scenic delights are the parkway's principal draw, but the cultural and historical significance of the area is also highlighted. A hiking trail at Humpback Rocks, milepost 5.8, takes visitors to a reconstructed mountain farmstead. Here you'll get a firsthand look at what life was like for those who had the courage to live in this wilderness. The homestead is furnished, and the occupants who "live-in" from May through October re-create the past.

One of the parkway's most popular spots is **Peaks of Otter**, milepost 85. Even before European exploration, this dramatic site attracted visitors. Iroquois and Cherokees following the "warrior's path" came here. The trail was later used by those carrying supplies for the troops fighting in the Revolutionary War. By 1845, there was an inn, or ordinary, operated by Polly Wood. She served travelers in this part of southern Appalachia until 1859. **Polly Wood's Ordinary** still stands, and on selected weekends the park hosts living history programs at the inn. Also still standing is the Johnson farm, built about 1850 and worked through the 1930s.

In 1867 Robert E. Lee climbed to the summit of the Peaks of Otter, named for the rocky promontory overlooking the valley. You can take one of the six trails or ride a bus to the summit. An easy and short walk is the Elk Run Loop, .08 miles, or you can have a more vigorous workout on the 3.3-mile moderately difficult Harkening Hill Loop.

Perhaps the most picturesque spot along the Virginia portion of the parkway is **Mabry Mill**, milepost 176. Ed Mabry was a West Virginia coal miner before he moved to the southern highlands of Virginia. He established a blacksmith shop in this rural region. During the summer months the Park Service operates the old blacksmith shop as part of its mountain industry exhibit. A tanner and shoemaker demonstrate their skills as well. But it is the weathered, gray frame mill beside the quiet stream that attracts visitors. No matter what the season, the banks of the mill stream are filled with amateur and professional photographers.

The Virginia portion of the parkway has four campgrounds (703)982-6490, and a lodge at Peaks of Otter (703)586-1081 and cabins at Rocky Knob, milepost 174 (703)593-3503. North Carolina has five camping spots plus Bluffs Lodge (919)372-4499 and Pisgah Inn (704)235-8228.

Several interesting mountain handicraft shops attract visitors along the North Carolina parkway. At milepost 258.6 there is the Northwest Trading Post; the Parkway Craft Center is at milepost 292.7 and the Folk Art Center is at milepost 382. Scenic spots in North Carolina include Linville Falls, the Cascades, Craggy Gardens and Crabtree Meadows. To obtain a calendar of events on the parkway, write the Blue Ridge Parkway Association, P. O. Box 453, Asheville, North Carolina 28802.

Directions: From the Beltway I-495/95 take Route 66 west and pick up Skyline Drive at Front Royal. Continue south until you hit the Blue Ridge Parkway at Rockfish Gap. Or take I-95 south from the Beltway to Richmond, then go west on I-64 to Waynesboro and pick up the parkway.

Carroll County Farm Museum

Rural Roots

There is something about autumn air that encourages city dwellers to head for the country. Colorful fall foliage beckons and roadside stands offer apples, pumpkins and the last of the summer vegetables.

It's also bracing to see what life used to be like on the farm. If you want to go way back to the colonial age, visit the National Colonial Farm and St. Mary's (see selections). The 19th century comes alive at Oxon Hill Farm (see selection) and here at the **Carroll County Farm Museum** in Westminster, Maryland.

Don't let the word museum mislead you; the Carroll County Farm Museum is not a stuffy, sterile exhibit of equipment. This farm museum re-creates the way of life of a land-owning, independent farm family of the 19th century. Families like the one depicted here grew enough crops to feed themselves and their livestock. They canned and preserved the excess food and saved the seeds to replant. The farmer and his sons worked the fields using old-fashioned horse power. They acquired mechanized equipment very gradually.

The farmhouse you'll visit was built in 1852 as a county almshouse. Workers tilled and planted the fields from the 1850s until 1965 when the house became a county museum. Six rooms of the farmhouse reflect the decorating style of the Victorian era. Every surface is either covered, draped, festooned or layered. Tables were covered by not one but three decorative cloths. Ornately framed pictures have lace swags; designers thought this drew the eye from one picture to the next.

There is a treasure trove of gadgets in the kitchen, many of them ingeniously specialized. Most visitors easily identify the apple corer, but few guess the use of the whipped-cream churner. The major difference between these devices and our modern kitchen tools is the power source.

Guides dressed in period costumes are available to answer questions and identify any of the old tools and equipment you can't place. After your house tour the guides will direct you to the craft barn. This two-story building has small workshops for weavers, spinners, quilters, tinsmiths, potters and blacksmiths.

The farm also has an assortment of farm animals and support buildings including a spring house, smokehouse, animal pens and barns. One barn houses a collection of horse-drawn and steam-powered machinery. Since Carroll County was one of the first regions to get rural free delivery in 1899, the exhibit includes one of the first mail wagons.

The farm museum is in the middle of a 140-acre park. The park offers nature trails and picnic tables under the trees beside a small pond.

The Carroll County Farm Museum is open Saturday and Sunday from NOON to 5:00 P.M. from May through October. During July and August it also opens Tuesday through Friday from 10:00 A.M. to 4:00 P.M. A gift shop sells items made by artisans who work in the craft barns. The shop is open Tuesday through Friday from 10:00 A.M. to 4:00 P.M. There are special weekend events scheduled throughout the year at the farm.

Directions: From the Beltway I-495/95 take I-95 north to the Baltimore Beltway, I-695, and go west to I-795. Take I-795 north to Route 140. Continue north on Route 140. When you are one mile south of Westminster turn left off Route 140 onto Center Street. Travel ½ miles and the Carroll County Farm Museum is on the right off Center Street.

Catoctin Mountains and Frederick

Sunshine and Moonshine

Autumn foliage provides a colorful frame for the 78-foot cascading Cunningham Falls in the **Catoctin Mountains** of Frederick County, Maryland. Sixteen trails cover 30 miles of Cunningham Falls State Park and adjoining Catoctin Mountain Park.

Even out-of-condition travelers can negotiate the short five-minute walk from the parking area off Route 77 to the falls overlook. Be sure to bring a camera, as the area is exceptionally photogenic, and bring binoculars for a closer look at the woodland birds. Two other trails to the falls begin at the William

Houck Recreation Area. The Lower Cunningham Falls Trail is moderately difficult; the Cliff Trail is strenuous.During the summertime, you can swim at the 40-acre Hunting Creek Lake. There is a bathhouse and two sandy public beaches. On weekends it gets crowded; arrive before 10:00 A.M. to find a parking spot. There is no admission to the park, but there is a per car fee at the beach area. Canoes are available for rent during the summer and into the fall months.

The mountain streams are popular fishing spots. Hunting Creek is a "catch and return" fly-catching stream. You can try your luck in the many mountain streams or the lake. Fishermen over 16 need a license. Other park options include camping, picnicking, sailing, horseback riding on designated trails, cross-country skiing and snowshoeing.

Across Route 77 from the falls is the Visitor Center for Catoctin Mountain Park. If you take the Blue Blazes Trail, you'll get to one of the area's most intriguing attractions, an old whiskey still. During the summer of 1929 revenue agents raided the Blue Blazes Still, one of the biggest Maryland stills ever destroyed, with an output of more than 25,000 gallons. Today, on weekends from NOON to 4:00 P.M. Memorial Day through October, volunteers retell stories about the dramatic raid and explain the still's operation.

Since 1970 National Park Service staffers have demonstrated how these old stills worked. They originally used a Smokey Mountain still seized by Treasury agents. But parts eventually wore out, and salvaged pieces were used to rebuild the model you see today.

Another reminder of bygone days is the remains of the Old Catoctin Furnace at the southern end of Cunningham Falls State Park just off Route 15, on Route 806. This was one of three furnaces that supplied munitions for the Continental Army during the Revolution. Posted signs explain how the furnace operated.

The Catoctin Mountain parks are located outside Thurmont. If you want to take a midday lunch break, you might stop at the town's Cozy Restaurant, at 105 Frederick Road. This spot has an international reputation because of the proximity of Camp David, the President's mountain hideaway, just eight miles away. They offer a hearty table with more than 65 items and an assortment of roughly 50 desserts. In 1979 Leonid Brezhnev visited Camp David, and many of his delegation stayed at Cozy's rustic motel.

Nearby **Frederick** has several interesting dining spots. On Market Street you'll find Bushwaller's. It looks like an old saloon but actually opened in 1981. The building was constructed in 1840 for a group of French refugees from the slave uprising in Haiti. The restaurant is relatively new, but the old photographs and memorabilia suggest a long history. Just up the street is the Provence, where the rear dining room overlooks the herb garden that provides fresh seasonings for the entrees.

If you want to return home with a taste of the country, stop at McCutcheon's Apple Products on S. Wisner Street and choose from mouth-watering country-style apple butter, pear butter, jellies, preserves and cider.

Include time to explore Frederick's historic district. In 1776, the Maryland legislature established a military post in Fredericktown. Hessian soldiers captured by the Continental Army were used to construct the barracks and supply depot. The barracks were used again during the Civil War, this time as a hospital for the wounded from the nearby Battle of the Monocacy. The Barracks are open by appointment; call (301)663-8687.

Frederick is immortalized in John Greenleaf Whittier's 1864 poem about Barbara Fritchie in which he wrote:

> The clustered spires of Frederick stand
> Green-walled by the hills of Maryland.

Barbara Fritchie is buried in Mount Olivet Cemetery, six blocks from her home at 154 West Patrick Street, where she reputedly waved her famous Union flag at the Confederate General Stonewall Jackson. The episode is recorded in the same poem:

> "Shoot if you must, this old gray head,
> But spare your country's flag," she said.

Other important figures from American history are buried in the same cemetery including Francis Scott Key, who wrote "The Star Spangled Banner." Key shared a law practice in Frederick with Roger Brooke Taney. Key eventually moved to Baltimore, but Taney, who had married Key's sister Anne, maintained a country home in Frederick. Furnished with family heirlooms, the Roger Brooke Taney House at 121 South Bentz Street can be toured by appointment.

Directions: From the Beltway take I-270 west to Frederick. Then take Route 15 to Thurmont where you will pick up Route 77 west. Take Route 77 west for both Catoctin Mountain Park Visitor Center and the parking turnoff for the easy trail to Cunningham Falls State Park. For Frederick continue on I-70 to the Patrick Street/Historic District exit and follow the signs to the Visitor Center.

Chincoteague National Wildlife Refuge

Watch the Waterfowl and Wild Ponies

As cold weather moves down the Atlantic coastline, so do the migratory birds. A major stop on their journey is **Chincoteague National Wildlife Refuge**, which comprises the Virginia end of Assateague Island. In fact, a large number of geese, swans and other waterfowl spend the winter at this refuge.

During Waterfowl Week in late November, a 7½-mile service road that is usually closed to automobile traffic is opened to allow motor access to the interior of the refuge. The road takes you past man-made fresh water ponds. These ponds, or impoundments, are diked to trap rain water. The vegetation that grows in the impoundments helps feed the thousands of waterfowl that visit each fall. The refuge was established in 1943 primarily for migratory waterfowl that stop here from November to March, but more than 300 other species of birds and animals have been identified within the refuge as well.

The advantage of exploring the refuge when the service road is open is that you are likely to get a close look at the **wild ponies.** These ponies were featured in the book and movie, *Misty*. One of the legends surrounding these horses maintains that they are descendants of survivors from a wrecked Spanish galleon. The ponies have a rounded appearance; it almost seems they have on saddles rather than extra girth. This weight is attributable to the large amount of salt in their diet of saltmarsh grasses. It is obvious that these wild ponies are strangers to curry combs. Their manes and coats are shabby and untrimmed. The forelocks on many cover their eyes. It is very important not to feed these ponies; a little bit of "junk" food multiplied by all the visitors to Chincoteague could lead to an unhealthy dependence. Also, it is not safe to feed or pet these wild ponies; every year some visitors are bitten or kicked.

Other residents of the island are the Sika deer, Oriental elk that were transported to the island by local residents in 1923 before the refuge was established. Chincoteague hardly needs exotic animals to attract visitors; just walking along the deserted, natural beach on a pleasant fall day can provide a relaxing change of pace. Should you tire of looking for your own shells, you can visit the **Oyster Museum** in the nearby town of Chincoteague. The museum is open on weekends from 11:00 A.M. to 5:00 P.M. and charges a nominal admission.

If you can't make the trip to Chincoteague during Waterfowl Week there are shorter automobile routes open all year, as well as hiking and bicycling trails. One interesting path leads to the Assateague Lighthouse, now more than 100 years old. Although visitors are not permitted to climb the tower, it offers a thrilling sight thrusting out of the flat marshland into the sky. Bicycles can be rented from several of the businesses in the town of Chincoteague, and interpretive tours are available on selected weekends. During the summer, on the last Wednesday in July, Chincoteague holds the annual pony swim and penning—one of the region's most popular events. The Virginia ponies swim across the Assateague Channel to Chincoteague. A community carnival adds to the fun.

While in the area you might want to stop at the **NASA/Wallops Flight Center** open for self-guided walking tours Thursday through Monday from 10:00 A.M. to 4:00 P.M. and on federal holidays except Thanksgiving, Christmas and New Year's. You can spend a few minutes or a few hours depending on your interest.

Wallops is responsible for preparing, assembling and launching space vehicles to obtain scientific information. There have been 19 satellites launched from Wallops Flight Center. The Visitor's Center offers a video presentation on the work of NASA as well as exhibits on America's space flight program. One of the most popular items is a moon rock collected during the *Apollo XVII* voyage.

Directions: Take Beltway Exit 19, Route 50, to Salisbury, Maryland. From there follow Route 13 to Virginia, five miles past the state line turn left on Route 175 to Chincoteague. Wallops Visitor's Center is on your right on Route 175. Take a left at the red light entering Chincoteague for the Oyster Museum. Then make a right on Maddox Boulevard and continue to the Chincoteague National Wildlife Refuge. The Visitor Center will be on your left as you enter the refuge.

Ellicott City

Change of Pace Place

Sometimes it's hard to appreciate the attractions of a new destination when you read about it. One man's "charming" may be another's "so what." A spot that to some may be picturesque may offer nothing of interest to others. A visit to **Ellicott City**, however, fosters a more uniform reaction—there's something for everyone.

The town has rebounded from disasters that would have signaled the end of a less determined community. The town was founded in 1772; not quite a century later, in 1868, a torrential flood washed away homes and businesses. The financial loss of over a million dollars was compounded by the death of 50 townsfolk. When Hurricane Agnes swept through Maryland in 1972, the waters of the Patapsco River once more flooded the streets of this low-lying town.

Yet another disaster struck on November 14, 1984, when a raging fire destroyed many shops along Main Street. But despite these setbacks, the town has endured, improved and prospered. Each time the residents rebuilt, they carefully maintained the old-fashioned appearance of the small stores, even the narrow streets and winding alleys.

On one side of Main Street an arcade of boutiques has a wide porch in the back overlooking a sparkling stream. Across the street, the antique and specialty shops, many dating back to the early 1800s, are built right into the granite hills. A few use natural niches in the rock wall as shelves for pottery and art objects. The walls, always moist, have a cavern-like appearance because of the presence of underground streams. The old stone buildings Ann Tongue built in the 1840s for the mill hands, now called **Tongue Row,** house antique and craft shops.

In many of the shops you can pick up a guided walking-tour map of Ellicott City. Things to see include an early settler's log cabin built in 1780 and the ruins of the Patapsco Female Institute, a finishing school for young ladies. This was one of four institutions of higher learning in town. The school, founded in 1837, was one of the finest in the country. Tuition was $300 a year. Another historic site is the old Colonial Inn and Opera House where John Wilkes Booth reputedly made his debut.

Three Ellicott brothers from Bucks County, Pennsylvania, founded the town. They called it Ellicott's Lower Mills. The brothers purchased 700 acres of land and water rights along the Patapsco River. They planted wheat and built a gristmill. To carry their crop to Baltimore they built roads; to ship their grain to more distant ports, they made a wharf.

In 1830 Ellicott City became the first railroad terminus in the country. Peter Cooper, working at the Mount Clare Station in Baltimore, developed an engine he called the "Teakettle" (others dubbed it the "Tom Thumb"). According to onlookers it resembled a water heater bolted to a farm wagon. The pipes were war surplus musket barrels.

Cooper's concoction first ran on August 24, 1830. Reports on the historic run marveled that the volunteers were able to take notes as they traveled, proving that the mind could function while moving at the dizzying speed of 14 mph. Four days later the Tom Thumb made its first journey to Ellicott City, 13 miles from Baltimore. This was not the run that fueled the story about the race between the iron horse and the gallant gray. There actually was such a race but it occurred a month later. During the latter run the fan belt broke, slowing the train, and that is how the horse won the race.

Even as late as 1850 when the Tom Thumb was making regular runs to Ellicott City scheduled trains were still far from the norm. There were only 50 miles of track in the country. The **B&O Railroad Station Museum** in Ellicott City's 1830 granite station captures these early years of railroading. Visitors to the museum particularly enjoy the scale model of the first 13 miles of track. As you watch the museum lights dim and lights begin to twinkle along the track, you are transported back in time. Children enjoy this authentic demonstration of a real "little engine that could."

The museum also presents an 18-minute audio-visual program on the early days of the B&O Railroad. There are displays of railroad memorabilia and the Freight Agent's Quarters are furnished to look as they once did. It is astonishing to learn that in the first few years, the agent's salary was only $400 a year, a meager sum even in the 1830s.

Most of the shops and eateries of Ellicott City are open daily. The B&O Railroad Museum is open Friday through Monday from 11:00 A.M. to 4:00 P.M. (the museum closes at 5:00 P.M. but admissions cease an hour earlier). It is closed on major holidays. Admission is charged.

Directions: From the Beltway I-495/95 take I-95 north and then exit on Route 175. Follow Ellicott City signs onto Route 108 and continue into the community.

Fallingwater

Mr. Wright Can't Be Wrong

Each year thousands of visitors travel to Mill Run, Pennsylvania, to see one of the country's most architecturally innovative buildings. **Fallingwater,** perhaps the most famous residence designed by Frank Lloyd Wright, lies within a day's journey of Washington.

Wright believed in organic architecture, and he incorporated the natural environment within the design of this private residence. Cantilevered out over the rushing mountain waterfall, Fallingwater seems to grow from the earth as naturally as the trees around which the rooms are angled. Huge boulders are used for the flooring and fireplace. One of the most felicitous touches is in the windows. They are designed to capture the sound of the falling water. A few of the narrow hallways in the house suggest the enclosed space of a cave, but the expanse of windows in the main living areas brings the outside in.

Wright built Fallingwater in 1936 as a summer weekend retreat for Edgar J. Kaufman, a Pittsburgh department store owner. Mr. Kaufman's son studied architecture at Wright's workshop in Taliesin, Arizona, and later gave the house to the Western Pennsylvania Convervancy.

It took a year to build Fallingwater and the contractor who built it was aghast at the design. He was reluctant to remove the supports and would do so only under Wright's personal supervision. Wright's vision was sound, and Fallingwater stood! Wright expended a great deal of attention on the interior and many of the furnishings are built in. They are very simple and fit the contours of the room.

Exhibits in the Visitors Center detail Wright's career. Guided tours of Fallingwater are conducted from April to mid-November from 9:00 A.M. to 4:00 P.M. Tuesday through Sunday. During the winter, tours are given on weekends from 11:00 A.M. to 3:00 P.M. Reservations are suggested, especially on weekends; call (412)329-8501. There is a restaurant at Fallingwater where you can enjoy a light lunch.

Not far from the harmony and beauty of Fallingwater is the natural beauty of **Ohiopyle State Park**. The Ohiopyle Falls divided the Youghiogheny River into the Middle and Lower Yough. Canoeing is popular on the 9-mile upstream Middle Yough. Below the falls, is the faster, more challenging 7.6-mile Lower Yough, where approximately 100,000 white-water enthusiasts raft each year. Within Ohiopyle's 18,719 acres there are 41 miles of hiking trails and 9 miles of bicycling trails. When winter snows cover the park the trails are used for snowmobiling, tobogganing and cross-country skiing.

Directions: From the Beltway, I-495/95 take I-270 west to I-70 and continue west to the Pennsylvania Turnpike. Take the turnpike west to Exit 9 and take Route 31 east to Route 381/741, which you will take to Mill Run. Continue south on Route 381 for Ohiopoyle State Park.

Fire Museum of Maryland

A Flaming Success with Small Fry

Most of us are familiar with modern fire-fighting equipment, but we have little idea of how it developed. A visit to the Fire Museum of Maryland, in Lutherville, fills in some of the missing details. The museum was founded in 1971 and houses a permanent collection of 60 fire-fighting vehicles dating from 1822. It is one of the country's largest fire museums, and anyone who has ever yearned to be a fireman will enjoy it.

One of the oldest pieces is the 1888 Clap and Jones horse-drawn, steam-pumping engine. This venerable piece was used to fight the Baltimore fire of 1904 that razed a great portion of the downtown area. Other interesting pieces are the 1908 American La France aerial ladder, the 1897 American steamer and a

1905 Hale water tower. Unlike some museums, this one offers more than a visual experience. Visitors ring the fire bell, sound the siren, listen to ongoing fire calls and operate an old pump engine. One thing you will discover is that fire equipment is neither strictly utilitarian nor always red. Many companies have special parade equipment. Some of the engines and trucks are white, green (what firemen use to call slime lime), or maroon. There is even an all-blue ladder wagon on display.

Volunteers will explain fire-fighting procedures at the watch desk. From desks like this communities were protected during the 1940s and 50s. You will learn who and what determines whether a fire is declared a single or a five-alarm fire. The museum contains smaller equipment such as hand lanterns that burned kerosene or whale oil, brass trumpets that were used to call the men to a fire and old fire buckets. A Wells Fargo safe, old fire alarm, telegraph equipment and an 1882 music box are all part of the memorabilia. In addition, two movies are shown at no charge: one on fire safety and the other on fire-fighting history.

The Fire Museum is a private collection, run by a nonprofit company manned by volunteers. It is open Sundays from 1:00 to 5:00 P.M. May through November. Special tours can be arranged by appointment; call (410)321-7500. A nominal admission is charged.

While you are in the area, continue on York Road for seven miles north and explore the Valley View Farms Country Store in Cockeysville. With its 100 Christmas trees decorated with more than 5,000 ornaments, it claims to be the country's largest and most complete Christmas shop. You can purchase ready-made ornaments or all the material needed to make your own. A large collection of music boxes, nutcrackers, carved nativity creches and numerous other holiday finery are also available. The Christmas Shop is open daily from mid-September through December 24.

Directions: From the Beltway, I-495/95 take I-95 north to Baltimore Beltway, I-685, and go west towards Towson. Get off at Exit 26 and go north on York Road, Route 45, for two blocks. You will see the Fire Museum on your right, behind the Heaver Plaza office building.

Ladew Topiary Gardens

Whimsical Delights

Hunting is a blood sport that often turns sensitive novices green, but not the deep hue you'll see at the Ladew Topiary Garden in

Monkton, Maryland. At **Ladew Gardens**, the horse, rider, fox and hounds are all clipped yews.

These whimsical figures are the creations of Harvey Ladew, an enthusiastic hunter who set a record for his day by fox hunting on two continents within a 72-hour period. Ladew hunted with renowned figures like England's King Edward VII.

The topiary camel is a reminder of another friend of his, T.E. Lawrence, better known as Lawrence of Arabia. Even when riding with the desert Bedouins, Ladew wore a dinner jacket against the evening chill, maintaining his reputation as one of the best-dressed men in America. This high-living lifestyle was possible because his family had made a fortune manufacturing leather belts used in heavy industry.

In 1929 Ladew purchased a 22-acre retreat in rural Maryland. He transformed the old farm house into a delightful country estate. He created a unique garden with 15 color-coordinated rooms, or garden areas. According to the Garden Club of America, Ladew's creations rank it as "the most outstanding topiary garden in America." Besides the hunt scene and camel, you'll see a topiary giraffe, goat, reindeer, rabbit, scotties and even an appealing unicorn.

To gain a perspective on Ladew's garden, stand on the terrace of the manor house and look down towards the Great Bowl. A corridor formed by a high green wall more than a third of a mile long draws your eye down the green expanse. Topiary swans, on top of the green wall, swim on waves of clipped yews. Arched doorways and windows in the wall hint at the wonders of the adjoining gardens.

Harvey Ladew liked to frame his vistas, to direct the eye of the beholder. In his garden tea house, he placed an ornate gold frame around one of the paneless windows. A label on the frame reads: "The Everchanging Landscape." The facade was once part of the ticket booth at London's Tivoli Theater.

Few gardens reveal so much about their creator. On the steps leading to the orchard, this life-long bachelor carved a Chinese proverb he evidently appreciated: "If you want to be happy for a week, take a wife. If you would be happy for a month, kill a pig; but if you would be happy all your life, plant a garden." The orchard, which he called the Garden of Eden, has a statue of Eve offering Adam an apple.

Many visitors say "amen" when they read the words inscribed on his sundial: "I am a sundial and I make a botch/Of what is done far better by a watch." The lighthearted approach that pervades the garden carries over into **Ladew's home** (both are included on the National Register of Historic Places).

This is clearly the spot to disabuse visitors of the idea that all historic houses are stuffy and dull. Ladew's home reveals a man of multiple interests and high spirits. You have to like a man who is so excited about his new home he invites guests to a party before the house renovations are complete. Some of the ladies at his first party were less enthusiastic when rough floor nails snagged their dresses, but few turned down an invitation from this eligible bachelor. Still their patience must have been tried when at another gathering he served both guests and his prize horse at the table, and from the same silver set!

His love of horses and hunting shows on the china, clocks and wall hangings as well as in paintings. Ladew did some of the art on the walls. In the suite used by his sister, a frequent if not always tidy guest, Harvey painted a chest of drawers with bits of lingerie dangling from the open drawers. He also painted two chairs on each side of the chest, which also have items strewn in disarray. More of Harvey Ladew's paintings are displayed in his studio.

Ladew rarely accepted the word impossible. On one of his trips to England, he purchased a massive oval desk that proved too big to fit anywhere in his home. He solved the problem by adding another room to the house. The oval library he built to accommodate the desk is included in Helen Comstock's book *100 Most Beautiful Rooms in America*. Being Harvey, he added certain whimsical touches like the secret panel he could use to escape dull parties. He also put a tennis net under his hunt table to hold his empties.

After touring Ladew's house and gardens visitors often remark that it must have been fun attending parties here. Ladew was a genuine Renaissance man; his was a world where imagination had free rein and price was no obstacle.

A framed note from T.E. Lawrence hangs on one wall. It reads: "Everything everywhere is changing." Ladew's death in 1976 did not seem to change the world he created, however.

Ladew Topiary Garden is open mid-April through October, Tuesday through Friday from 10:00 A.M. to 4:00 P.M. and on weekends NOON to 5:00 P.M. The last house tour starts one hour before closing. The Ladew Cafe serves lunch. Admission is charged. You can purchase a combination ticket that includes house and gardens or you can just tour the gardens. For additional information call (410)557-9466.

Directions: From the Beltway I-495/95 take I-95 to the Baltimore Beltway, I-695, and take that west to Exit 27, Dulaney Valley Road, Route 146. At a fork in the road, Route 146 will become Jarrettsville Pike. Ladew is five miles past Jacksonville on the right at 3535 Jarrettsville Pike.

Land of Little Horses and Gettysburg National Military Park

Horseplay and Sabre Rattling

Although most travelers head for Gettysburg to see the battlefield and historic monuments, you should add to your outing a stop at a different attraction—the **Land of Little Horses**.

Young children who are often unenthusiastic about trekking across a battleground are charmed by these toy-size horses. The Lilliputian steeds, only slightly bigger than German shepherds, come in all breeds and colors: Appaloosa, Clydesdale, Arabian, English trotter, pinto, palomino, black and many others. As the horses are gentle and well-behaved, children can pet their long, silky manes. You can put youngsters on one for a quick picture at no charge. A ride around the compound, even if on a lead-line, is a genuine adventure. Other farm animals like goats and sheep are in the paddock beside the nature trail.

This farm is living proof that travel is broadening. When ex-sea captain Tony Garulo visited Argentina he became fascinated with the miniature horses bred by Julio Cesar Falabella and his family who had been developing their breeds since the 1860s. One of their prize stallions was the 20-inch-high Napoleon, who sired the parents of many of the horses you'll see when you visit this farm. After Garulo obtained an agreement with the Falabellas to be their exclusive representative in the United States, he brought 51 horses to his Gettysburg farm in 1971. Over the years interest in these picture-perfect horses has grown as has the farm; only the horses have remained small. The delightful miniatures are natural performers. They jump and dance and respond to commands. One of the stars can untie knots in handkerchiefs. The counting horses will answer math problems by scratching a hoof against the ground. The small Clydesdales pull wagons just like their full-size look alikes. (Wagon rides are available for a nominal fee.)

Falabellas are endearing, and a list of their owners reads like a roster for the "Lifestyles of the Rich and Famous": Princess Grace, Lord Mountbatten, the Aga Kahn, Charles de Galle, Aristotle Onassis as well as Frank Sinatra, Queen Elizabeth and the Dutch royal family. Demand for the horses is as high as the price.

You can see the miniature horses from April to November from 9:00 A.M. to 5:00 P.M. During the summer the farm stays open until 6:00 P.M. In the spring and fall shows start in the 800-seat arena at 11:00 A.M., 1:00 and 3:30 P.M. From July through Labor Day shows are at 11:30 A.M. and 2:30 and 4:30 P.M. Admission is charged and picnic tables are available. There is also a gift shop and snack bar.

Don't leave the area without driving through the **Gettysburg battlefield** where in July 1863 the forces of North and South met in one of the bloodiest battles in American history. It was the turning point of the Civil War, the second and last time that Lee attempted to invade the North. It takes about two to three hours to cover the entire battlefield with the help of an auto-tour tape. A stop at the Visitor Center will orient you to the events that happened here and the various means for learning about them. The Visitor Center has an Electric Map orientation program, at a nominal charge, on the three-day battle. Just next door is the Cyclorama Center and a free 10-minute film about the battle. For a small fee you also can see the sound-and-light program shown against the backdrop of the 356-foot cyclorama painted in 1881 by Paul Philoppoteaux. This is one of only three cycloramas in the country. Gettysburg Park roads open daily from 6:00 A.M. to 10:00 P.M. The Visitor Center and Cyclorama are open from 9:00 A.M. to 5:00 P.M. Closed on major holidays.

If time permits include a visit to the **Eisenhower National Historic Site**—the only home that Dwight D. Eisenhower ever owned. The Eisenhowers purchased the 189-acre farm in 1950, but it wasn't until after John Kennedy's inauguration in 1961 that they retired here.

The farm, intact since they left it years ago, looks like the Eisenhowers have just stepped out on an errand. The comfortable home gives you an intimate look at the country's 34th president.

In the fall the Gettysburg area is appealing because it lies in orchard country. Markets are well stocked with apples and apple products like cider and apple butter. You can watch the apples being picked, then purchase a basketful at a discount from the orchard's stand.

Directions: From the Beltway I-495/95 take I-270 to Route 15W. Continue on Route 15W until it intersects Route 30W. Once you are on Route 30W you will see signs. From Route 30W make a left onto Knoxyln Road. To return by an alternative route through the apple fields, take a right out of Gettysburg onto Route 116. When you reach the Ski Liberty trails, turn left. This road will take you through the orchard area and back onto Route 116 at Fairfield. Continue west on Route 116 to the intersection with Route 97 and take that into Emmitsburg. Take a right on Route 15 and follow this to I-270 at Frederick.

Lexington

Lessons From the Past

George Washington, Robert E. Lee, Stonewall Jackson, George Marshall and Matthew Maury all had connections with **Lexing-**

ton, Virginia. And all wanted to share their ideas and ideals with future generations.

George Washington endowed the Lexington college that now bears his name. In the **Washington & Lee University** Chapel there is a museum on the lower level where you see his faded christening dress. There is also a letter written by the college in 1796 thanking Washington for his $40,000 endowment of James River Canal Company stock. University students to this day receive a small residual from this stock.

When Robert E. Lee accepted the presidency of the college less than six months after the surrender at Appomattox, he was 58 years old and his annual salary was $1,500. When he first arrived, Lee lived in the president's house that Stonewall Jackson had shared with his in-laws during his 14-month marriage to Elinor Junkin, the president's daughter.

Before Lee embarked on the construction of a new president's house, he supervised the construction of the college chapel. Helping him with this project was his son, General George Washington Custis Lee, a professor at neighboring Virginia Military Institute. Work began on the chapel in early 1867, and it was completed in time for the commencement ceremonies of 1868. Lee attended daily worship services with the students for the rest of his life.

Lee's office was on the lower level of the chapel. When you see it today it looks just as it did on September 28, 1870, when illness forced him to take to his bed. The remains of his beloved horse Traveler are buried on the grounds outside his office. Traveler spent the last years of his life sheltered in the brick stable adjoining Lee's house. After the Civil War, newspaper accounts reported that souvenir hunters pulled so much of Traveler's mane and tail the old war horse shied away from visitors and needed a refuge. The college museum exhibits mementoes from the Lee years.

The Lee family crypt is beneath the chapel. Three days after Lee died on October 12, 1870, the college was renamed Washington and Lee University. The Lee Chapel and Museum are open Monday through Saturday from 9:00 A.M. to 4:00 P.M. from mid-October to mid-April. The rest of the year it is open until 5:00 P.M. Sunday hours are 2:00 to 5:00 P.M. The campus is off Main Street.

Stonewall Jackson lived and taught in Lexington before the Civil War. At the **Jackson House** you can see a short slide program introducing the young, handsome Virginia instructor who once memorized his lectures standing at his desk in this house. His students thought he was a dull lecturer and nicknamed him "Square Box," but after his legendary feats during the war he was called Stonewall. The house is furnished with personal possessions and period pieces to match the inventory taken after Jackson's tragic death following the Battle of Chancellorsville in 1863.

The Stonewall Jackson House at 8 East Washington Street is open 9:00 A.M. to 5:00 P.M. Monday through Saturday and Sunday 1:00 to 5:00 P.M. During the summer the house stays open until 6:00 P.M. The last tour is given a half hour before closing. Admission is charged.

The first 23 cadets at **Virginia Military Institute** reported to their sole instructor on November 11, 1839. This was the country's first state-supported military college. Over the next 150 years VMI-trained officers made significant contributions to our country's history. In the VMI Museum you can see the spartan living quarters of the young cadets. The museum includes a uniform Jackson wore while teaching at VMI and the battlefield raincoat he was wearing when he was accidentally shot in the arm by his own men on May 3, 1863. The bullet hole is clearly visible in the rubber coat. There are also reminders of the 157 young cadets who joined Breckenridge's troops at the Battle of New Market. Ten cadets died in this battle on May 15, 1864.

Another illustrious professor was Matthew Fontaine Maury who taught physics. He closely followed Jackson's years at the college; in fact, he used the same microscope that Jackson had used. Maury was known as the pathfinder of the seas because of his detailed sea charts. John Mercer Brooke, who also taught at VMI, designed the armor for the ironclad *Merrimac*. An outstanding graduate remembered in the museum is George Catlett Marshall; his museum and library is located elsewhere on the parade grounds.

The VMI Museum is open at no charge Monday through Saturday 9:00 A.M. to 5:00 P.M. and Sundays 2:00 to 5:00 P.M. The museum is in the Jackson Memorial Hall on the VMI parade grounds just off Lexington's Main Street.

George C. Marshall selected VMI over West Point because he wanted to be near Virginia's Civil War battlefields. He spent his spare time studying the military strategies of the war, especially the tactics of former VMI instructor Stonewall Jackson.

As a staff officer in the Philippines in 1913 and four years later in France, Marshall's military genius was compared to that of Jackson's. At the **George C. Marshall Museum** exhibits trace Marshall's military career through World War II. Marshall was the only professional soldier to be awarded the Nobel Peace Prize, and his service as a statesmen and diplomat is also documented.

The museum is open at no charge Monday through Saturday from 9:00 A.M. to 5:00 P.M. From November through March the museum closes at 4:00 P.M.

You have to enjoy a town that doesn't take itself too seriously even in the midst of this wealth of historic landmarks. The house next to the Jackson House has its own plaque. It reads: "N.O.N. Historic Marker, On This Spot, February 20, 1776, Absolutely Nothing Happened."

Directions: From the Beltway I-495/95 take I-95 south to Richmond. At Richmond take I-64 west to Lexington. Take the Route 11 exit off I-64. Just outside Lexington, Route 11 forks to the right onto Main Street. All of the city's historic sites are well marked. For information on additional Lexington attractions stop at the Lexington Visitors Center at 102 East Washington Street, or call (703)463-3777.

Mercer Mile

Concrete Creations

Henry Mercer's awesome concrete structures transport visitors to another world and another age. They appear to belong in medieval England, not contemporary Bucks County, Pennsylvania.

The imaginative Mercer took the maxim "a man's home is his castle" literally. Like a young boy playing with blocks, Mercer arranged clay pieces on a table until he had constructed a castle-like structure with 30 rooms, 12 baths and soaring towers, gables, parapets and chimneys. Once he found a pleasing layout he created a plaster of Paris model then started to build it in earnest. He used no architect drawings, no diagrams, nothing to indicate scale—just his own inner vision.

When Mercer began construction of **Fonthill** in 1908 he used a small stone farmhouse built in 1742 as the nucleus of his project. Over it and around it, he poured concrete to create three powerful arches strong enough to support the concrete ceiling. Mercer worked for four years on his castle, using eight to ten unskilled local laborers at $1.75 a day—they worked for ten hours, six days a week.

Innovative architectural features include the elaborate vaulted tile ceilings and the split-level design that allowed a viewer in the large salon to see stairways and rooms all merging at different levels. Mercer incorporated intricate tile designs throughout the house. Visitors marvel at the brocade tiles that decorate the fireplace in the morning room and the arrangement of Persian tiles in the central hallways. One of Fonthill's most engaging areas is the Columbus Room where Moravian tiles depicting the discovery of the New World swirl across ceiling, floor and walls. Mercer, in fact, once called his home "a castle for the New World."

Long before Mercer completed Fonthill, this restless creator embarked on yet another extraordinary project, a tile factory. The cloister-like design of Mercer's concrete **Moravian Pottery & Tile Works** is reminiscent of California's Spanish missions. Parts of this structure are copied from the San Juan Capistrano, Santa Barbara and San Luis Rey missions. The factory is busy once more as the old equipment, tools and molds are still being used to turn out Mercer's unique designs. Tours provide a deeper appreciation of his artistic genius.

Mercer completed both his home and factory in 1912 and waited two years before beginning the **Mercer Museum**, his third and last concrete extravaganza. It too was a castle, this one designed to display Mercer's collection of 15,000 pre-industrial tools, including such oversize items as a Conestoga wagon, a whaling boat and a stagecoach.

Mercer organized his tools by crafts and by use, like those needed for building shelters, preparing food and making clothes. After primary needs were met, there were tools for learning, amusement, transportation, law and a myriad of other subjects. Brightly painted tavern signs and intricately crafted weathervanes fill the halls. Everywhere you look there is an abundance of objects. At Mercer's death the collection numbered 25,000 items, and it has since grown to 40,000. Every bit of space is used. You'll see a fire engine dangling from a balcony and baskets and cradles hung in profusion. Henry Ford remarked in 1922 after a tour that this was "the only museum I've been sufficiently interested in to visit."

It takes all day to cover these three concrete creations. They are open daily from 10:00 A.M. to 5:00 P.M. Admission is charged. It is easy to see the tile factory and museum on a walk-in basis, but reservations are advisable for Fonthill where guided tours are given on the hour, with the last beginning at 4:00 P.M. To make reservations call (215)348-9461.

Directions: From the Beltway I-495/95 take I-95 north to Philadelphia then head north on Route 611 to Doylestown, where it becomes S. Main Street. After entering town turn right onto Ashland, then make another right onto Pine Street where you will see the Mercer Museum on your right. Less than a mile away and well marked are the Moravian Pottery & Tile Works on Swamp Road, Route 313, and Fonthill Museum on East Court Street.

New Castle

Old Riches in New Castle

New Castle has escaped the incursions of commerce and change; it remains a microcosm of Delaware's historical past. The four flags flying over the Old Court House only hint at the town's fascinating beginning. Historically, **New Castle** suffered an identity problem; in its first 30 years its name changed four times and its sovereignty five times. It was settled by the Dutch who lost, regained and again lost control. Other colonial powers that vied for this territory were the Swedes and the British. Each time it changed hands the name changed. Finally, it became part of the newly emerging United States.

To untangle this rich cultural mix, take the New Castle Heritage Trail that begins beneath the four flags. The **Old Court House** was built on Delaware Street in 1732, the year George Washington and Delaware leader John Dickinson were born. Reflecting these early years are a fully restored pre-Revolutionary courtroom and a colonial assembly room.

As you leave the Old Court House you will see the town green, which was literally pegged out by Peter Stuyvesant, the town's one-legged founder and first administrator. Stuyvesant built Fort Casimir, his name for the settlement, in 1651 on land purchased from the Indians. Three years later the fort fell to the Swedes, but Stuyvesant recaptured it in 1655 when the Dutch gained all of the territory Sweden claimed in America.

Their triumph was brief because soon England claimed all of the Dutch possessions in the New World. New Castle and the surrounding area became part of the crown's grant to William Penn. In fact, it was at New Castle that Penn landed when he reached America in 1682.

It is the brick British courthouse that survives; the wooden Dutch courthouse on the village green was burned to the ground by a prisoner during an attempted escape. New Castle lost a landmark, but justice wasn't entirely thwarted; the prisoner was hanged from a tree on Stuyvesant's green.

A landmark from the days of Dutch settlement that has survived is the **Old Dutch House Museum,** on Third Street facing the green. The sloping eaves of this cottage make it look more Old World than New. The house is furnished with interesting oddities. In the parlor you'll see an assortment of *klumpin,* Dutch wooden shoes. A 1665 ship's chart hangs on the dining room wall; modern sailors may have trouble getting their bearings on this outdated map. This is the oldest of the three house museums in New Castle. The second, the **Amstel House Museum,** at fourth and Delaware Streets, dates from 1738. Antique collectors appreciate the teapots that line the cupboard shelves, but the real conversation piece is the battered blue umbrella resting in the parlor corner. Cross-stitched on the umbrella is William Read's name, giving substance to New Castle's most beguiling legend. The story is that William Read was carrying this umbrella one stormy night when the wind loosened his grip and carried the umbrella out into the Delaware River where it became entangled in the sails of a clipper ship bound for China. A year later the ship returned, the captain called on Mr. Read and returned the umbrella. This tale is the basis for a children's book sold in New Castle.

A story rooted more firmly in documented history recounts the details of George Washington's visit to the Amstel House for a wedding reception on October 30, 1784. New Castle Judge James Booth described the occasion: "The Great Man stood upon the hearthstone and kissed the pretty girls—as was his wont."

William Read's family home is the third and most elegant house museum in town. Known as the **George Read II House,** 42 The Strand, it was built between 1794 and 1803. This is New Castle's most impressive property with interior and exterior fanlights, intricately carved woodwork crafted in the punch-and-gouge style and a perfectly proportioned entrance hall with arches ever so slightly reduced as the series progresses to create a harmonious visual impression.

Two distinct decorative periods, a full century apart, are used at the Read house. Some rooms reflect the 1820s when the Reads lived here, while others are in the style popular in the 1920s when the home belonged to the Philip Lairds. The gardens have also been restored.

These three properties are only a few of the lovely homes that line the streets of New Castle's historic district. As you stroll along the highly irregular brick sidewalks (do be sure to wear walking shoes) you'll see homes that date from the 1690s to the 1830s.

There are several dining establishments where you can continue to enjoy New Castle's Old World ambience. The historic David Finney Inn, (302)322-6367, facing the village green is decorated with antiques and old ship models. The lunch and dinner menus change daily. The 1809 Arsenal, also facing the green, is now the New Castle Inn, (302)328-1798. You can enjoy colonial and regional fare at this historic spot.

The Old Dutch House and Amstel House are open March through December on Tuesday through Saturday 11:00 A.M. to 4:00 P.M. and Sunday 1:00–4:00 P.M. They are open weekends only in January and February. The George Read II House opens an hour earlier. Admission is charged at each house.

Directions: From the Beltway, I-495/95, take I-95 north. Just before the Delaware Memorial Bridge take Route 141 south. This leads into New Castle.

Skyline Drive

Oh, Shenandoah!

Riding the crests of Shenandoah National Park is the aptly named **Skyline Drive**. It stretches 105 miles through the Shenandoah National Park from Front Royal to Waynesboro, Virginia, where the Blue Ridge Parkway begins (see selection).

This famed mountaintop drive has only four entrances—Front Royal, Thornton Gap, Swift Run Gap and Rockfish. The speed limit is a leisurely 35 miles per hour, so this is not a drive to take when you are in a hurry. It is impractical to stop at all 71 outlooks, but most travelers do stop often, lured from their cars by the breathtaking vistas. Skyline Drive is at its best in the fall when nature's palette bedecks the trees with burnished gold, rich russet, pumpkin orange, brilliant scarlet and mellow yellow.

The recreational facilities within Shenandoah National Park and Skyline Drive were created during Franklin D. Roosevelt's administration by the Civilian Conservation Corps. Over-settlement had depleted the game and shrunk the forest, but in the years after Congress established the park in 1926, the land and wildlife returned to their former glory. There are more than 100 species of trees and abundant game. Deer are a common sight. In addition to the forested area, **Big Meadows,** an expansive open area, is resplendent in the spring when the wildflowers bloom. Later in the summer the berry bushes bear fruit.

Driving Skyline Drive is undoubtedly the best way to cover the park, but try to plan your day so you have time to hike. There are over 500 miles of hiking trails in **Shenandoah National Park**. You can take short walks or opt to trek part of the 95-mile Appalachian Trail, which runs roughly parallel to Skyline Drive. A popular favorite is the **Old Rag Mountain Trail**, considered by many hikers the most spectacular in the northern Blue Ridge. This trail has a 1.2-mile obstacle-strewn course around and under boulders and natural tunnels. If you want to cover part of the **Appalachian Trail**, take the 6.25-mile hike from Fishers Gap to Skyline Drive. This trail offers incredible views from Franklin Cliffs. You also can branch off and take a side trail to the top of Hawksbill, the highest elevation in the park at 3,860 feet.

Horseback riding on the 150 miles of trails is another way to explore the park. Horses can be rented from stables at Skyland Lodge and Big Meadows. Other recreational options are canoeing, tubing or rafting the **Shenandoah River.** There are several outfitters in the region including Shenandoah River Outfitters (703)743-4159, Blue Ridge Outfitters (304)725-3444 and River and Trail Outfitters (301)834-9952.

Some of the interesting trails are beneath the surface in huge limestone caverns. There are seven such formations in the area, but the best is **Luray Caverns** where amazing, dripping stalactites still grow as they have for millions of years. The base rock in the cavern was formed over 400 million years ago in the Paleozoic age. No colored lights or special effects mar your appreciation of the soaring formations and quiet crystal pools. The one major man-made addition is viewed by almost all visitors as a plus; in fact the Great Stalacpipe Organ was featured on "Ripley's Believe It or Not" television show.

At Luray you can hear a recital on the 47 bells of the Luray Singing Tower built atop the caverns. These 45-minute programs are given during the summer on Tuesday, Thursday, Saturday and Sunday at 8:00 P.M. In the spring and fall they are given on weekends at 2:00 P.M. Luray Caverns also operates a Historic Car and Carriage Caravan, which stays open one-and-a-half hours after the last cavern tour. This museum showcases 75 vehicles including a 1927 Rolls Royce that once belonged to Rudolph Valentino. Luray Caverns is open daily year-round at 9:00 A.M. During the summer the last tour is at 7:00 P.M.; in the autumn it is at 6:00 P.M. and in the winter months it is 5:00 P.M. on weekends and 4:00 P.M. during the week.

If you want to include one more cavern, stop at **Skyline Caverns** near Front Royal. These are claimed to be the world's only known anthodites, called the "orchids of the mineral kingdom." The anthodites are slow growers, gaining only an inch every 7,000 years. Shenandoah Caverns near New Market has its fans who appreciate the sparkling Diamond Cascade and the immense Grotto of the Gods.

Civil War buffs will want to stop at **New Market Battlefield Park**. This 260-acre park has a Hall of Valor where you get an overview of the Civil War battles that took place in Virginia. A movie tells the story of the 247 Virginia Military Institute cadets who joined General John Breckinridge's troops to win the last Confederate victory in the Shenandoah Valley. Outside is the Bushong Farm around which the battle was fought. The farmhouse is open in the summer. The battlefield park is open daily 9:00 A.M. to 5:00 P.M. On the Sunday before May 15 the Battle of New Market is re-enacted.

You can extend your outing by staying overnight at the Skyland Lodge or Big Meadows Lodge, both within Shenandoah National Park (703)999-2221. There are also two resorts just outside the park, Bryce Mountain (703)856-2121 and Massanutten Village (703)289-9441.

Directions: From the Beltway I-495/95 take I-66 west to Front Royal and pick up Skyline Drive.

Strasburg Rail Road

Ride the Rails to Paradise

How can you resist a trip to Paradise? Steam trains departing daily from **Strasburg Rail Road**, the nation's oldest short-line railroad, travel to a quiet picnic spot in Paradise, Pennsylvania. This is an ideal getaway for the extended family; grandparents can regale the younger generation with tales of traveling on the network of rails that crisscrossed America. It is also a chance to experience an authentic operational railroad in contrast to the cars that carry crowds around most of the larger theme parks.

You can't stay in Paradise, alas. The 45-minute round trip takes you through the picturesque Lancaster farmland. From the train's windows you will glimpse straw-hatted Amish farmers working the fields with plows drawn by horses and mules. The somber clothes of the Amish hang neatly on the wash line outside the immaculate white farmhouses, and in front of the barns you'll see their black buggies. The entire experience provides a sense of slipping into a time warp.

There are reminders of the past wherever you look. Trains depart from a 1892 Victorian railroad station. Adding to its visual appeal is an old water tower and several pieces from the line's rolling stock. The entire panorama seems designed for a period movie, and indeed several of the railroad cars have been used in films. An open observation car and several others made a colorful backdrop in the movie *Hello Dolly*. The world's oldest standard-gauge coach, called the Willow Brook, shared billing with Elizabeth Taylor in *Raintree County*.

You can climb aboard several of these interesting old cars, including the private coach of the president of Reading Railroad, which once epitomized traveling elegance. With its separate sitting, dining and sleeping areas the car cost $100,000 to build in 1916. Designer touches include cut-glass ceiling lamps, lace-curtained windows and mahogany paneling inlaid with rosewood. There are those who claim that Harry Truman used this car in his famous 1948 whistle-stop campaign across the country.

Preservationists restored the cars in the Strasburg collection to the way they looked in the late 1800s. They have puffer-belly engines, plush seats, inlaid wood paneling, kerosene lamps and potbellied stoves. When you ride aboard one of these coaches, the conductor will move down the aisle punching your ticket. He'll also answer your questions and tell stories about the early days of rail travel. If you want, you may disembark for a picnic, but you have to bring your own supplies.

It's easier and more in keeping with the train theme to eat at the nearby Red Caboose, a local restaurant located in an actual dining car. There are rooms available in coach cars for overnight guests. Each converted caboose has either regular or bunk beds plus a fully equipped, though tiny, bathroom. There are even television sets hidden in the potbellied stoves. Call (717)687-6646 for details.

This area is a Mecca for train enthusiasts. Directly across from the Strasburg Rail Road is the **Railroad Museum of Pennsylvania** that offers a treasure trove of railroad memorabilia plus a substantial collection of rolling stock. The best vantage point to get an overview of the museum's collection is from the second floor observation bridge. From there you can see all the cars on the museum's four tracks. More than 31 classic locomotives and railroad cars date from 1835 to the present. Platforms give you a glimpse into the windows of these old Pullmans, passenger cars, mail and baggage cars. There are still more cars behind the museum although many of these will go indoors once the museum completes its expansion project. You can easily spend hours wandering around this fascinating museum.

If the life-size cars remind you of the train sets from your childhood then head over to the nearby **Toy Train Museum** opposite the Red Caboose. Here you get a miniaturized view of railroading as you study the cases filled with train models. Three layouts show standard gauge, American Flyer "S" gauge and "O" gauge trains. About 200 toy trains chug around the tracks. This museum also serves as the headquarters of the Train Collectors Association.

Another spot you shouldn't miss is the **Choo Choo Barn** and its elaborate 1,700-square-foot model train layout. Thirteen trains travel through some 130 animated scenes. Every 20 minutes the scene switches to a nightime view. The shop that sells tickets sells just about everything a model train enthusiast could possibly want. This is a great spot to visit at Christmas time.

If time remains be sure to explore **Strasburg's Main Street,** part of the town's National Historic District. This street was once part of the Conestoga Highway, the first westward route from Philadelphia. The district has at least a dozen log houses; the Christopher Spech House dates back to 1764. Other historic buildings date from the 18th and 19th centuries. On a hot day there's no better place to stop for a treat than the Strasburg Country Store and Creamery where old-fashioned ice cream is served at an 1890 soda fountain.

The Strasburg Rail Road is open daily from mid-March through November. Closed on Thanksgiving. There are special Santa Claus runs the first two weekends in December. Call (717)687-7522 for current steam train schedule. The Railroad Museum of Pennsylvania is open 9:00 A.M. to 5:00 P.M. Monday through Saturday and NOON to 5:00 P.M. on Sundays. From November through

April the museum closes on Mondays. The Toy Train Museum is open Monday through Sunday 10:00 A.M. to 5:00 P.M. from May through October and on weekends only at that time in April, November and the first two weekends in December. The Choo Choo Barn is open daily 10:00 A.M. to 5:00 P.M. from late March until mid-November. During the summer months it stays open until 6:00 P.M., and it is open weekends only in November and December.

Directions: From the Beltway I-495/95 take I-95 north to the Baltimore Beltway and head northwest towards Towson. Take Exit 24, I-83 north to York, Pennsylvania. At York take Route 30 east through Lancaster, then turn right on Route 896 to Strasburg.

Sugar Loaf Mountain

Sweetens Nature

The goal of many day trips is to find a good vantage point from which to enjoy and appreciate nature's bounty. One of the best views, particularly during the autumn foliage display, is from the top of the 1,283-foot **Sugar Loaf Mountain** near Dickerson, Maryland.

You can see to the south Virginia's Bull Run where the first battle of the Civil War was fought; to the west, Catoctin and the Blue Ridge Mountains; and to the north, the Frederick Valley. Numerous historic records contain reports of action on or near Sugar Loaf. In 1775, General Braddock passed by on his way to the disastrous Battle of Fort Duquesne where he lost his life. The mountain was used as a Union lookout post during the Civil War, and in 1862 a Union sentry atop Sugar Loaf spotted General Robert E. Lee leading his men across the Potomac before the Battle of Antietam. After that bloody encounter, wounded men from both north and south were treated in log cabins that still stand at the base of the mountain.

Sugar Loaf Mountain rises up in dramatic contrast to the farmland at its foot. It was charted as early as 1707 and named by early pioneers. Its shape recalled to them the sugar loaves their wives and mothers prepared.

The mountain was acquired by Gordon Strong after he discovered it while on a vacation in 1902. He bought the property gradually over the years, and by 1912 he had built a Georgian colonial estate high on the mountain slopes. He named his home, and the land on which it stood, Stronghold. The Strongs entertained many distinguished guests. When President Franklin Delano Roosevelt visited in the early 1940s he wanted to acquire the mountainside estate as a presidential retreat. He was persuaded instead to turn his attention to the 10,000 acres in Thurmont, which the government already owned. There he built his presidential retreat and named it, at Gordon Strong's suggestion, Shangri-La. President Eisenhower renamed it Camp David, in honor of his son.

When you visit you'll understand why President Roosevelt was so taken with Sugar Loaf Mountain, now preserved as a Registered National Natural Landmark. There are three walking trails and one horse trail. The 5½-mile trail across the mountain peak was devised and is maintained by the local chapter of the Appalachian Trail Club. There's a shorter hike along a winding road with a number of overlooks that extends up the mountain about a mile. At the end of the paved road a ¼-mile trail leads to the mountain top.

You can visit Sugar Loaf Mountain at no charge from 7:00 A.M. to sunset daily. A snack bar operates on summer weekends and on holidays and there are picnic tables and restrooms.

Directions: Take the Beltway I-495/95 to I-270 exit and drive west for about 28 miles to the Hyattstown exit. Turn right onto Route 100. Pass under I-270 and go another 3.3 miles to Comus. Turn right on Route 95 and go 2.5 miles to Sugar Loaf Mountain.

Surratt House Museum

Conspirator in Crinoline

The **Mary Surratt House** in Clinton, Maryland, calls to mind the tragic past of its owner. The house was one of the stops on the blood-stained trail of John Wilkes Booth after he assassinated Abraham Lincoln. For her role in that criminal conspiracy Mary Surratt was the first woman executed by the federal government. Who was she and how did she become involved in one of the blackest crimes in the annals of American history?

You'll discover the answer to these questions when you tour the restored house built in 1852 by John Surratt. The house served as a home, tavern, post office, polling place and general gathering place for the community. It was perhaps inevitable that southern Maryland dissidents, unhappy with their state's northern status, would gather here. By 1862 John Surratt had died and Mary had sole responsibility for her three children. Her youngest son, John Jr., left college to help her run the tavern and fell under the sway of the Confederate sympathizers; in time the tavern became a safe house for agents of the Confederacy.

It was this involvement that led to the day when Mary Surratt left field glasses and "shooting irons" hidden in the ceiling of the tavern for John Wilkes Booth. They were originally to be used in a plot to kidnap Lincoln; but when, after shooting the president, Booth and an accomplice stopped to retrieve the guns, her

157

complicity cost Mary Surratt her life. She was executed on July 7, 1865. When her son John was tried for virtually the same crime in 1867, the court decided it did not have sufficient evidence to convict him.

Both floors of the Surratt House Museum are furnished with antiques from the early to mid-Victorian era. Costumed docents give guided tours of the house from March through December on Thursday and Friday from 11:00 A.M. to 3:00 P.M. and on weekends NOON to 4:00 P.M. A nominal admission is charged.

In the spring and fall the Surratt Society sponsors a day-long excursion on the route Booth took from Ford's Theatre to the site of the farm, now the Fort A.P. Hill military base, where the assassin was finally cornered and shot. For details of the John Wilkes Booth Escape Route Tour, call (301)868-1121.

If you want to follow Booth's route on your own, then venture farther down Branch Avenue to the **Dr. Samuel A. Mudd House**. On April 18, 1865, Booth left the Surratt Tavern and stopped at the Mudd farm. The house you'll visit looks exactly as it did when Booth rode to the door and changed forever the lives of Dr. Mudd and his family.

Since John Wilkes Booth was acquainted with Dr. Mudd—indeed, he had even been entertained at this farm—he and his accomplice, David Herold, took the precaution of using false names when they arrived at Mudd's doorstep. Some reports claim that Booth, and accomplished actor, wore a false beard. Dr. Mudd helped Booth to the red velvet couch (now returned to the house after a long absence). After examining Booth's injured leg, the doctor helped him upstairs to a bedroom, then cut off Booth's boot and tossed it under the bed. It was this boot that was used as evidence in Dr. Mudd's trial.

The two conspirators remained at the farm for only one night, and the Mudds maintained they never recognized Booth. The doctor also insisted he had not learned of Lincoln's death when he treated Booth. Despite his testimony, Mudd was convicted by a military court of aiding and harboring a fugitive. He was, however, found innocent of any role in the assassination conspiracy.

Dr. Mudd was sent to Fort Jefferson Prison in the Dry Tortugas off Key West, Florida. After he attempted to escape, he was subjected to the additional agony of chains. A yellow fever epidemic that swept through the prison population gave Mudd a chance to practice medicine again and ultimately to gain his freedom. His work to save lives was rewarded by a presidential pardon granted by Andrew Johnson. Dr. Mudd returned to his Maryland farm but frequently traveled around the country lecturing on yellow fever. Family furnishings and mementos bring back the tragedy of this long-ago drama.

The Dr. Samuel A. Mudd House is open on weekends from

NOON to 4:00 P.M. Admission is charged. For more information call (301)645-6870.

Directions: From the Beltway I-495/95 take Exit 7A, Route 5, Branch Avenue, to Woodyard Road, Route 223, in Clinton. Take a right on Woodyard Road and turn left at the second traffic light, where you turn onto Brandywine Road. The Surratt House Museum is on the left at 9110 Brandywine Road. For the Dr. Mudd House continue south on Route 5 past Waldorf and then turn left on Route 382. Make a right on Route 232 and look for the Mudd farm on the right.

Theodore Roosevelt Island

Rough, Ready and Rustic

An 88-acre wilderness preserve nestles between two booming metropolitan areas—Arlington, Virginia and Washington, DC. The natural terrain of **Theodore Roosevelt Island** has been left undisturbed, the underbrush tangled, the trees untrimmed; if you ignore the jets coming in to land at nearby National Airport, you can have a peaceful retreat. On any visit you are likely to see people hiking and bicycling on the trails. It's also a popular place with pet owners because dogs may be taken along the trails if they are leashed.

The island park was presented to the American people in 1932 as a living tribute to one of the country's most conservation-minded presidents, Theodore Roosevelt. During his administration he created the U.S. Forest Service, 5 national parks, 51 bird sanctuaries and 4 game reserves. Roosevelt deplored the despoliation of our natural resources and focused attention on the wanton destruction that had already occurred. When asked late in his life of what he was most proud, he unhesitatingly cited his preservation of 150 million acres of forest and other natural areas.

A large standing sculpture of Theodore Roosevelt dominates the northern section of the island. The 17-foot bronze statue in front of a 30-foot granite shaft stands at the center of terraced areas with boxwood plantings and urn-shaped fountains. Surrounding all is a water-filled moat spanned by marble footbridges.

On Saturday and Sunday mornings at 10:00 there are guided nature walks. At 2:00 P.M. the park guides offer a history talk on Theodore Roosevelt followed by an optional walk. The well-marked trails, however, enable anyone to be his own guide. Signs deal with various environmental aspects—the weathering process, the swamp, the fall line and many others. Any questions you might have will be answered by the park guides.

Be sure to inquire about the early history of the island. Many Washingtonians are surprised to learn that George Mason, whose lovely estate, Gunston Hall, is well worth visiting, also built a home here, and the Mason family inhabited the island for 125 years.

There are three trails: the Swamp Trail, the Upland Trail and the Woods Trail. These are all short walks. The total trail length on the island is only 2.5 miles. The Swamp Trail provides a number of scenic vistas. From a perch on the large boulders at the water's edge, you can watch scullers on the Potomac River. Or you can sit on a bench and enjoy a delightful view of the Kennedy Center and the Lincoln Memorial framed by the Theodore Roosevelt Bridge.

The marsh area with its cattails, pickerelweed and arrow arum provides the perfect terrain for marsh wrens, red-winged black-birds and kingfishers. Muskrats, turtles and frogs are common. The mudflats are rooting grounds for willows, red maples and ash trees and are home to the raccoons. More than 200 wild-flowers thrive on the island. Theodore Roosevelt Island is right off the Atlantic Flyway, and in spring and fall black ducks, mallards, great blue herons, grosbeaks and many other birds rest here.

The Upland and Woods Trails wander through elm, tulip trees, maples and oaks. Here you can see downy woodpeckers, chickadees and wood thrushes with their neighbors the grey squirrels, chipmunks, red and grey foxes and cottontail rabbits. The island is a wildlife sanctuary and the plants, animals and birds are protected.

Theodore Roosevelt Island is open daily at no charge from 8:00 A.M. to dusk. For more information call (703)285-2600.

Directions: Theodore Roosevelt Island is inside the Beltway. From Washington take either the George Mason Memorial Bridge or the Theodore Roosevelt Bridge onto the George Washington Memorial Parkway. The park entrance and parking lot is well marked and is on the east side of the Parkway near the Theodore Roosevelt Bridge in Virginia. Arlington National Cemetery is directly across the Potomac River from Washington via the Arlington Memorial Bridge.

U.S. Army Ordnance Museum and Havre de Grace

Old Havre Graces the Susquehanna

If you want to visit a spot sure to be a hit with masculine travelers head for the Aberdeen Proving Grounds 21 miles north of Baltimore. History buffs, adventure movie enthusiasts and military veterans find much to enjoy at the **U.S. Army Ordnance Museum.** And for good reason. They see many weapons here that are not exhibited anywhere else. This is the world's most complete weapon collection.

The rows of tanks, armored cars, Howitzers and artillery on the museum grounds fascinate visitors. As you tour you're apt to hear veterans regaling younger family members with stories about the days when their lives depended on this equipment. But even when veterans embellish their stories, they are unlikely to be more fascinating than the factual accounts of some of these field pieces.

One famous piece is Anzio Annie, the name the Allies bestowed on the German Leopold gun that trapped them on an Italian beach south of Rome. Allied officers could not understand how a gun large enough to fire a 550-pound shell could remain undetected. The Allies sent air strikes and strafed the area, but the gun continued to hold the troops on the beach. The Allies solved the mystery when they finally fought their way off Anzio beach. They discovered that the gun was on railroad wheels and was rolled into a mountain hideaway when not being fired. This sanctuary had protected the gun—the only German railroad gun to survive the war.

This is by no means the only piece with a past; there is also the 166,638-pound atomic cannon developed in the early 1950s. This high-tech weapon fired conventional and atomic munitions at targets up to 18 miles away. Even this deadly weapon did not inspire the widespread terror caused by the frequently fired V-2 rockets that the Nazis trained on London. While most visitors to the museum have read about the V-2, few have ever seen one. They'll see that as well as exhibits on the history and development of ammunition, the evolution of the combat helmet and a comprehensive array of rifles, rocket launchers, machine guns, submachine guns, chemical weapons, uniforms and transport vehicles. Visitors who are turned off by military hardware may very well be intrigued by the human and historical details.

After visiting the museum, if you continue north on I-95 for one more exit you'll reach **Havre de Grace**, along the banks of the Susquehanna River. It's a charming spot to take a stroll into the past. The town's history is divided into six periods with the houses reflecting a wide range of architectural styles.

The earliest years, 1780 to the early 1800s, are represented by only a few scattered homes. The British burned the town on May 3, 1813, and 60 percent of Havre de Grace was destroyed. You'll see many examples from the years 1830 to 1850 when both the railroad and the canal linked the area with other parts of the state and country. The Concord Point Lighthouse was finished on May 21, 1829, just in time to herald the new era of prosperity for Havre de Grace. The lighthouse is an excellent vantage point from which to view the town, the Susquehanna River and the Chesapeake Bay. On weekend afternoons the tower is open to climbers.

Between 1850 and 1880, canal traffic declined and the Civil War diverted attention to broader matters. It was in the Victorian years following the war that Havre de Grace acquired the delightful architecture that visitors still enjoy. You will see an assortment of gingerbread-bedecked homes embellished with bay windows, towers, gables, turrets, stained glass and ornamented porches.

The fifth period between 1910 and 1940 saw an influx of vacationers, hunters and weekend residents who built bungalows and second homes. Lastly, there are a few homes and businesses that reflect the contemporary period. In all, a few short blocks will give you an overview of American architectural styles spanning the nation's history.

Havre de Grace also has two museums. The **Susquehanna Museum** is in the 1840 lock house, formerly the home and office of the canal lock tender. Furnishings in the parlor, kitchen and bedroom reflect the canal era and exhibits provide additional information. The museum is open on Sunday afternoons from April through October.

The Havre de Grace **Decoy Museum,** open daily 11:00 A.M. to 4:00 P.M., exhibits a wide array of both commercial and decorative decoys. The town bills itself as the decoy capital of the world.

The U.S. Army Ordnance Museum is open at no charge from NOON to 4:45 P.M. Tuesday to Friday. Weekends hours are 10:00 A.M. to 4:45 P.M. The outdoor exhibits can be seen daily from 9:00 A.M. to sunset.

Directions: From the Beltway I-495/95 take I-95 north to the Aberdeen exit. Take Route 22 to the Ordnance Museum. For Havre de Grace continue north on I-95, exit on Route 155 and head south into town.

Virginia Living Museum and Virginia Air and Space Center

Master of All You Survey

Hampton Roads has two museums that open windows on the natural world both near and far. The **Virginia Living Museum** in Newport News is part native wildlife park and part science museum and aquarium. A small planetarium and abundant botanical specimens provide a multi-discipline introduction to Virginia's natural worlds. The new Virginia Air and Space Center takes visitors from the sea to the stars.

The Virginia Living Museum, modeled on the renowned Arizona-Sonoran Desert Museum in Tucson, opened in May 1987. None of the wildlife exhibited at this museum were taken from the wild; they came from other zoos, nature centers, museums, rehabilitation facilities and breeders.

The museum's exhibits start with a living cross-section of Virginia's James River; it covers 340 miles in 60 feet. It begins with the plants, fish and wildlife found in a mountain stream, then moves to a sluggish tidal river, next to the Chesapeake Bay and on into the Atlantic Ocean. The ocean tank has a loggerhead sea turtle. Young turtles are given to the museum, grow to maturity and then are released to the wild and the cycle begins again.

Young children enjoy reaching in and handling the specimens in the Touch Tank. They also enjoy "On the Track of the Virginia Dinosaurs," an exhibit that opened in October 1990. Visitors can place their hands on an authentic track made by a Kaynentapus that roamed in this area over 210 million years ago. These bipodal dinosaurs were 126 inches high and 10½ feet long. A sample of their footprint is nine inches long. These tracks were discovered by workers at the Culpeper Stone Company in a quarry near Stevensburg.

Another section of the museum concentrates on "How Life Survives," focusing on such basics as food, defense, reproduction and shelter. Creatures as diverse as a black widow spider, an octopus and a kestrel demonstrate various aspects of these vital functions. You will discover that if the kestrel could read it would be able to peruse a newspaper 100 yards away.

Certainly one of the most popular indoor areas is the two-story glass songbird aviary. These injured, abandoned and hand-raised birds have no fear of visitors, and it's easy to get excellent close-up photographs of the colorful specimens. You'll see such elusive birds as cedar waxwings, summer tanagers and quail.

From there the walkway leads outside along Deer Park Lake and past the habitats of native water animals like river otters, raccoons and beavers. In May 1991 a striking outdoor Wetlands Aviary opened. Within this haven you can see glossy ibis, elegant herons and a variety of multi-hued ducks and other waterfowl. The aviary's overlook has three observation points so that you can see habitats representing marsh, swamp and bog. Only four percent of Virginia land is wetlands, but within that area live one-third of the endangered species in the state.

The outdoor exhibits also include such woodland creatures such as bobcats, deer, fox, opossum and skunk. You also can get a close look at a pair of bald eagles.

Depending on the time and length of your visit you may be

able to take in one of the museum's daily planetarium shows. During the summer there are three shows every afternoon and another on Thursday evening. The rest of the year there is only one afternoon show during the week. There is an extra charge for these shows. Another way to explore space is through the museum's telescope. The observatory offers solar viewing during regular museum hours and a chance to look at the stars on Thursday evening.

The Virginia Living Museum is open from Memorial Day to Labor Day from 9:00 A.M. to 6:00 P.M. Monday through Saturday and Sunday 10:00 A.M. to 6:00 P.M. The rest of the year hours are 10:00 A.M. to 5:00 P.M. Monday through Saturday and 1:00 to 5:00 P.M. on Sunday. Thursday evenings the museum is open from 7:00 to 9:00 P.M. Closed on major holidays. For information on the planetarium shows call (804)595-1900.

Space and man's achievements in conquering it are the main themes at the state-of-the-art **Virginia Air and Space Center** in Hampton that opened April 5, 1992. If you want an overview of the exhibits be sure to watch the short video at the Orientation Theater. You begin your self-guided tour in a large open space area where an array of small models trace the evolution of the airplane from its earliest days while full-size examples hang suspended from the ceiling.

One of the exhibited aircraft is a F-4E Phantom II that saw combat in Vietnam; it actually has 1½ MIG kills to its credit. The suspended planes also include prototype YF-16 like the Thunderbirds fly and a Corvair F-106B, a huge aircraft with a 38-foot wing span. These planes can be seen from several levels; you can even look down on them from a gantry that crosses high above the museum's ground floor.

The first floor has a 300-seat IMAX theater and the Hampton Roads History Center. Hampton was an official Royal Port for the Virginia colony. A wharf exhibit focuses on the importance of trade and tobacco to the area. In colonial times the Bunch of Grapes Tavern stood on this site, and it was here that irate patriots would gather to discuss their unhappiness with English rule. The American Revolution, War of 1812 and Civil War are explored as they relate to this region. There is a full-size replica of the casement of the *Merrimac* (also called the *Virginia*). There is also a large scale portion of the *Monitor*. It surprises many visitors to discover that the *Merrimac*, at 275 feet in length, was more than twice the size of the space shuttle.

On the second floor there is a gallery devoted to space. At the entrance of this exhibit, there is a cradle with a infant dressed not in traditional infantwear but in a space suit. The legend over the cradle reads: "Earth is the cradle of mankind, but we cannot live in the cradle forever" (Konstantin Tsiolovsky). In this gallery

164

you'll see actual Mercury and Lunar Orbiter spacecraft. Inter-active displays let you play at being an "astronaut for a minute." There is also a simulated space launch. Other topics exhibited include the planets, science fiction, the history of the Air Force and rocketry.

The Virginia Air and Space Center is open daily. For additional information call (804)727-0800.

Directions: From the Beltway I-495/95 take I-95 south to Richmond. Then take I-64 east to Newport News, use Exit 62A, the J. Clyde Morris Boulevard. A sign indicates the museum on your left at 524 J. Clyde Morris Blvd. For the Virginia Air and Space Center take I-64 to Hampton, use Exit 68, turn right on Settlers Landing Road. Across the bridge, look for the Center on the left.

Washington Monument State Park

It's Monumental, by George!

Maryland can boast that it has the first county in the country named in honor of George Washington and the first monument built in his honor. The monument stands on land reportedly surveyed in 1748 by 16-year-old George Washington for Lord Fairfax.

The people of Boonsboro in Washington County were not satisfied simply to raise money to build a monument; they were determined to build it themselves as a gesture of respect and appreciation for the country's first president. On July 4, 1827, about 500 townspeople met in Boonsboro at seven in the morning and marched to the summit of South Mountain to begin their labor of love.

South Mountain was well supplied with "blue rocks," and these were used to construct the tower. The stones were cut and laid, without benefit of mortar, to form a circular wall. After a full day's work the Boonsboro residents had erected at 15-foot tower. Work was not resumed until after the crops were harvested, but before the end of the year the remaining 15 feet were added. It was proudly proclaimed that, "As monuments go, none was ever built with purer or more reverent patriotism."

Unfortunately, the workers' enthusiasm was greater than their skill, and their mortarless monument began to crumble. It was reduced to rubble with 55 years. In 1882 the Boonsboro Odd Fellows Lodge rebuilt the monument, adding an iron canopy to the tower. Barely a decade passed before the monument was once more in ruins; this time a lightning strike is thought to have caused a crack that crumbled the structure.

The third tower, the one you see today, was built between 1934 and 1936 by the Civilian Conservation Corps. You will be glad they persevered in their rebuilding when you climb the 34 steps to the top of the monument. The panoramic view encompasses three states—Maryland, Virginia and West Virginia. The sight of the Potomac River winding through the rolling countryside is splendid.

The land immediately beneath and around the monument is all part of the 106-acre **Washington Monument State Park.** There is a circular hiking trail in the park and the Appalachian Trail passes through. The park stays open April through October from 8:00 A.M. to sunset and November through March, from 10:00 A.M. to sunset. There are facilities for family camping.

At the exhibit center you can see displays and hear a taped account of the building of the monument. You'll also see exhibits on the geology and flora and fauna of South Mountain. This area is on the flyway for migratory birds, and each year bird-watchers gather to compile a count of passing hawks and eagles.

The park's exhibit center is also a good spot to find out about the Civil War battle that occurred on South Mountain on September 14, 1862—a delaying action before the confrontation at Antietam. General James Longstreet, commanding a major section of Lee's Army of Northern Virginia, held the mountain passes, preventing the far larger army of General McClellan from crossing the mountain.

Confederate General D.H. Hill used a nearby inn as his headquarters during the Battle of South Mountain. The inn had also figured in an earlier episode in 1859 that contributed to the breakdown of civilities between the North and South; it was captured and held as a meeting spot by John Brown's raiders in their unsuccessful attempt to arm themselves and rally the slaves to their banner (see Harpers Ferry selection). Old South Mountain Inn is still open, and you can dine amid the echoes of history at this picturesque spot on the National Road. Reservations are recommended; call head to (301)432-6155.

Directions: From the Beltway I-495/95 take I-270 west, intersect I-70 and continue west past Frederick to Exit 49, Alt. Route 40. Take Alt. Route 40 west five miles past Middletown to the top of South Mountain, Turners Gap. At Turners Gap you will find Old South Mountain Inn on your left and the Washington Monument State Park entrance road, Monument Road, on your right.

Waterford

The Fairest Fair

To paraphrase George M. Cohan, **Waterford** is only 45 minutes from the Beltway but oh, what a difference that makes. This mountain hamlet is centuries removed from the modern city ambience and appearance.

Waterford's charm stems from the fact that the village is neither restored nor re-created; it is preserved. The houses, churches, shops, schools and farms have survived, faded and chipped but true to an earlier age. The Department of Interior in 1970 designated the entire village The **Waterford Historic District** and listed it as a National Historic Landmark. It is one of the few entire villages so honored.

Located in the foothills of the Blue Ridge Mountains, Waterford was founded in 1733 by Quaker settlers from Pennsylvania. A surprising number of buildings date from those early years. Because of their religious scruples few Waterford inhabitants took part in the American Revolution, but during the Civil War the only organized troop of Virginians to fight for the North were the independent Loudoun Rangers, organized by Waterford miller Samuel Means.

Once a year the tumultuous Civil War days are brought to life with a re-creation of the skirmish that occurred in Waterford in 1863. It is staged as part of the Waterford Homes Tour and Crafts Fair held for more than 45 years in early October. Several militia groups set up camp during the fair to demonstrate musketry, engage in military maneuvers and provide a bit of living history.

Waterford's annual fair is the oldest fair in Virginia and one of the best on the East Coast. More than 100 craftspeople are chosen from many applicants to demonstrate and sell their wares. Visitors are often able to try their hand at spinning, weaving or making shoes, candles and brooms. In addition to those actually practicing their craft, there are hundreds of exhibitors selling handcrafted items. For those able to get organized early, this is an ideal place to start Christmas shopping.

The fair is also noted for what is called "the largest collection of weeds this side of the Mississippi"; dried wildflowers, straw flowers and decorative weeds literally fill a barn. The fair sponsors a juried art show and a photography exhibit.

The added incentive to visit Waterford during this popular three-day event is the chance to tour a sampling of the town's private homes, a few of which are open as bed-and-breakfast spots. The **James Moore House** (703/882-3342) was built by a descendant of the Irish poet Thomas Moore. It was Moore who persuaded his neighbors to change the town's name from Milltown to Waterford, commemorating that Irish city. The current owner is a noted quilter and her work decorates the bedrooms. You can also overnight at the Waterford Inn (703/882-3465) nestled quietly in the center of town.

Waterford is hilly, with irregular brick sidewalks. Whether you choose to explore during the annual fair or another time, you should wear comfortable walking shoes. The only time you can find a variety of food available is during the fair when you'll be tempted by the smell of an open-pit barbecue as well as a wide variety of home-made desserts. For information on the Waterford Fair call (703)882-3018.

Directions: From the Beltway I-495/95 exit on Virginia Route 7 and head west past Leesburg to Route 9. Turn right on Route 9 and proceed a half mile to Route 662 and turn right for the fair parking lot.

Wheaton Regional Park and Brookside Gardens

Fragrance, Flora and Fauna

Wheaton Regional Park has so much to offer you can spend an entire day exploring. Park options include Brookside Gardens, Old MacDonald's Farm, Wheaton Lines Railroad, Pine Lake, Brookside Nature Center, plus riding stables, ice rink, playground area, pony rides and hiking trails.

Once discovered, **Brookside Gardens** lures visitors back again and again. The conservatories and grounds change with the seasons. The 50-acre garden is inviting in the fall when chrysanthemums line the paths. In early autumn you can see the last of the colorful summer annuals. Before the onset of hard frosts, the fragrance garden with its representative herbs test visitors' olfactory keeness. Herbs are planted here for their aroma not their visual appeal. It's fun to try to identify oregano, peppermint and lavender from their smell; if you have trouble, the labels help.

As the outdoor blossoms fade, the indoor conservatory chrysanthemum exhibit comes into bloom, peaking in November. Multi-hued blossoms are trained into lavish flowering cascades, upright columns and miniature trees. The conservatory has a permanent collection of hibiscus, azalea, bird of paradise and a wide array of lush foliage plants. Following the fall exhibit the garden mounts an equally dramatic poinsettia holiday display.

Even in late fall and on mild winter days Brookside's Japanese garden is worth a visit. There is a ceremonial tea house surrounded by tranquil ponds, trees, shrubs and ornamental gates. Be sure to return in the spring when the outdoor azaleas bloom and in the summer when the rose collection peaks.

Brookside Gardens' conservatories are open daily 9:00 A.M. to 5:00 P.M., and the grounds open from 9:00 A.M. to sunset. It is closed on Christmas Day. There is no admission. For more information call (202)686-5807.

After visiting the garden, take the path from the parking lot to the **Brookside Nature Center.** Here you'll find exhibits on the flora and fauna found along the park's forest trails. The park staff schedules guided walks and shows nature films.

A favorite with young visitors is **Old MacDonald's Farm,** a typical Maryland farm re-created on a small scale. The farm has a barn, smokehouse, brick oven, windmill, silo and a wide variety of farm animals. Behind the farm is the five-acre Pine Lake where from 10:00 A.M. to sunset you can fish from the shore for bass, bluegill, crappie and catfish. Fishermen of all ages are welcome to try their luck, and those 16 and under do not even need a license.

Young children also will enjoy the **Wheaton Lines Railroad** that wanders on its two-mile track around Pine Lake and through meadow and woodland. The train is a reproduction of an 1865 steam engine with vintage cars, switch and signals. The ride over bridges and tunnels is a real adventure for beginning train buffs. There is also a carousel for youngsters. (Budget cuts have temporarily closed the farm, railroad and carousel.)

Wheaton has miles of hiking and bicycle trails through the unspoiled interior of the park. Trail maps are available and bicycles can be rented during the summer months. Athletes will find the ice rink, athletic fields and tennis courts well suited to their needs. There is also a riding stable with horses for rent and woodland bridle trails. The park has the latest in innovative playground equipment plus conveniently located picnic tables.

Directions: From the Beltway I-495/95 take Exit 31A, Georgia Avenue north. Make a right on Shorefield Road for the playground, farm, train station and athletic areas. For the entrance to Brookside Gardens stay on Georgia Avenue to Randolph Road and make a right. Then make another right on Glenallan Avenue for the garden parking lot.

Woodlawn Plantation and Frank Lloyd Wright's Pope-Leighey House

Dual Dream House

An interesting architectural contrast between the old and the new can be seen at Woodlawn Plantation. On the rolling hills of this gracious southern estate you can see a plantation built in the early 19th century and a Frank Lloyd Wright suburban house from the mid-20th century.

The **Pope-Leighey House** is the unexpected surprise. It was moved to the Woodlawn grounds in 1964 from its original location in Falls Church, Virginia. Built in 1940, this house was the second of Frank Lloyd Wright's Usonian (standing for the

United States of North America) houses, built for families of modest income. Five Usonian houses were built along the east coast. As Wright explained it, "To give the little family the benefit of industrial advantages of the era in which they live, something else must be done for them than to plan another little imitation of a mansion. Simplifications must take place. They must themselves see life in somewhat simplified terms."

Although this Usonian house is made of cypress rather than concrete like Wright's later models, it does demonstrate his contributions to modern architecture. The house has unplastered cypress paneling both inside and out. It is built on a concrete slab and blends cypress, brick and glass. The flat roof and carport have since become standard features on suburban homes. Wright's ability to achieve organic unity and use space and light are very much in evidence in the design of the Pope-Leighey House. These modest houses were built for $7,000 and needed little maintenance; there was no need for repainting, repapering or replastering.

It is fortunate that the landscape at **Woodlawn Plantation** resembles the house's original surroundings 15 miles away because the integration of a building with its natural setting was an important consideration for Wright. It was fortunate that when the construction of an interstate highway necessitated the relocation of the house, the same master craftsman who had built it was available to oversee the dismantling and reassembly of the house and its built-in furniture. It is important to remember when visiting that his house was indeed a prototype.

The Woodlawn Plantation that shares the grounds was, on the other hand, a deliberate copy. The house was designed to resemble Kenmore, the Fredericksburg family home of Lawrence Lewis, son of George Washington's sister, Betty. It was furnished with family pieces collected by his bride, Nelly Parke Custis, from her home, Mount Vernon. Nelly was the foster granddaughter of George Washington (she was Martha Washington's natural granddaughter and at the death of Nelly's father, Martha's son by a previous marriage, George and Martha raised her), and he gave her the land for this home as a wedding gift.

Nelly and Lawrence were married on George Washington's last birthday, February 22, 1799. The grief Nelly felt for the only father she ever knew is apparent in the placing of a bust of Washington on a pedestal raised to his exact height. Nelly's presence is still felt in the Music Room where her sheet music rests on the pianoforte, and a taped recording of one of her favorite pieces can be heard at a push of a button.

Woodlawn, in addition to being attractively furnished with period pieces, has one special room for youngsters, the **Touch**

and Try Area. Old fashioned games and toys are available to be used and enjoyed, not displayed as museum pieces.

Woodlawn Plantation is open daily 9:30 A.M. to 4:30 P.M. year-round. The plantation is closed only on Thanksgiving, Christmas and New Year's Day. The Frank Lloyd Wright's Pope-Leighey House is open daily 9:30 A.M. to 4:30 P.M. from March through October.

Directions: From the Beltway take Exit 1, U.S. 1, south for 14 miles to the Woodlawn Plantation and Frank Lloyd Wright's Pope-Leighey House. They are located at the intersection of U.S. 1 and Virginia Route 235 in Mount Vernon, Virginia.

Yorktown

Streets of Old

A rich tapestry of American history unfolded in and around **Yorktown** from 1691 through 1991. During the 1600s, settlers moved into this Virginia peninsula, and Yorktown gradually evolved into a thriving colonial seaport. The town's most significant moment coincided with the demise of Britain's colonial claims in America. It was in Yorktown in 1781 that Lord Cornwallis fought his last campaign. When his siege of the city ended on October 19, 1781, more than half of the buildings in Yorktown had been destroyed.

The city never fully recovered from its brush with history, but today that long sleep adds to its charm. It is possible to catch a glimpse of old Yorktown by strolling down the main streets. But to grasp what it was once like, you must visit the **Yorktown Victory Center**.

In 1991 the Center redesigned their major exhibits, another reason to revisit this popular attraction. Restyled displays trace the development of York and Gloucester, directly across the river, from the colonial period to their pivotal role at the conclusion of the American Revolution. An associated exhibit concentrates on the ships sunk off Yorktown and shipboard life during the Revolution. Those with a keen interest in this subject must plan to stop at the **Watermen's Museum** (open Tuesday–Saturday 10:00 A.M.–4:00 P.M. and Sunday 1:00-4:00 P.M.) located in a replica of a colonial plantation house on the Yorktown waterfront.

In another exhibit at the Yorktown Victory Center you'll hear firsthand accounts from participants and observers of the Revolution. One section explores the motivations of a black patriot, white Loyalist and Quaker pacifist as they chose sides in the struggle. The views of officers and enlisted men are also presented. A section on the homefront gives the civilian story; another covers the role of blacks in the Revolution and the events that led to the last major military campaign in Yorktown.

During the summer and on weekends in the fall and spring there is a re-created Continental army camp on the grounds of the museum. Soldiers and women representing family members who traveled with the troops bring to life the daily routines of the Revolutionary War years. The Yorktown Victory Center is open daily 9:00 A.M. to 5:00 P.M. and admission is charged.

After absorbing the background presented at the Victory Center, you're ready to appreciate the Yorktown Battlefield where you can still see remnants of the siege lines. Also remaining is the **Moore House** where officers negotiated surrender terms. The house was restored to its 18th-century appearance, and the park service presents living history programs that dramatize the tense negotiations that occurred here. The battlefield may be visited at no charge daily 8:30 A.M. to 5:30 P.M. (Mid-June to Labor Day the park stays open until 6:00 P.M.)

Another house closely associated with the siege of Yorktown is the **Nelson House**, the home of Declaration of Independence signer and Virginia governor, Thomas Nelson, Jr. During the war, Nelson was a Brigadier General, and his loyalty to the Revolutionary cause was sorely tested during the siege of his hometown. Unfortunately for Nelson, Cornwallis made Nelson's house his headquarters. (There is also a cave along the waterfront where Cornwallis supposedly took refuge.) Nelson ordered his men to fire at his own home. The two cannonballs in the east wall were placed here in the 20th century to fill scars left from the 18th-century attack. During the summer months there is a living history program here. (Budget considerations may result in the cancelation of this outstanding program. Call (804)898-3400 for up-to-date information.) The Nelson House is open at no charge daily from 10:00 A.M. to 5:00 P.M.

Thomas Nelson, Jr., is buried in the churchyard of Grace Church, one of 50 remaining churches that served the colonists during the Revolution. During the Civil War the church was badly damaged by nearby fighting. Today it stands serenely on the bluffs above the York River, a quiet reminder of tumultuous times.

Directions: From the Beltway I-495/95 take I-95 south to Richmond then head east on I-64 to the Colonial Parkway. Follow the Colonial Parkway to Yorktown. For information and maps on Yorktown and the surrounding region call the Virginia Peninsula Tourism and Conference Bureau (800)333-RSVP.

172

Autumn Calendar of Events

SEPTEMBER

Early:

Gunston Hall Car Show—Gunston Hall Plantation, VA (703)550-9220. This popular car show features more than 200 collectors' cars. Trophies are awarded and drivers are encouraged to wear costumes. Music, refreshments and tours of the gracious colonial mansion add to the fun.

Steam Show Days—Carroll County Farm Museum, Westminster, MD (410)848-7775. Antique farm equipment, steam and gas engines are exhibited and demonstrated. Flea market, country food, crafts and a guided tour of the farm house round out the weekend.

Fall Pennsylvania Crafts Fair—Brandywine River Museum, Chadds Ford, PA (215)388-7601. Arts and crafts are demonstrated and sold at this fair. You can also obtain dried natural plants to use for holiday decorations.

Battle of Hagerstown—Jonathan Hager House & Museum, Hagerstown, MD (301)739-8393. Living-history program re-creates military encampment as well as reenacting the battle with over 100 participants.

John Wilkes Booth Escape Route Tour—Surratt House, MD (301)868-1121. The second tour of the year sponsored by the Surratt Society retraces Booth's route after his assassination of Lincoln.

Boonesborough Days—Boonesboro, MD (301)582-2034.This weekend-long event features more than 125 old-fashioned crafts in a juried show. The work is demonstrated, judged and sold. Folk music, square dancing, barbershop quartets and home cooking are part of the festivities.

Traditional Frontier Festival—Museum of American Frontier Culture, Staunton, VA (703)332-7850. Enjoy entertainment and crafts that stem from Germany, England, Ireland and America.

Mid:

Defenders Day—Fort McHenry, MD (410)962-4299. Military pageantry marks the celebration of the 1814 Battle of Baltimore. There are patriotic music and drills, a mock bombardment of Fort McHenry and the raising of a replica of the Star-Spangled Banner. A fireworks display brings the event to a close.

Neptune Festival—Virginia Beach, VA (804)498-0215. Sandcastle building, an air show, sailing, surfing, a grand parade, arts and craft and fireworks add to this celebration.

Autumn's Colors—Longwood Gardens, Kennett Square, PA (215)388-6741. From mid-September through October the conservatories of Longwood are filled with thousands of chrysanthemums.

Candlelight Walking Tour of Chestertown—Chestertown, MD (410)778-3499. The only time during the year that the private homes of this community open their doors to the public.

Reenactment of the Battle of the Brandywine—Brandywine Battlefield National Historic Park, Chadds Ford, PA (215)459-3342. Life during the Revolutionary War is re-created. Soldiers march in formation while families follow. Both American and British regiments are represented. Eighteenth-century crafts are demonstrated.

College Park Airport Open House and Air Fair—College Park, MD (301)864-5844. Air show, airplane and helicopter rides, exhibits and refreshments are all part of the festivities.

18th-Century Autumn Market Fair—Claude Moore Colonial Farm, McLean, VA (703)442-7557. Colonial merchants, period craftsmen and country cooking are part of this weekend-long event.

National Capital Trolley Museum Fall Open House—Wheaton, MD (301)384-6088. The museum's collection of American and European trolleys are brought out of the barns so that visitors can photograph them. You can also take a trolley ride.

Historic Ellicott City Country Fair—Ellicott City, MD (410)313-2762. Juried country crafts, living history, hands-on craft workshops, entertainment and country cooking.

Late:

Maryland Wine Festival—Carroll County Farm Museum, Westminster, MD (410)848-7775. Wine tasting and country cooking are the main draws, but there is also entertainment and crafts.

Colonial Day—Montpelier Mansion, Laurel, MD (301)953-1376. Colonial crafts and 18th-century music can be enjoyed and this rural Maryland estate toured. They also have historic reenactments.

Fall Farm Festival—National Colonial Farm, Accokeek, MD (301)283-2113. Woodcarving, spinning, quilting, corn-husk doll making, apple cider pressing, blacksmithing and candle dipping are demonstrated. There are also children's games and refreshments.

Fall Harvest Festival—Steppingstone Museum, Havre de Grace, MD (410)939-2299. Make your own scarecrow, take a hayride or ride a pony, purchase fresh-made apple butter and join the square dancing at this country party.

OCTOBER

Early:

Fall Festival—Rose Hill Manor, Frederick, MD (301)694-1648. There are three museums to see at Rose Hill Manor Park while you enjoy this country festival. A carriage museum, farm museum and children's touch-and-see museum are all part of the ongoing fun at this Frederick, Maryland attraction. During the festival crafts will be demonstrated and exhibited.

Blessing of the Fleet and Historical Pageant—St. Clement's Island, Colton's Point, MD (301)769-2222. Reenactment of the landing of the first settlers in Maryland. Nautical displays, boat rides and seafood are also part of day's fun.

Autumn Traditions—Colvin Run Mill, Great Falls, VA (703)759-5241. Traditional folk music, old tool demonstration, apple butter boiling and cider pressing plus tours. Children can play in the haystacks.

Victorian Craft Fair—Surratt House, MD (301)868-1121. Rediscover domestic life in the 19th century at this fair featuring such crafts as weaving, spinning, rug looming, braiding, English smocking, quilting, lacemaking, needlework, bookbinding, caning, woodworking and basketry.

Waterford Fair—Waterford, VA (703)882-3018.This festival is held in the 18th-century National Historic Landmark Village of Waterford. It is a marvelous chance to walk along the quaint streets of this charming community and explore the craft booths of artisans from all across the country. Music, military encampments and country cooking add to the fun.

Chesapeake Indian Culture Day—Chancellor's Point, St. Mary's City, MD (301)862-0990. One of the most unusual local annual events lets you discover what it was really like to live on this continent before the coming of the Europeans. You can take part in stone tool making, help start a fire by friction, listen to stories and try Indian food.

Carriage Drive and Competition—Morven Park, Leesburg, VA (703)777-2412. This annual steeplechase is also a perfect opportunity to tour this lovely estate. There are seven races.

Mid:

Oktoberfest—Town Point Park, Norfolk, VA (804)627-7809. Be transported to a German Festhaus with authentic German oompah bank, dancing, singing, beer barrel races and ethnic food.

Needlework Show—Oatlands, Leesburg, VA (703)777-3174. Over 250 needlework pieces are customarily displayed at this gracious estate.

Autumn Glory Festival—Oakland, Deep Creek Lake, MD (301)334-1948. Up around Deep Creek Lake where the autumn leaves provide their own glory this annual festival is a popular weekend event. There is a parade, an arts and craft bazaar, antique show and musical performances.

White House Fall Garden Tours—Washington, D.C. (202)456-2200. A chance to see the famous Rose Garden at its fall peak.

Yorktown Day—Yorktown, VA (804)898-3400. The town celebrates the surrender of the British to the American forces in 1781 with a parade, colonial music, military drills, tours of historic properties and 18th-century refreshments.

Catoctin Colorfest and Cozy's German Festival—Thurmont, MD (301)271-4432 and 271-4301. The Thurmont community park has roughly 350 craft booths while Thurmont's Cozy Restaurant features live entertainment, crafts and German food.

Late:

Chesapeake Appreciation Days—Sandy Point State Park, Annapolis, MD (410)269-6622. Celebration for working watermen with skipjack races, plenty of seafood plus entertainment.

Harvest Days—Sully Plantation, Chantilly, VA (703)759-5241. Historic activities, craft demonstrations, folk music and dances plus country cooking make for a fun-filled day.

Olde Towne Ghost Walk—Portsmouth, VA (804)399-5487. A lantern-led walking tour of the historic Olde Towne with actors re-creating tales of ghostly visitations.

Monster Tour of Historic District—Frederick, MD (301)694-7433. A special tour at Halloween lets you cover the historic district with some unusual company. Carriage rides are also available.

Halloween Spook Trail—Cape Henlopen State Park, Lewes, DE (302)645-6852. More than the ocean roars on this spooky walk in this picturesque park. If you arrive early while it is still light, you might want to try the frisbee golf layout. It's one of the best around.

NOVEMBER

Early:

Veteran's Day Ceremonies—Arlington National Cemetery, Washington, D.C. (202)619-7222. The President or a high-ranking official lays a wreath at the Tomb of the Unknowns, and there is a service in the Memorial Amphitheater.

Chrysanthemum Display—Brookside Gardens, MD (301)949-8230. This is the most spectacular display of the year at Brookside Gardens conservatory. The display features Japanese cascade mums, upright columns, hanging baskets, miniature tree mums and bedding mums.

Christmas at Oatlands—Oatlands Plantation, Leesburg, VA (703)777-3174. For over a decade visitors have found inspiration for their own holiday decorations while enjoying the arrangements at Oatlands which re-creates celebrations of the 1880s. Throughout the 13 exhibit rooms at Oatlands the Christmas finery is re-created based on records kept by the family.

Oyster Day—Chesapeake Bay Maritime Museum, St. Michaels, MD (410)745-2916. You can watch tonging and nippering, enjoy oyster shell-skipping contests plus purchase oysters prepared a myriad of ways.

Virginia Thanksgiving Festival—Berkeley Plantation, VA (804)272-3226. Two years before the Pilgrims landed at Plymouth Rock the colonists in Virginia celebrated a Thanksgiving ceremony. On the first Sunday in November at Berkeley Plantation this historic first Thanksgiving is reenacted with Captain Woodlief and his companions again coming ashore from their replica of the *Margaret*. Indians, too, are on hand to take part in this ceremony.

Mid:

Waterfowl Festival—Easton, MD (410)822-4567.You can see waterfowl art, decorative and working decoys, nautical artifacts, antique guns and an old-fashioned auction at this yearly festival.

Anniversary of Lincoln's Gettysburg Address—Gettysburg National Cemetery, PA (717)334-6274. On the Saturday closest to 11/19 a Remembrance Day is held with a parade of Civil War troops and a wreath-laying ceremony.

Yuletide at Winterthur—Winterthur Museum, DE. (302)888-4600/ 3883. Christmas arrives early at this museum of American decorative arts. Reservations are a must for these popular tours.

18th-Century Threshing Day—Claude Moore Colonial Farm at Turkey Run, McLean, VA (703)442-7557. Help with the fall chores, you can make yeast cakes, work in the fields as the staff does the threshing and winnowing of the wheat and then enjoy period music.

Late:

Waterfowl Week—Chincoteague National Wildlife Refuge, VA (804)336-6122. This is a once-a-year opportunity to use normally closed park roads at Chincoteague National Wildlife Refuge. It gives you a great chance to get close to the wild ponies of Chincoteague, as well as the opportunity to see a wide range of waterfowl. This event occurs during the migration of Canada and snow geese.

Thanksgiving Conservatory Display—Longwood Gardens, Kennett Square, PA (215)380-6741. You can't beat this annual display of chrysanthemums. Longwood has more and bigger flowers than you will see in other gardens or conservatories.

Historic Alexandria Show—Old Colony Inn, Alexandria, VA (703)838-4554. About 40 dealers from 16 states display their wares. They offer appraisal clinics and lectures.

Holidays in the City, Grand Illumination and Street Parade—Norfolk, VA (804)623-1757. Miles of white lights in downtown Norfolk create a glowing ambience for the Christmas street parade. The celebration continues the next weekend with a lighted boat parade.

George Washington and 12,000 troops endured the long, severe winter of 1778 at Valley Forge, Pennsylvania, chosen as an encampment site because the terrain provided suitable defense positions. Courtesy: National Park Service.

Alexandria

Art and History Along the Waterfront

Many residents of the Washington area are geographic victims, blinded by their proximity to interesting historical and cultural sites. They overlook many nearby attractions like **Alexandria**, Virginia. In one day the visitor here can absorb art, architecture, history, antiques and crafts from around the world.

Start by taking a leisurely walking tour along Alexandria's cobblestone streets, some of which were surveyed in 1748 by George Washington, then still a teenager. The best place to get your bearings is at the **Ramsay House Visitor Center**, on the corner of Fairfax and King Streets. This is the oldest house in Alexandria, built 24 years before the town was founded. William Ramsay, who became a prosperous merchant, wanted to get established before his competitors. Rather than spend the time to build a new residence, in 1749 he barged his house up the Potomac River, probably from the Scottish settlement at Dumfries.

The Ramsay tartan hangs on the door welcoming curious visitors. Brochures, maps, up-to-date information on special events and a free film provide extensive background on all the things to do and see in Alexandria. The Visitor Center is open daily 9:00 A.M. to 5:00 P.M. except on major holidays.

Just five doors away is the **Carlyle House**, 121 North Fairfax Street, built three years after Ramsay's house was moved to town. John Carlyle modeled his home on elaborate Scottish manor homes. Built before the town developed city ordinances, it is the only house in Alexandria that was not in line with the street. The Carlyle House found its place in history three years after completion. General Braddock, who was using the Alexandria house as his headquarters, invited five colonial governors to join him for a conference. When the talk turned to taxation, young George Washington maintained that it would be easier to raise the dead than to raise taxes. Ten years later when the Stamp Act became the symbol of taxation without representation, this issue became a leading cause of the colonists' fight with England. The Carlyle House is open at a nominal fee on Tuesday through Saturday 10:00 A.M. to 4:30 P.M. and Sunday NOON to 4:30 P.M.

As you wander from one interesting attraction to another you will pass houses and businesses built in a variety of architectural styles. The 100 block of Prince Street, known as Captain's Row, was popular with the sea captains who visited this bustling port. The 200 block is called Gentry Row because of the elaborate homes built by the town's prosperous residents. Be sure to note the "spite houses," alley houses built to gain control of the narrow passageways or alleys. You can see examples at 205 King Street, 523 Queen Street and 316 South Royal Street. These are all private homes and cannot be toured.

There are two homes here associated with the Lee family. After the first presidential election, Washington was riding out of town on the way to his inauguration in New York. When he passed the **Lee-Fendall House**, at 614 Oronoco Street. Lighthorse Harry Lee, who was dining there that night, went out to the front steps and delivered a moving farewell address to Washington from the citizens of Alexandria. Since then 37 Lees have made the Lee-Fendall House their home and filled it with family heirlooms. Tours are given Tuesday through Saturday from 10:00 A.M. to 4:00 P.M.; they begin at NOON on Sundays. Admission is charged.

Across the street, at 607 Oronoco Street, is the **Boyhood Home of Robert E. Lee** where young Robert lived from 1811 to 1816. His family moved back again from 1820 to 1825. One of the bedrooms is decorated to look as it did when young Robert lived here. Lafayette was entertained here in 1824 when he returned to America to celebrate the Revolutionary victories. Tours are Tuesday through Saturday 10:00 A.M. to 4:00 P.M.; they begin at 1:00 P.M. on Sunday. Admission is charged.

Several public and commercial buildings have an interesting historical past. At 118 North Washington Street you'll find **Christ Church** where George Washington had a pew. Lee worshipped here and was confirmed on July 17, 1853. Most 20th-century presidents have worshipped here during their terms of office. You can visit Christ Church daily 9:00 A.M. to 4:00 P.M. Sunday services are offered in the morning, and tours start at 2:00 P.M.

Alexandria can justifiably be termed George Washington's hometown. He not only worshipped here, he patronized the local establishments. He was a steady customer at the **Stabler-Leadbeater Apothecary Shop**, at 107 South Fairfax Street. After one in Bethlehem, Pennsylvania, this is the second oldest drugstore in the country. Now the shop displays the country's largest collection of apothecary jars in their original setting. The museum also has early medical implements and patent medicines. Legend has it that Lee was shopping here when he learned that he was ordered to Harpers Ferry to handle John Brown's raid on the federal arsenal. The shop can be visited Monday through Saturday 10:00 A.M. to 4:30 P.M.

On his visits to Alexandria, Washington was accustomed to stopping at **Gadsby's Tavern** for a meal and the latest news. Now the tavern is both a museum and an inn that serves colonial as well as other fare. The museum tour includes a look at the bedrooms used by lodgers, the ballroom and the ice house. Tavern owner, John Gadsby, dug an ice cellar in 1805 and sold blocks of ice from the Potomac River for eight cents a pound. The tavern is open Tuesday through Saturday from 10:00 A.M. to 5:00 P.M.; on Sunday it opens at NOON. An admission is charged for tours.

Alexandria deserves credit for its efforts to uncover the past; it is one of the few cities in the country to undertake a major archaeological study beneath its visible historic structures. Artifacts recovered in this program are displayed at the Alexandria Archaeology offices on the second floor of the **Torpedo Factory Art Center**. The latter is another must on any excursion to Alexandria. Studios and workshops for nearly 200 artists showcase a wide range of work here, daily from 10:00 A.M. to 5:00 P.M.

The Visitor Center has a brochure listing many excellent restaurants in Alexandria. Options include a wide variety of ethnic fare—Greek, Spanish, French, Italian—seafood specialties and traditional cuisine. You also can pack a picnic lunch and take a midday break at the waterfront park right next to the Torpedo Factory Art Center on North Union Street. Specialty shops and boutiques offer an abundance of handcrafted and international wares from around the world.

Directions: From the Beltway I-695/95 take Virginia Exit 1, U.S. 1 north into Alexandria. Make a right on King Street for the Ramsay House Visitor Center.

Annapolis

Christmas Cheer in Colonial Capital

Annapolis, the 18th-century Maryland capital, was considered for restoration by the same foundation that restored Williamsburg, the colonial capital of Virginia. Williamsburg was chosen instead, but some people feel Annapolis gained from her loss. Instead of representing only the past, the city is an aesthetic blend of the 18th, 19th and 20th centuries.

Annapolis's mixture of old and new is particularly felicitous during the Christmas season. Fine 18th-century homes are garlanded for the holidays in authentic colonial style. Specialty shops along Main Street brim with tempting items. In between purchases, shoppers investigate delicious smells and delicacies at the City Dock Market.

Decorating Annapolis's old homes is like adding tinsel to the Christmas tree; it isn't necessary, but it adds a final note of splendor. The shining star of Historic Annapolis's restoration is the **home of William Paca**, a signer of the Declaration of Independence. Each Christmastime the Georgian mansion is decked with ribbons, fruit and greenery—swatches, garlands and wreaths. By mid-December the tables are laid for a colonial feast, and on selected weekends you can enjoy colonial cooking demonstrations in the Paca kitchen. In all seasons the rooms are decorated to suggest activities that might have been going on in the 18th-century, from an afternoon tea party to an evening card game. The house does not need the bright greens and reds of the holidays to lend color to its rooms. After peeling 22 layers of paint and wallpaper from the walls, restorers found a brilliant Prussian-blue color scheme. Tours of the Paca House, 186 Prince George Street, are from 10:00 A.M. to 4:00 P.M. Tuesday through Saturday and NOON to 4:00 P.M. on Sunday. The garden is also open Monday from 10:00 A.M. to 5:00 P.M. If you visit during the spring or summer months don't miss Paca's pleasure garden. You get a bird's-eye glimpse of it from the upstairs windows of the mansion.

In 1760 Samuel Chase, one of the more radical and outspoken signers of the Declaration, also built here. Economic reverses forced him to sell his unfinished home to Edward Lloyd IV, who then hired William Buckland to complete the exterior and design the interior. Buckland's work was done with breathtaking detail as you can see when the house is open for tours Tuesday through Saturday from 2:00 to 4:00 P.M. The **Chase-Lloyd House** at 22 Maryland Avenue is now a home for elderly ladies, and only the first floor is open for tours. It too is specially decorated for the holidays.

Another Annapolis gem is the **Hammond-Harwood House**, directly across from the Chase-Lloyd House. This historic home always has a Christmas Greens Show and Sale as well as refreshments, music, decorations and candlelight tours. The Hammond-Harwood House is the only house Buckland, who was called the tastemaker of the colonies, both designed and built. Many consider this his finest work. Located at 19 Maryland Avenue, the house is open Tuesday through Saturday from 10:00 A.M. to 4:00 P.M. and Sunday from 1:00 to 4:00 P.M.

Another Historic Annapolis property is the **Victualling Warehouse** at 77 Main Street, where the Maritime Museum is located. Victualling means provisioning a ship with food, new sails, rope and other equipment, and items pertaining to these responsibilities are displayed here. Hours are 11:00 A.M. to 4:30 P.M. daily. Across the City Dock area from the maritime museum is the **Tobacco Prise House** where tobacco was once pressed into hogsheads to be rolled to the dock for shipping. The details of this important colonial activity are explained Tuesday through Sunday from 11:00 A.M. to 4:30 P.M. from mid-April through October. Combination tickets to tour these historic buildings can be obtained at Historic Annapolis headquarters in the Old Treasury on State Circle (410)267-8149.

The **Governor's Mansion** opens its state rooms for tours by reservation only on Tuesday, Wednesday and Thursday. Each First Lady of the state can influence the decor of these rooms, so return visits are interesting. To arrange a tour call (410)261-2961. The Governor traditionally holds an Open House in early December. At the same time there is a candlelight tour of the State House. This is always interesting to see because it was here in the Senate Chambers that George Washington appeared before the Continental Congress in December 1783 and resigned his commission.

U.S. naval history is deeply entwined with Annapolis because of the **United State Naval Academy**, where so many naval officers trained. You are welcome to visit the Yard, or campus, from 9:00 A.M. to 5:00 P.M. daily. Enter through Gate 1, at the end of King George Street, as that will take you directly to the Visitor Center parking lot. In the Center, located in Ricketts Hall, pick up a self-guided walking tour brochure of the academy. While touring don't miss the stained-glass windows of the chapel. Each window depicts a biblical passage about the sea. John Paul Jones is buried in the crypt. The Academy Museum is open Monday through Saturday from 9:00 A.M. to 4:45 P.M. and Sunday from 11:00 A.M. to 4:45 P.M. A one-hour escorted walk is given daily on the hour.

The spirit of Annapolis is demonstrated with flair by the annual holiday **boat parade** sponsored by the Eastport Yacht Club. Each year between 50 and 100 boats, each decorated with thousands of lights, participate in this glittering Christmas present to the city. The tradition started in the early 1980s and has grown into a not-to-be-missed holiday event. The parade passes through Annapolis Harbor and Spa Creek. You can best view the spectacle from the City Dock, the Spa Creek Bridge or from the many restaurants along the water.

Directions: From the Beltway I-495/95 take Route 50 east. Take Rowe Boulevard exit, Route 70, into Annapolis and continue to State Circle where you can find the Old Treasury Building and obtain maps and information.

Baltimore Museum of Industry

How People Worked

Baltimore's Inner Harbor reflects the city's fun side; across the harbor, the Baltimore-Locust Point Industrial District reflects the working side of the city and is an appropriate location for the **Baltimore Museum of Industry**.

The museum's motto is "A working museum for a working city." The weekend bustle within the museum's three work areas replicates the weekday bustle on this side of the harbor. The museum is in the 1865 Platt Packing Company, an oyster cannery. Marking its location is the last crane from the recently dismantled Key Highway shipyards. This industrial-endangered species serves as a visual reminder of one of Baltimore's vanishing industries.

Those who think industry is exclusively steel, smokestacks and workers in coveralls will get a new perspective at this hands-on museum. Here you can see the jobs—past and present—Baltimoreans held and the tools and equipment they used in their work. This is not a dry, scholarly presentation; visitors of all ages enjoy working the vintage machines.

One work environment is the turn-of-the-century machine shop, which now makes parts for the museum's antique equipment. Floor-to-ceiling belts, turning flywheels and planing machines bear an uncanny resemblance to Rube Goldberg's cartoon contraption. One old piece is a Simplex time clock used by the payroll master to determine how many hours each employee worked.

Another re-created work setting is an old-time print shop where visitors can help "pull the devil's tail." One try at the difficult lever and you'll understand why so many printers developed muscular left arms. Another popular hands-on option is the 1900 Poco Proof Press; few visitors leave without printing their own souvenir that reads: "I Printed This."

Your visit will bring to life many commonly used expressions. For example, a printer had to "mind his Ps and Qs" as he picked the type from his composite case. The printer's ability to select the correct type was like a touch typist's technique, and a good printer had to be as fast as a good typist. (There is, however, another explanation of this expression that suggests it referred to bartenders pouring pints and quarts.) The phrase "hot off the press" takes on new meaning when you learn that printers dried wet ink by holding the freshly printed page over a candle flame.

In the printing work area you'll see the evolution of printing machines. The collection includes cumbersome early models like the 1870 Baltimore Jobber press and more modern pieces like the 1952 version of the linotype.

Visitors also get a chance to participate in the garment shop. You'll really get the feel of the job—you can try your hand, and your foot, working the vintage treadle sewing machines. Many young girls once spent their daylight hours in Baltimore lofts working at these sewing machines. The specialization of these

184

vintage models surprises many visitors. You'll see a belt looper, a hand-operated button sewer and a large and small basting machine. There are also irons used in the garment business that are so heavy many visitors are unable to lift them from the table.

Youngsters have their own special activity areas. There is an activity center called motor works where kids punch out paper cars on an assembly line and work in an 1880s cannery. Performing specialized tasks, children become shuckers, labelers and printers. These programs and others that give children a feel for social history are run on weekends; call ahead for specific times.

Other exhibits remind young and old of Baltimore's canning and shipping industry. This was the first city in America to have a gas company. The earliest gas fixtures were gas lamps; these rings of fire were invented by painter Rembrandt Peale. The museum's re-created tinsmith's shop is gas-lit. You also can visit an 1895 drugstore that once stood on the corner of Eastern Avenue and Conkling Street in Baltimore. Another shop is the electric repair shop stocked with a myriad of old-fashioned household appliances.

The museum has its own dock space, and moored there is the **S.S. *Baltimore***, a 1906 steam engine tugboat. This tugboat is one of the last of its type to operate on the East Coast. It was recovered from the bottom of the Sassafras River on Maryland's Eastern Shore. Again operational, the S.S. *Baltimore* now serves as the museum's floating ambassador of goodwill. The Tadpole Clipper, a prototype seaplane made in 1937 by the Glenn L. Martin Company, is undergoing restoration.

The Baltimore Museum of Industry at 1415 Key Highway is open Saturdays 10:00 A.M. to 5:00 P.M. and Thursday, Friday and Sunday from NOON to 6:00 P.M. Admission is charged. For details on special programs call (410)727-4808.

If you have time extend your excursion and visit nearby **Fort McHenry** National Monument and Historic Shrine. The fort figured prominently in the War of 1812. It was the flag flying over this fort that inspired Francis Scott Key to write our national anthem. At the Visitor Center there is an inspirational film about the "star" fort. You also can visit the reconstructed barracks, guardhouses and powder magazine. The fort is open daily; it is closed on major holidays. There are picnic tables and a mile-long waterfront path.

Directions: From the Beltway take Exit 22, the Baltimore-Washington Parkway, into Baltimore. It will become Russell Street. Continue up to Pratt Street and then make a right to the Inner Harbor. Turn right at Light Street and follow signs for Fort McHenry. For the Baltimore Museum of Industry turn left at Key Highway to the museum. For Fort McHenry continue on Key

Highway to Lawrence Street and turn right. Take Lawrence to Fort Avenue and turn left and proceed to the gate of Fort McHenry.

Capital Children's Museum

"I Do and I Understand"

One of Washington's most captivating, but all too frequently overlooked, attractions just keeps improving. **Capital Children's Museum** is geared to children 2 to 12, but older youngsters, as well as parents will find it a place that stimulates both the mind and the senses. The working philosophy here reflects the Chinese proverb:

> I hear and I forget
> I see and I remember
> I do and I understand.

This is definitely a hands-on museum. Youngsters paint with a computer, bake a tortilla, launch a satellite, crawl through a manhole, print a poster, read an electronic newspaper, move water with an Archimedean screw, fashion a yarn necklace, experiment with lasers, send messages on a ship's blinker and much, much more.

In one of the museum's major exhibit areas, Communications Hall, exploration begins in an Ice Age cave, reproduced with ancient drawings like those found in caves in southern France. A sound-and-light show introduces the complexities of communications. Youngsters are given a try at communicating with such antiquated means as the Greek torch, African drums and picturograms. The exhibit continues with displays of coding, on through computers and sound tapes. A game called Orbit allows children to simulate a satellite launch.

The **Hall of Information** highlights inventive techniques that have been used to store information, from painting on hide and clay tablets to use of knotted string and wooden tally sticks, on through computer codes and punch cards. To reach the Mass Communication section, visitors walk through the arcade of a 1906 nickelodeon, the last one to operate in Washington. To illustrate the vast difference the printing press has made in mass communication, an 18th-century print shop with working press is shown adjacent to a scriptorium. Children experience the extent of this progress for themselves when they write with a quill pen, then operate the press.

The second major exhibit area, **International Hall,** provides a tantalizing introduction to Mexico. At the Marketplace children don sombreros and serapes and dance to traditional Mexican music. An authentic Sierra Mountain cabin is re-created, and the daily life of the people is explained while youngsters prepare and sample tortillas. On a simulated Mexican farm Rosie the goat enjoys attention and helps focus the children's attention on rural life. In a Oaxacan kitchen, young visitors help to make a regional chocolate drink using lava-rock utensils.

In the **Think Metric Room,** kids weigh and price fruits and vegetables using a metric scale. The long jump, calculated in centimeters, provides a more active learning opportunity. After exercising, children weigh themselves on metric scales. In Science Hall over 20 hands-on activities deal with light and color. Another exhibit introduces the science of sound and the world of the deaf. Youngsters can try sign language, practice reading lips and experience sound through vibrations.

The **City Room** brings metropolitan life down to size—kid size. Manholes lead to a maze of underground pipes and circuitry that young explorers can investigate. To get the feeling of a cross section of city jobs, children may try on a policeman's or fireman's uniform, a mail carrier's jacket, a construction worker's hard hat, a motorman's cap and also fiddle with various job-related gear.

There is so much to do that one visit will serve only as an introduction to this innovative place. Temporary exhibits continually bring in something new, and there are varied weekend workshops and special events. There is a gift shop and a cafeteria. The museum is open daily 10:00 A.M. to 5:00 P.M., closed on major holidays. Admission is charged.

Directions: The Capital Children's Museum is located inside the Beltway at 800 3rd Street, N.E., three blocks from Union Station.

Dupont-Kalorama Museums

Capital Treats

Like a foil-wrapped bonbon, the setting of the mansion museums in the Dupont-Kalorama district is part of the treat. The area surrounds Dupont Circle, where New Hampshire, Connecticut and Massachusetts avenues meet, and extends north up Kalorama Road. It's an elegant district filled with embassies, gracious private homes, restaurants, sidewalk cafes, art galleries and specialty shops.

The **Dupont-Kalorama Consortium** was formed in the early 1980s to assist visitors in savoring the high spots of this district by combining them in a walking-tour guide that is available at each Consortium member. You can also obtain a museum-walk guide by calling (202)387-2151. Consortium members are the

Phillips Collection, the Textile Museum, Fondo del Sol Visual Arts and Media Center, Anderson House, the Heurich Mansion, Woodrow Wilson House and Meridian House (see Dupont-Kalorama Houses selection).

In 1921 Duncan Phillips opened America's oldest museum of modern art in two rooms of his Georgian Revival mansion at 1600-1612 21st Street, N.W. Phillips described his collection as a "museum of modern art and its sources." His family made their fortune in the Pittsburgh steel industry, and he dedicated the museum to his father and brother who died within thirteen months of each other. Duncan started collecting Impressionist and Post-Impressionist work in 1916. As he and his wife, Marjorie, continued to accumulate paintings, art filled the house, forcing them to move to another residence.

The Phillips Collection, which now extends into a modern annex, is administered by Duncan Phillips's son Laughlin. The rooms in the mansion wing still retain a home-like appearance while the upstairs galleries have comfortable settees and chairs for sitting and drinking in favorites. The list of artists exhibited is formidable: Monet, Cezanne, Matisse, El Greco, Goya, Renoir, Kandinsky, Klee, O'Keefe and others. Some of the famous works include Renoir's *The Luncheon of the Boating Party* (purchased for $125,000 in 1923), El Greco's *The Repentant Peter*, Degas's *Dancers at the Bar*, Van Gogh's *The Road Menders*, Klee's *Little Moe*, Archipenko's *Standing Woman* and Marjorie Phillips's (Duncan's wife) *Night Baseball*. The latter, one of the museum's most popular works, depicts Joe DiMaggio at bat against the Washington Senators in Griffith Stadium. The exhibited work changes continuously as only 100 items can be displayed at one time from the permanent collection of 2,500. The museum also hosts temporary exhibits and presents gallery talks, lectures, concerts and special programs.

The Phillips Collection is open Tuesday through Saturday from 10:00 A.M. to 5:00 P.M. and Sundays from 2:00 to 7:00 P.M. Closed on holidays. An outstanding museum shop stays open until a half hour before closing. Admission is by donations. A cafe is open until 45 minutes before closing time. For information on special programs call (202)387-0961.

George Hewitt Myers amassed a very different type of collection. In 1896, Myers, a sophomore at Yale, purchased an Oriental rug for his college room. This was the start of an extensive collection that now includes rugs and textiles from Turkey, Persia, Egypt, India, China, Indonesia, Spain and Peru. Myers's collection is housed in the mansion built for him in 1916 by John Russell Pope. Myers purchased the adjoining house and renovated it to provide additional gallery space. The **Textile Museum**'s permanent collection includes more than 1,000 rugs and

10,000 textiles plus more than 13,000 volumes in the library related to textiles. The collection is exhibited on a rotating basis augmented by special exhibits. Ethnic art, costumes, quilts, rugs, tapestries and numerous other items are displayed. The public can bring in examples and staff experts will explain their provenance, that is, the ethnic and geographic history of the item. No monetary value is assigned during these evaluations done from 11:00 A.M. to 1:00 P.M. the first Wednesday of each month. The museum has a shop with an extensive collection of books on textiles plus artistic handcrafted specialty items.

The Textile Museum, 2320 S Street, N.W., is open Tuesday through Saturday from 10:00 A.M. to 5:00 P.M. and Sunday from 1:00 to 5:00 P.M. Walk-in tours are given on Saturdays from 1:00 to 3:00 P.M. The library is open Wednesday through Friday during museum hours and on Saturday until 2:00 P.M. You are welcome to enjoy a picnic lunch in the picturesque garden behind Myers's stately brick Georgian mansion. There is no admission, but $2 donations are suggested.

Fondo del Sol Visual Art and Media Center is more modest in appearance and scope. Housed in a row-house with a front bay window that provides a bright exhibit room, this museum, whose name means center of the sun, offers changing art shows featuring Hispanic, Caribbean and Native American work. The museum, founded by artists and community members in 1973, also has a permanent collection of pre-Columbian, folk and contemporary art. There is an uncatalogued video collection that includes performance art by musicians from the Americas. Fondo del Sol, 2112 R Street, N.W., is open Tuesday through Saturday from 12:30 to 5:30 P.M. Admission is by contribution.

Directions: The Dupont-Kalorama district is in the Dupont Circle area.

Ephrata Cloister

Radical Religious Reminder

Ephrata Cloister undoubtedly is at its scenic best in the spring or autumn. It is in winter, however, when the biting wind whips through the quiet valley along the Cocalico Creek that visitors are more apt to get a feel for the magnetism of Conrad Beissel. Only a man with his forceful personality and strong beliefs could have persuaded his fellow Seventh-Day Baptists to live at this spartan settlement.

The Ephrata Cloister in Lancaster County is the country's most outstanding example of European medieval architecture. Craftsmen slightly modified Old World building techniques to re-create this rustic frontier settlement. All but one of the eleven surviving buildings (the stone academy) are log or frame structures. The buildings' whitewashed clay interiors cover a core of hand-split oak beams.

Ephrata Cloister had three orders: the brotherhood, sisterhood and married householders who worshipped but did not live within the cloister. Beissel's followers attempted to reproduce the primitive Christianity of the Old Testament by living an austere, simple, meditative life. In theory, even the architectural details of the buildings centered the Brethren's attention on spiritual matters. The narrow hallways suggested the straight and narrow path members were to follow, while the low doorways reminded all to practice humility.

A brief slide presentation on the background and beliefs of the sect precedes the escorted portion of your tour of the cloister. The first building you are taken to is the **Saron**, a three-storied house built for the sisterhood in 1743. The sect grouped the women according to the work they did at the cloister—writing, singing or weaving. Two groups shared a workroom on each floor. The sisters slept in small individual cells with a wooden bench around two sides that served as both seat and bed. A small wooden block served as a pillow. In one sister's cell you'll see a huge woven basket. It was too big to remove when it was finished.

You might think it would be impossible to sleep in such uncomfortable conditions. After learning about the daily schedule you might believe that members would have been happy to sleep on the floor, so exhausting was their regime. The day began at 5:00 A.M. and both men and women worked all day at chores necessary to maintain their existence. The one real meal of the day, served at 6:00 P.M., was "pearled barley boiled in milk, with bread broken into it," plus "pumpkin mush, with slices of small crusted bread on a plate." The members could partake of bread, water and fruit at any time during the day. In the evening from 7:00–9:00 members would study, or attend singing or writing classes. Their rest would be interrupted after three hours for the midnight service that would last until 2:00 A.M., giving them three more hours of sleep before beginning the schedule again.

Members worshipped in the **Saal**, the second building you visit on your tour. This meetinghouse, built in 1741, first served as a place for the married members to worship, but gradually the entire sect gathered here. The sisters filled the second balcony. The regular service consisted of scripture reading, preaching and a capella singing. Special services included communion and foot washing, followed by a love feast of lamb stew. This was the only time members ate meat.

After seeing these two buildings you are on your own to explore the remaining cloister structures. A householder's residence shows you how married members lived. It would look spartan in other surroundings, but in comparison with the austere cells of the celibate members the house is well appointed. Married members had a real bed and chairs with backs and other household utensils that gave their home more style and comfort. It is interesting to see the simple cabin the brothers built in 1748 for their leader, Conrad Beissel, who lived here the last 20 years of his life.

At its peak the group numbered 300, and its fame spread from the New World to the Old. Voltaire and the noted French thinker Raynal wrote about the cloistered community. Respected colonial political figures visited Ephrata including Proprietor Thomas Penn, Declaration of Independence signer George Ross, Governor William Denny and Governor George Thomas. The latter liked the bread made at the cloister, and he had it supplied to him the rest of the time he was in the Lancaster area. It was not only the famous who were welcome at the cloister; all who found their way to the community were given food and shelter.

The community also gained notice from the printing press they set up in 1745. It was one of the earliest complete publishing centers in the colonies. The press was first in the Brothers' House (no longer standing), then moved to the building you see today. The Brethren printed original manuscripts by Beissel and other members and translated noted volumes into German. Their most ambitious project was the translation from Dutch of the *Martyrs' Mirror*. It ran to 1,512 pages, making it the largest book printed in Pennsylvania before the Revolution. Fifteen brothers worked on the book for three years, yet the price was only one pound, about $2.50. In 1990 Ephrata Cloister acquired one of these valuable old volumes for its collection. The elaborate bookplate done by brothers skilled in Frakturschriften, an ornate style of calligraphy, make this a prized addition to Ephrata's collection. When the cloister was operating, the work of the Fraktur, or writing school, filled the walls of the cloister. A few faded examples remain.

The cloister was also noted for its style of singing and its musical compositions. Conrad Beissel was one of America's first composers. He developed an unusual rhythmic style and a peculiar falsetto intonation. Listeners described the otherworldly, ethereal music as music for the soul, not for the ear. You can hear Beissel's music on summer Saturdays from July to Labor Day in the musical drama *Vorspiel* which depicts cloister life.

If you want to look like a character in the drama, stop at the **Solitary House** where you can try on the robes sect members wore. The white habits suggest those worn by Capuchin friars. After you put on the robe try lying on the wooden rack that served as a bed and place the block pillow beneath your head.

This hands-on experience reinforces the impression of a group of people who dedicated their lives to their spiritual existence without any consideration for bodily comfort.

The complex includes other buildings such as the bake house, craft house, carpentry shop, stables, barn and academy. As you leave be sure to stop at the sales shop where there is an interesting collection of books and hand-crafted items.

Ephrata Cloister is open at a nominal charge Monday through Saturday 9:00 A.M. to 5:00 P.M. and Sunday NOON to 5:00 P.M. For more information or ticket queries for the *Vorspiel* call (717)733-6600.

While in the area be sure to stop at another religious sponsored spot, the **Mennonite Self-Help Crafts of the World Shop** at 240 N. Reading Road (Route 272 north) in Ephrata (there is also one in Bird-in-Hand). This shop buys quality handicrafts from 37 countries and sells them at surprisingly reasonable prices. Try to time your arrival so that you can lunch in their tearoom, which features the cuisine of a different country each week. The varied fare has so impressed local diners that shop volunteers have compiled a cookbook of favorite recipes. Shop hours are Monday through Saturday 9:00 A.M. to 5:00 P.M. (on Friday it stays open until 9:00 P.M.). The tearoom closes at 4:00 P.M. except on Friday.

Another unique shopping experience awaits at **The Artworks at Doneckers**, once an old shoe factory and now a collection of artists' studios and workshops. The shops are filled with everything from pottery and furniture to jewelry and fine arts. The huge building also has a lunch spot plus exhibit space for scheduled special events. The Artworks at Doneckers is located at 100 North State Street in Ephrata and is open daily 11:45 A.M. to 5:00 P.M., Saturdays 10:00 A.M. to 5:00 P.M. and Sunday NOON to 4:00 P.M. Closed on Wednesdays.

Directions: From the Beltway I-495/95 take I-95 to the Baltimore Beltway I-695 and head west to I-83. Take that north to the York area and then pick up Route 30 east to Lancaster. At Lancaster take Route 22 north to the Ephrata Cloister on your right.

Folger Shakespeare Library, Explorers Hall and Union Station

As You Like It

A visit to Stratford-on-Avon evokes Elizabethan times, but you can experience that same era closer to home. The **Folger Shakespeare Library** in Washington gives visitors a glimpse of Merrie England during the 16th and 17th centuries. The Exhibition Gallery with its mellow oak paneling and barrel-vaulted ceiling replicates the interior of a great Elizabethan hall. The Queen's coat of arms is carved over the door. The heraldic banners and coats of arms also include Shakespeare's family emblem. Shakespeare's fictitious characters are immortalized in Thomas Sully's 1835 painting of Portia and Shylock and Benjamin West's 1793 rendering of Lear and Cordelia. Exhibits include scripts annotated by noted Shakespearean actors, a model of the Globe Theater, 79 copies of the First Folio, an extensive collection of playbills plus costume and set drawings.

The Shakespeare Theater is a replica of a public playhouse of the Bard's day. The Tudor-style timber-and-plaster inn-yard theater has a series of balconies, a canopy over the stage area and a trap door through which actors rise to heaven.

The Folger is the repository for the world's largest collection of Shakespearean material. Henry Clay Folger, president and chairman of the board of the Standard Oil Company of New York, and his wife, Emily Jordan Folger, amassed this collection on their many trips abroad between 1889 and 1919. It also contains an outstanding collection on English and continental history from 1476 to 1700. The library is administered by Folger's alma mater, Amherst College. The reading room is open to qualified scholars but not to the general public. The Folger Shakespeare Library is open at no charge Monday through Saturday from 10:00 A.M. to 4:00 P.M. It is also open during the same hours on Sunday from mid-April to Labor Day. The public can tour the **theater** and **Exhibition Gallery.** Be sure to note the building's exterior bas relief sculpture depicting scenes from Shakespeare's plays. For information call (202)544-4600. The box office number is (202)546-4000. The Shakespeare Theatre group that performed at the Folger for many years is now at the Lansburgh Theater at 450 Seventh Street, N.W.

While you are downtown, make your own discoveries at **Explorers Hall** at the National Geographic Society. The Hall has a permanent, computer-interactive center called Geographica that demonstrates multiple aspects of the Earth using the beautiful photographs and videos that have made National Geographic world renowned. The nerve center of Geographica is Earth Station One, a 72-seat interactive amphitheater that simulates an orbital flight 23,000 miles above the earth. Explorers Hall's 11-foot globe represents the earth. A computer program that runs several times an hour gives visitors traveling on the space station a chance to answer questions posed by the captain. The answers are instantly analyzed and displayed on twin video walls.

Although Explorers Hall has been revamped in recent years, you still see old favorites like the giant Olmec head, Admiral Peary's sled, the hominoid skeleton and Henry the macaw, always popular with young visitors. The south end of the hall has changing exhibits. The shop in Explorers Den sells books, atlases, globes and nature-related items.

Explorers Hall is open daily at no charge from 9:00 A.M. to 5:00 P.M.; on Sunday it opens an hour later. Closed on Christmas Day.

If you want to make a full day of your downtown foray, why not head for **Union Station**, once the largest train station in the world and now splendidly restored. The gold-leaf ceilings and columns glitter anew and the white granite walls shine.

Union Station is still an active railroad depot for Amtrak and commuter trains. If it no longer equals its once daily average of 40,000 passengers, it is still a bustling transportation hub. But now revamped and refurbished Union Station is itself a destination. Lunch in one of the many tempting eateries and browse through the sophisticated shops.

Directions: The Folger Shakespeare Library is at 201 East Capitol Street, which runs between Constitution and Independence avenues in southeast Washington. Explorers Hall is at 17th and M streets in northwest Washington. Union Station is on Columbus Plaza at 50 Massachusetts Avenue in northeast Washington close to the Capitol.

Ford's Theatre National Historic Site and Petersen House

Comedy and Tragedy

The audience expected light comedy, but they saw high tragedy. It was the night of April 14, 1865. There was a full house for **Ford Theatre**'s production of *Our American Cousin*. President and Mrs. Lincoln watched from Box Seven. In the balcony, a young actor followed the play line by line, waiting for his entrance. The actor was John Wilkes Booth, and he had written his own part into the production. Booth waited until late in the play when there was only one actor on stage and the audience was laughing; that was the moment he chose to enter the President's box from the Dress Circle and put a pistol to Lincoln's head. Major Rathbone, attending the play with the Lincolns, tried to hold Booth, but the agile actor jumped to the stage. Although Booth injured his leg in his leap, he still made good his escape.

The audience was paralyzed, but quick thinking doctors in the audience rushed to the President's box and carried the wounded Lincoln across the street to Petersen House where he died the next morning. Booth escaped as far as Port Royal, Virginia, where he was shot 11 days after the assassination.

The tragedy forced Ford's Theatre to close. The federal government purchased the building and used it to house the files of Union soldiers and the Army Medical Museum. This ill-fated building suffered yet another tragic incident on June 9, 1893. The third floor collapsed, killing and injuring a number of federal employees.

Exhibits connected with Lincoln's assassination have been exhibited at Ford's Theatre since the 1930s. Many years were to pass, however, before the theater was restored to its appearance on that fateful night. In 1968 Ford's Theatre reopened. Box Seven had reproductions of Lincoln's rocker and his wife's straight-back chair. The red sofa is original; so also is the framed engraving of George Washington on the front of the box. Although plays are again performed at Ford's Theatre, this box bears silent witness to its last patrons.

You don't have to attend a performance at Ford's Theatre to explore the **Lincoln Museum** in the basement. Here you'll see the Oldroyd Collection that has been on display since the 1930s plus farm tools from the time when Lincoln tilled the soil in Illinois, some of his books and pieces of his surveying equipment. The most significant item is the single-shot derringer Booth used to slay Lincoln. The display includes the clothes Lincoln and Booth were wearing, the flag that draped Lincoln's coffin and photographs of the funeral.

Ford's Theatre is open 9:00 A.M. to 5:00 P.M. daily. There is no admission. If Wednesday and Sunday matinees are being performed the theater is not open, but the Lincoln Museum can still be toured.

After touring Ford's, cross the street to **Petersen House**. When the wounded President was carried out of the theater, a boarder staying at the Petersen House suggested they bring Lincoln into the empty back bedroom. The President, because of his height, was placed diagonally on the small cottage bed. His wounded head rested on the pillow over the edge of the bed. Mrs. Lincoln spent the long night in the parlor of the boarding house. She was joined by her eldest son and close friends who stood vigil with her. Dr. Charles Leale, who had been at the theater, monitored the dying President. During the night, Secretary of War Edwin Stanton also established himself at the Petersen House, using another bedroom as a command post as he began an investigation of the assassination. Government officials stopped at the house all through the night to pay their respects to the dying President.

At 7:22 A.M. on April 15 Lincoln died. His body was taken immediately to the White House. A boarder took a photograph of the bed on which Lincoln died. This picture, which was not circulated until 100 years after Lincoln's death, was used in the restoration of Petersen House in the 1930s.

The Petersens did not profit from their brush with history, despite the public's interest in Lincoln's assassination. William

Petersen died of a drug overdose in 1871. His wife died later that same year from a heart attack. Their boarding house was sold to the government in 1896. The Petersen House is open at no charge 9:00 A.M. to 5:00 P.M. daily except Christmas Day.

Directions: Ford's Theatre and the Petersen House are located inside the Beltway in downtown Washington. Ford's Theatre is at 511 10th Street, N.W. The Petersen House is directly across the street at #516.

Hillwood Museum

Old World Elegance

Magazines and television stories about the lifestyles of the rich and famous are always popular. Visiting the home of one of America's untitled aristocrats is even more appealing than the tantalizing, vicarious glimpses the media offers.

In and around Washington there are many private homes that pique the public interest. A few of these are open to the public, and one of the most interesting is Marjorie Merriweather Post's **Hillwood Museum**. This estate was originally owned and developed by Isaac Peirce, grandson of George Peirce who is known for his work on the arboretum and park at Longwood Gardens in Kennett Square, Pennsylvania (see selection). In 1955 Mrs. Post acquired Hillwood and put her distinctive stamp on it inside and out.

The mansion showcases a priceless art collection in a royal setting. Many of the furnishings and bibelots were, in fact, created for the royal families of Europe. An enthusiastic collector of French pieces, Mrs. Post was particularly fond of the matching sofas and chairs in the drawing room. Louis XVI and Marie Antoinette commissioned this set as a gift for Prince Henry of Prussia, the brother of Frederick the Great. Also in the drawing room a portrait of Empress Eugenie, consort of Napoleon III, hangs between two wall cases filled with Sevres porcelain.

In the dining room the walls are covered with an 18th-century French carved paneling from a Parisian town house. The porcelain tableware commissioned by Catherine the Great, reflects Mrs. Post's fascination with Russia. In the breakfast room the striking green and clear glass chandelier once lit Catherine's suite at Tsarskoe Selo, the Romanov estate outside St. Petersburg.

Mrs. Post's husband, Joseph E. Davis, was the U.S. ambassador to the Soviet Union in 1937 and 1938. The new Soviet government confiscated art and furnishings from aristocrats and church prelates and sold them to finance Russia's industrialization. The priceless Russian treasures were sold by the gram, without any consideration for their artistic worth. Silver chalices were priced at five cents a gram. Mrs. Post purchased many of the rare items in her collection during this period. She acquired additional items after she returned to the United States, building one of the most comprehensive collections outside the Soviet Union.

When you visit Hillwood you will see an impressive array of Russian porcelain, glass, silver and jewel-studded objects. Many of the exquisite items were created by Carl Faberge for members of the Romanov family. He made the lovely diamond-studded crown worn by the last three czarinas at their weddings.

The Russian influence extends to the grounds where you can see a one-room dacha. This wooded cottage resembles those used by the Russian aristocracy for weekend retreats. In Hillwood's dacha you will see additional items from Mrs. Post's 5,000-object collection.

There is a second country house on the grounds. It resembles Topridge, Mrs. Post's vacation house in the Adirondacks. In this upscale rustic cabin, you can see the collection of American Indian art and artifacts that Mrs. Post once displayed at Topridge. The collection was donated to the Smithsonian, but many items have been loaned to Hillwood indefinately. The C.W. Post wing displays the Victoriana and memorabilia collected by Mrs. Post's father.

The family connection is strongly felt at Hillwood. Mrs. Post's daughter, actress Dina Merrill, narrates a new 30-minute film about her mother. The film includes Post family home movies.

If you visit in the dead of winter be sure to return in another season to explore the gardens. Mrs. Post, working with landscape architect Perry Wheeler, created a charming mix of garden areas on her 25-acre estate. In the introductory film, Mrs. Merrill confides, "She'd think nothing of having an 80-foot tree moved merely five feet in order to improve the view." There are more than 3,500 plants and trees on the Hillwood grounds, and Mrs. Post's taste led to considerable rearranging before the gardens reached their present felicitous appearance.

You can appreciate Mrs. Post's attention to the perfect placement of each plant when you stand on the portico of Hillwood. From this perspective you gaze down the Lunar Lawn, and six miles in the distance you see the Washington Monument.

A springtime visit is particularly delightful because the mountain laurel, azalea and rhododendron planted throughout the wooded setting are in bloom. From spring through fall the formal garden planted around a Moorish water canal is enjoyable. There is also a Japanese garden with waterfalls, bridge and lanterns. Two rose gardens put on a splendid show in early summer and again in the fall.

One flower-filled area that is enjoyable year round is the greenhouse. Here you'll see an impressive collection of orchids. The greenhouse sells plants for those who would like a living reminder of Hillwood.

You need to make advance reservations for the two-hour house tour. Tours are offered Tuesday through Saturday; call (202)686-5807 to arrange a visit. No children under 12 are allowed. The gardens are included with the house tour, but you can explore the gardens without touring the house. You do not need advance reservations to tour the gardens or exhibit buildings on the grounds. Admission is charged for house and gardens. There is a cafe where you can have lunch or tea.

Directions: From the Beltway I-495/95 take the Connecticut Avenue exit into Washington. From Connecticut Avenue turn left on Tilden Street and then left on Linnean Avenue. Hillwood is at 4155 Linnean Avenue, N.W.

Maryland Science Center

Invitation to Action

When Alice fell down the hole into Wonderland, she landed in a place where even ordinary things like doors and drinks had signs inviting her to "Try This!" Lewis Carroll would undoubtedly be amused to see the same signs in the **Maryland Science Center** at Baltimore's Inner Harbor.

This science wonderland is a hands-on museum that encourages participation; in fact, it is better if there are two participants. If parents don't want to get in on the action, they'd better bring two youngsters. Each scientific experiment has easy-to-understand instructions; then a "what's going on" message explains the scientific significance.

There are three floors of exhibits covering energy, television production, fish, architecture, the Chesapeake Bay, probability, metrics and space exploration. In addition there are long-running special exhibits.

Maryland may not have slot machines anymore, but you can still find them at the Science Center. There is a machine you can play that asks questions about the Chesapeake Bay. If interacting with a machine sounds like something Alice would have done in Wonderland, wait until you see the educational funhouse. An illusion-filled room with a slanted floor tests your optical perception. Anti-gravity mirrors, telescopes, lights, sounds and optics combine to make learning fun in the science arcade.

The games continue in the energy exhibit where children can play a metric tick-tack-toe that challenges them to convert one form of energy to another. Throughout the exhibit areas there are "explainers" who present programs on the weekends dealing with optical illusions, chemical experiments, combustion reactions and other topics. There are also encounters with live specimens such as the museum's snakes, turtles, ferrets and other animals.

For young children, ages four to seven, a special area on the third floor called **K.I.D.S. Room** (Key Into the Discovery of Science) opens on weekend afternoons. The staff gear the experiments specifically for this younger group.

Within the Science Center you'll find the **Davis Planetarium.** Thirty-minute shows are presented in a 144-seat theater that boasts 125 projectors, a four-channel sound system and laser graphics. The special effects created by this technical wizardry are astounding. Programs often focus on space and astronomy though they cover other scientific concepts.

There is also an **IMAX theater,** one of only a select few in the country. These IMAX theaters, including the one in Baltimore, are among the biggest in the world with screens more than 55 feet high and 75 feet wide, more than five times the size of a standard movie-house screen. This immense size gives you a feeling of being right next to the astronauts in space or to the divers exploring the deep; you become part of the action. For information on IMAX programs and the shows at the Davis Planetarium call (410)685-2370 or (800)843-9779. If you are calling outside Maryland, (800)843-9978.

The Maryland Science Center is open Monday–Friday 10:00 A.M. to 5:00 P.M., Saturday 10:00 A.M. to 6:00 P.M. and Sunday NOON to 6:00 P.M., extended hours during the summer. There is an admission to the Science Center and additional charges for both the planetarium and the IMAX shows.

Directions: From the Beltway I-495/95 take the Baltimore-Washington Parkway into Baltimore. Turn right on Pratt Street and then left on Light Street. The Maryland Science Center is at 601 Light Street on the southern shore of Baltimore's Inner Harbor.

NASA's Goddard Space Flight Visitor Center

An A-OK Place

Dr. Robert H. Goddard, the "Father of American Rocketry," dreamed of conquering space through the use of rocket propulsion. He, as much as anyone, is responsible for the dawning of the Space Age. On March 16, 1926, Goddard launched the first successful rocket at Auburn, Massachusetts. His liquid-fuel rocket stayed aloft for only two-and-a-half seconds, but history was made in that brief flight.

Only 33 years later, on May 1, 1959, the National Aeronautics and Space Administration, NASA, established the **Goddard Space Flight Center** in Greenbelt, Maryland, the first major scientific laboratory operating solely for the exploration of space. In May 1976, the Visitor Center opened.

On entering the center you are greeted by a full-scale sculpture of Dr. Goddard with his rocket. The center has a state-of-the-arts exhibit hall. But amid all the high-tech displays there are light touches, like the spacesuit cutouts where aspiring astronauts can have their picture snapped—more like carnival than Canaveral.

Wandering like Alice through Wonderland, visitors discover answers to such intriguing questions as: Why and how is man exploring outer space? Why will a space station contribute to this exploration? How will the astronauts survive long space voyages? They even see a special ecosphere, a sealed environment designed to make extended periods in space possible.

The color photographs that illustrate many of the audio-visual tracks are astonishingly beautiful. There is also space hardware on display. Although you don't see an actual space shuttle you do see examples of the small Get Away Special (GAS) the shuttles transport. You can even sign a guest book that may one day be carried aloft in a 2½-by-5-foot metal GAS.

The Hubble telescope, a tool of the 1990s, is here in model form only, but it gives you the idea of the expansion of man's knowledge of space. First you see what the planets, galaxies and star clusters look like when seen by the naked eye, then through an earth-based telescope and lastly through the Hubble space telescope. The model of the Hubble only hints at its vast dimensions, which one staff member describes as "roughly the size of a Greyhound bus."

Not all of the visual impressions are from still shots; the center also shows movies and short subjects on the hour and half hour. If you want a closer look at the work done at Goddard, visit on Thursday afternoon and join the 2:00 P.M. free one-hour grounds tour of the Control Center, Building 14, the computer and communications nerve center for NASA's satellites.

After covering the exhibits within the center, check out the oversize rockets on the grounds. NASA launches roughly 50 sounding rockets a year, each carrying a payload that may weigh as little as 12 pounds or more than a ton. Sounding rockets surrounding the center include a Nike-Tomahawk, an early Iris, a huge Javelin rocket and the two-stage Nike-Black Brant. Also displayed is an early Delta Launch Vehicle and a full-scale model of an Apollo space craft.

You can watch rocket launches, though they are only models, on the first and third Sunday of each month at 1:00 P.M. The model rockets are fired from the hillside behind the Goddard Visitor Center.

The Center is open Wednesday through Sunday from 10:00 A.M. to 4:00 P.M. There is no admission.

Directions: From the Beltway I-495/95 take Exit 22 and bear to the right for Greenbelt Road. Take Greenbelt Road past the main entrance to Goddard and follow the signs for the Visitor Center. You will turn left on Conservation Road and then left again into Goddard.

National Aquarium in Baltimore

A Sure Lure

Since the **National Aquarium in Baltimore** opened August 8, 1981, it has been Maryland's premier paid tourist attraction, drawing more than a million visitors annually. It fully deserves its popularity. The aquarium is a huge water wonderland with more than 5,000 marine and freshwater animals, including 500 different species.

The self-guided tour takes two hours, even longer if you watch the 25-minute marine mammal presentation in the Pier 4 pavilion. The first exhibit you will see is "Wings Under Water" in the central tank on level one. The country's largest ray exhibit includes six different types of rays. Swimming with the rays are black-tipped sharks and guitar fish.

The trip through the aquarium is one way; the escalators only go up. To exit you circle back down through the Atlantic coral reef exhibit. You can, of course, retrace your steps. Level two explores Maryland's water habitats from the mountains to the sea. Some of the live specimens, like the killdeers in the coastal beach section, are so still it's startling to discover they are alive. But records indicate these birds are quite active; they've raised numerous chicks in their glass home. The gray-necked wood rails have reared more than 55 offspring.

On level three an assortment of exotic, and often colorful, fish demonstrate how well they can adapt to different environments. Memorable specimens found in the section on evolving include the yellowhead jawfish and the red-backed cleaning shrimp. Equally fascinating is the strikingly colored clownfish, which attract prey for the sea anemone, the host plant in the feeding exhibit.

The aquarium is a multi-sensory experience. The sound of the whales is piped into the exhibit area, and the microphones in the sea cliff exhibit on level four let you hear the puffins, murres and razorbills. Touch comes into play at the children's cove where in the North American tidal pools children can handle hermit and horseshoe crabs, starfish and other specimens. Volunteers monitor the children's activities and answer questions.

The top level, level five, houses the glass-roofed South American rain forest. In January, its warmth, colorful feathered denizens, and constant activity prompt visitors to find a bench and linger to enjoy the tropical ambience. If you have a keen eye, you may spot the lizard that walks on water, the pair of two-toed sloths (their names are Rapunzel and Slow-Moe), and the brilliant Amazon parrots. The best vantage point is the observation deck, which gives you a bird's-eye view of the Inner Harbor and rain forest birds.

The tiny, brilliantly colored dart-poison frogs you see as you exit the rain forest are as rare as the small jewels they suggest. Their bright hues warn enemies of their venom. The aquarium with 21 species has one of the world's most comprehensive collections of these frogs.

The route down is no letdown. Indeed, the aquarium's Atlantic coral reef, which you pass through, is one of the most popular exhibits. This multi-level, 335,000-gallon donut-shaped tank gives you a scuba diver's view of the reef fish. Three times daily a diver enters the tank to feed the fish by hand to insure that all get a fair share. During these feedings the normal placid circular route of the fish is replaced by eager feeding patterns. While in the tank the volunteer divers clean the windows so visitors have maximum visibility. Descending visitors reach the 200,000-gallon open ocean ring that accommodate four varieties of sharks—lemons, sand tigers, sandbars, and nurses—plus six rays and large game fish. The number of the latter changes, depending on the appetite of the former.

In 1990 the aquarium added a 35-million dollar **Marine Mammal Pavilion** with a 1.2 million-gallon pool for dolphin and belugas. Sitting in the 1,300-seat amphitheater the audience can see all the action in the pool thanks to the transparent pool walls. With the harbor water clearly visible outside the pavilion, it almost seems as though you are watching the mammals in their natural environment.

The charming, crowd pleasing belugas (or white whales), Anore and Kia, formerly the stars of the central tank on Pier 3, are now in the new pavilion on Pier 4. They are joined by Sikku, another beluga, plus five Atlantic bottlenose dolphins. During the 25-minute presentation given throughout the day, staff enter the water with the mammals. Playful interaction develops as the whales learn how to present a pectoral or fluke on request or respond to a command to roll over. The whales certainly communicate with each other as visitors quickly learn. Belugas are nicknamed "canaries" because they bark, whistle, squawk, chirp and make clicking sounds; in all they have 11 different calls. More about whale communication is conveyed on the giant video screens flanking the tank. Throughout the interactive presentation videos of whales in the wild complement the action in the tank.

The admission price is slightly higher than a first-run movie fare (1991 adult fare was $11.50), but it is certainly worth the price. For current rates call (301)576-3810. Winter hours, mid-September through mid-May, are daily 10:00 A.M. to 5:00 P.M., and on Friday evenings until 8:00 P.M. Summer hours are Monday through Thursday 9:00 A.M. to 5:00 P.M. and Friday through Sunday 9:00 A.M. to 8:00 P.M. The aquarium has a well-stocked gift shop and restaurant.

There are often long lines. You can plan ahead, however, by calling Ticket Center at (800)448-9009 and by obtaining advance, timed tickets. If you want to take a chance, the best times to avoid crowds are late afternoon and in the evening.

Directions: From the Washington Beltway I-495/95 take I-95 north into Baltimore. Take the Inner Harbor exit, make a right on Conway Street and then left onto Light Street. Bear right on Pratt Street and follow the signs for the Aquarium. Pay parking is available at Piers 5 and 6 and at the Inner Harbor Center Garage on Pratt Street across from the Aquarium.

National Capital Trolley Museum

Streetcars You Will Desire

From Lincoln's administration to Kennedy's, streetcars traveled the streets of Washington. The first cars were drawn by horses that clip-clopped at a leisurely pace. The last were electric streamliners that skimmed fast and smoothly along their tracks. The age of the trolley ended in the capital on January 28, 1962.

But not all of the cars were lost to Washington: a few have been kept running thanks to the efforts of transit company vice-president A.E. Savage, who hid them in the Navy Yard Car House to save them from the scrap yard. When you visit the **National Capital Trolley Museum** you can ride No. 766, the car that made Washington's last run. Trolley enthusiasts have repaired the 14 streetcars in the museum's collection, some of which make regularly scheduled runs on the 1¾-mile track.

The 14 have been collected from near and far. Several are European cars, including three from Austria and two from Germany. The 1924 gray-and-white Berlin car that ran during the flower festivals in Karlsruhe, Germany, looks appropriately festive with red and white parlor curtains and shiny brass fittings. One of the Austrian cars has a measuring stick on the wall because children were charged by age or height, whichever was the greater. Closer to home there are six cars from Washington as well as cars from New York and Pennsylvania. Older city residents may recognize car No. 1101, Washington's first streamliner, introduced in 1937.

The trolleys go on parade during the trolley festivals held on the third Sunday of every September and April (unless that's Easter in which case April's festival is held on the fourth Sunday). There is always at least one trolley running. It departs every half-hour from the Visitor Center, which is built to resemble an old-time railroad station. A nominal fee is charged for the ride. At the end of the track a volunteer reminisces about the days when you could travel anywhere in Washington by trolley. He'll also answer questions and punch your ticket before the return trip.

The museum hosts musical programs, special movies and model car exhibits. For information on these programs call (301)384-6088. On the museum grounds you'll find a gazebo and picnic tables. Hours are weekends NOON to 5:00 P.M. year-round. In July and August the museum also opens from 1:00–4:00 P.M. on Wednesday. It is open on Memorial Day, July Fourth and Labor Day. On December weekends the museum hosts "Holly Trolley Illuminations" featuring outdoor lighting displays and Santa on the streetcars.

Directions: From the Beltway I-495/95 take Exit 28, New Hampshire Avenue, north for 5.4 miles. After the road narrows go to the second traffic light, which is Bonifant Road, turn left and proceed 1.9 miles to the trolley museum on your right at 1313 Bonifant Road in the Northwest Branch Regional Park.

National Shrine of the Immaculate Conception

Not Just for the Religious

Washington is noted for its many religious denominations, and you can achieve the equivalent of a course on comparative religion by visiting the capital's temples, mosques, cathedrals and churches. One site you must see, regardless of your own religion, is the National Shrine of the Immaculate Conception. It is the largest Catholic church in the United States and the eighth largest in the world, but its enormous size in no way diminishes its innate grace.

Like medieval cathedrals it is built of stone, brick, tile and concrete. The design is a blend of Byzantine, Romanesque and contemporary architecture.

Inside are two distinct areas, the Crypt Church, which opened in 1926, and the large Upper Church, which opened in 1959. The Crypt Church preserves the atmosphere of the ancient Roman catacombs, but religious artifacts and sculpture make it a museum.

The Upper Church with its towering walls and great arch-supported dome is an impressive sight. It contains many valuable mosaics, tapestries, glowing stained-glass windows and fine pieces of contemporary American sculpture, as well as objects donated by the Vatican. Side chapels dedicated to the Virgin and commemorating her reported appearances throughout the world flank the main nave.

The National Shrine of the Immaculate Conception is open free to the public from 7:00 A.M. to 7:00 P.M. from April through October. It closes at 6:00 P.M. from November through March. There are guided tours Monday through Saturday from 9:00 A.M. to 3:00 P.M. and on Sunday from 1:30 to 3:00 P.M. Tours begin at Memorial Hall and last approximately 45 minutes. The shrine is handicapped-accessible.

The great organ of the shrine can be heard at the Masses on Sundays and Holy Days. These Masses regularly bring together visitors and pilgrims from throughout the United States.

Directions: The shrine is located inside the Beltway at 4th Street and Michigan Avenue in northeast Washington. It borders on the Catholic University of America. Plenty of free parking is available. The shrine is a two-minute walk across the Catholic University campus from the Brookland Metro Station.

Navy Yard Museums

Sailors' and Marines'

From the moment visitors drive through the gates, the Navy Yard captures their attention. First, there are the omnipresent uniformed personnel. Then, when visitors reach the parking lot they are surprised by the submarine that seems to be surfacing from the pavement. This photogenic spot with the conning tower rising from the concrete is an inviting introduction to the **Navy Memorial Museum**.

The outdoor display continues in Willard Park in front of the museum where you'll see a collection of captured guns, Civil War cannons, shipboard missile launchers, tanks and a huge propeller from the battleship *South Dakota*.

Building 76, which houses the indoor exhibits, was originally the Breech Mechanism Shop of the old Naval Yard Gun Factory. The Navy Yard began operation in 1799 and built the first ships for the young American navy. This cavernous building (at 600 feet it is the longest hall in Washington) is often called the Navy's attic. The military pieces that fill the huge space offer young visitors a chance to climb on cannons and into the bathyscaphe. When youngsters sit behind the barrel of the massive cannon they can crank the heavy brass wheel to swing the barrel. Kids are apt to provide their own sound effects, as they quickly realize this isn't the kind of museum where they must talk in whispers.

While younger visitors man the guns, older visitors can read the fascinating commentary that accompanies the exhibits. There is a simulated gun deck from the *Constitution*, the oldest commissioned ship in the Navy, that explains the origin of the nickname *Old Ironsides*. The seven-inch oak timbers from which the hull was constructed were so thick cannon balls seemed to bounce off. The museum also has the fully-rigged foremast of the *Constitution*, taken off the ship when it was overhauled in 1976.

It would take hours to fully appreciate all the items included in the collection. Among the more interesting pieces is Admiral Byrd's Antarctic hut, a 19th-century cat-o-nine tails, a full-size submersible, a model of an Apollo spacecraft and a collection of ship models.

The models range in size from exquisite ivory miniatures to oversize battleships. Old World crafts include early Viking ships, Spanish galleons, Korean tortoise boats and ancient Chinese fighting boats. There are models of distinguished ships of the United States Navy including the *Tennessee*, *Panay*, *Ranger*, *Fletcher*, *Missouri* and *Forrestal*. The models and artifacts fill cases, walls and corners. They even hang from the ceiling like the World War II *Corsair* and the huge underseas exploration vehicle *Trieste*.

If you're visiting with children be sure to pick up the scavenger hunt brochure and the activities' booklet when you enter the museum as they make exploring even more fun. There's a computer game to decode messages that's sure to challenge older children. The game also teaches players the history of cryptanalysis.

There is still more to see in the **Navy Museum Annex** next door in Building 70. This houses the museum's collection of rare and unusual submarines. Another option is the **Navy Art Gallery** in Building 76, a one-room collection of 32 paintings by Navy combat artists.

The Navy Memorial Museum and Annex are open Monday–Friday 9:00 A.M. to 4:00 P.M. and in the summer and on weekends and holidays from 10:00 A.M. to 5:00 P.M. The Navy Art Gallery is open Wednesday–Sunday from 9:00 A.M. to 4:00 P.M. All are free.

There is one more "must" stop and that is the USS *Barry*, a destroyer decommissioned in 1982. It's been on visiting duty at the Navy Yard for over seven years. Launched in 1956, the *Barry* was on active duty during the Cuban missile crisis and in the Vietnam War. As you tour the 424-foot ship (remember the difference between ships and boats is that ships carry boats, like the life boats, whale boat and Captain's gig aboard the *Barry*), it's hard to imagine a crew of 315 enlisted men and 22 officers operating in this small space. The officers' quarters are spartan, yet they look more appealing after a visit to the compartment that 63 crewmen shared. They called the three-tiered bunks "coffin racks." Once you see the mess where the men not only ate meals—in 15 minute shifts—but also watched movies and played cards, you'll realize that there is not a single place to be comfortable aboard ship. There is no lounge area and only the officers' chairs have backs.

There is, however, some very sophisticated equipment. When your tour reaches the Captain's Bridge and the Combat Information Center, the brains of the ship, you'll be impressed by the array of hardware. You'll see a terminal that controls the ASROC launchings; this will mean more when you arrive on the stern and see the anti-submarine launcher that fires the RTTs, or rocket-thrown torpedoes. Like all military personnel, your Navy guide speaks in acronyms that he explains during the 20-minute tour of the ship. The *Barry* can be boarded at no charge on weekdays from 9:00 A.M. to 4:00 P.M., on weekends and holidays from 10:00 A.M. to 5:00 P.M. During the summer months hours are from 9:00 A.M. to 5:00 P.M.

If you have more time there is one more museum at the Navy Yard and that is the **U.S. Marine Corps Historical Center and Museum** in Building 58. Although this is not hands-on, it still appeals to both young and old visitors, particularly its corridor of Marines in Miniature. Lighted dioramas capture a series of battles and confrontations from 1800 to 1918. You'll see reminders of nearby conflicts like the Battle of Bladensburg during the War of 1818 and more far-flung missions like the June 10, 1918, Battle of Belleau Woods where Gunnery Sergeant Dan Daly led his men forward with the shout, "Do you want to live forever?"

Daly was decorated for his valor. Other Marine heroes and officers are remembered in a display along another wall. A collection of uniforms, weapons and other artifacts represents all the major conflicts in which the Marines have fought since the Revolution. On your way out you'll see an exhibit featuring the Pulitzer Prize-winning photograph Joe Rosenthal shot at Iwo Jima.

The Marine Corps Historical Center and Museum is open at no charge Monday–Saturday 10:00 A.M. to 4:00 P.M. and Sundays and holidays from NOON to 5:00 P.M.

Directions: The Washington Navy Yard is inside the Beltway at 9th and M Streets, S.E.

Octagon, Decatur House and Cedar Hill

Span the Centuries

A trio of Washington's historic homes spans the decades from the time the capital was established into the 19th century. The Octagon House dates from 1801, Decatur House from 1819 and Cedar Hill from 1855.

It was George Washington who persuaded fellow Virginia planter, Colonel John Tayloe, to build a town house in the new capital city. When city-planner Pierre L'Enfant was laying out lots, Tayloe picked a challenging, irregular plot. Using the ship-builder's art of curved walls, windows and doors to adapt the house to the oddly shaped lot, William Thornton, architect of the U.S. Capitol, designed a six-sided mansion. Miscounting resulted in its being incorrectly called the **Octagon House**.

The Octagon became the nation's first temporary White House when President James Madison and his wife, Dolly, returned to Washington after the British burned the executive mansion during the War of 1812. The Madisons lived at the Octagon House from September 1814 until March 1815 while Benjamin Latrobe oversaw the repairs of the White House.

In his circular office on the second floor, Madison signed the Treaty of Ghent on February 17, 1815, ending the War of 1812. The Treaty Room still holds the table where Madison signed this historic document.

A wide, oval staircase leads to the second floor. This is the architectural centerpiece of the house, which figures prominently in a ghostly tale told about the Octagon's first owners. According to the story Colonel Tayloe had an argument with one of his daughters over a suitor. During their heated exchange she fell over the stair railing to her death (a few yarns hint she was pushed). Since then, some claim to hear her crying on the stairs.

The Octagon House is now the headquarters for the American Institute of Architects Foundation. The house contains handsome Federal furnishings that belonged to the Tayloe family. It is also worth visiting for its architectural interest and the decorative interior design work including the original Italian marble floors and the ceiling molding in the Treaty Room. The house is open Tuesday through Friday 10:00 A.M. to 4:00 P.M. and on weekends 1:00 to 4:00 P.M.

There is another downtown historical house, **Decatur House**, that owes its prominence, indeed its very existence, to the War of 1812. Naval hero Stephen Decatur built his home on one of the 19 lots he purchased with prize money he won fighting the Barbary Pirates and the British. When the American navy was created he dropped out of college to enlist. His father also joined the fledgling navy and achieved early fame by capturing the French ship *Le Croyable* and bringing her to Philadelphia as a prize of war.

Young Stephen soon followed in his father's footsteps. In 1804 during the war with the Barbary Pirates, he was credited by the famous British Lord Nelson with "the most daring act of the age." Decatur's fame stemmed from the raid he led with roughly 70 volunteers into the harbor of Tripoli to burn the captured U.S. frigate *Philadelphia* to prevent it from being used in battle against other American ships. Later during the War of 1812 he captured the *Macedonian*.

Stephen Decatur moved to Washington early in 1816 to serve on the Navy Board of Commissioners. He hired the noted architect Benjamin Latrobe to design his three-story brick house. Latrobe's drawings are preserved in the Library of Congress, and the house has been restored to its original appearance. It is the only private residence designed by Latrobe that has survived the vicissitudes of time. Over the years the house has been owned by George M. Dallas, Vice President under Polk and three Secretaries of State—Henry Clay, Martin van Buren and Edward Livingston. Both France and Russia used it as a legation.

Stephen Decatur and his wife, Susan, lived in their Washington town house for only 14 months. At age 41 Decatur was killed in a duel by Commodore James Barron, who blamed Decatur for ruining his naval career. Congress adjourned for his funeral, and he was mourned throughout the country.

The first floor rooms at the house reflect the Federal style popular during the Decaturs' brief residency. The upstairs is furnished in the opulent Victorian style of the Beales, the last residents. It was Beale who spread the news of the discovery of gold in California across America.

The Decatur House is open Tuesday through Friday 10:00 A.M. to 2:00 P.M. and weekends and holidays from NOON to 4:00 P.M. Admission is charged.

The third private house, **Cedar Hill**, takes visitors to the threshold of the 20th century. Frederick Douglass's journey from fugitive slave to U.S. Marshall brought him to Washington in 1877. He was born in 1817 not too far from the capital in Easton, on Maryland's Eastern Shore. Although he was a slave he taught himself to read and write, despite his owner's objections. At age 21 he was sent to Baltimore to learn ship caulking and, seizing his opportunity, Douglass escaped north. He then took his name, married Anne Murray and began fighting for the abolitionist movement.

Frederick Douglass was such an articulate spokesman for the antislavery movement that many doubted he had once been a slave. He published his life story in 1845 even though this put him at great personal risk since he was still a fugitive slave. Compelled to flee the country, he moved his struggle for abolition to England. There he gained supporters who provided financing for the abolitionist newspaper, *The North Star*, that Douglass began publishing on his return to the U.S. in 1847.

Douglass continued his newspaper work when he moved to Washington and edited the *New National Era*. Several years after arriving in the capital he became the District's Register of Deeds. Eighteen months after his wife died, he married a secretary for the Office of the Recorder of Deeds. Theirs was an interracial marriage, but she was a staunch supporter of black human rights. After Frederick Douglass's death on February 20, 1895, his wife spent the rest of her life preserving their Washington home as a memorial to his life and work.

In 1962 the National Park Service took over the Cedar Hill property (also called the Frederick Douglass Memorial Home). The two-story brick house, built in 1855, sits on a hill overlooking the capital. The furnishings and grounds reflect the Douglass years, and many of his personal belongings fill the rooms. His 2,000-volume library has been preserved. You'll see a brief film on Douglass's life before you begin exploring the house. Cedar Hill is open at no charge from 9:00 A.M. to 5:00 P.M. daily, although from October through March it closes an hour earlier.

Directions: All of these historic houses are inside the Beltway in downtown Washington. The Octagon House is located at 1799 New York Avenue N.W., at 18th Street (202/638-3105). The Decatur House is at 748 Jackson Place, N.W., on Lafayette Square across from the White House (202/842-0920). Cedar Hill is at 1411 W. Street, S.E. (202/426-5961).

Odessa and the Winterthur Houses and Hotel

Nostalgic Noel

How things change. In the 18th century prosperous **Odessa** residents would take an excursion to shop and socialize in the city. Now city residents from Washington, Baltimore and Philadelphia enjoy a day trip to this picturesque community. Early December is one of the best times to visit; not even Scrooge could resist Christmas in Odessa.

Odessa once sounded like a mythical land. During 1654–56 a traveler recorded in his journal that dragons existed here. He wrote of other things too: "rattlesnakes, a kind of large horrible and abominable snake, they have jaws like a dog, they (can) cut and bite off a person's leg, as if it has been cut off with an ax." Fortunately, this colorful and imaginative description was never verified.

The Odessa area was not developed until 1731 when Richard Cantwell built a bridge across the Appoquinimink Creek. In its heyday there were six large granaries in the town, and the port at Cantwell's Bridge shipped 400,000 bushels of grain each year. The continued growth of the town was jeopardized when the railroad bypassed it, crossing through nearby Middletown instead. To emphasize its importance as a shipping center, the town changed its name to Odessa, after the Ukranian grain port that had become well known during the Crimean War.

Odessa, as well as other towns in this part of Delaware, enjoyed the fruits of the "peach boom." Peach orchards created prosperity until "the yellows," a virulent blight, wiped out the crop at the end of the 19th century. The town then entered a Rip van Winkle phase—falling asleep, to awaken virtually unchanged as a historical attraction under the aegis of the Winterthur Museum.

One senses the past most romantically during the annual Christmas festival in Odessa traditionally scheduled for the first weekend in December. The entire community joins the celebration, and wreaths and garlands bedeck the doors and windows of the 18th- and 19th-century homes of the historic district. This is one of the few times during the year that the town's private homes join the three Winterthur properties (described below) in opening their doors to visitors. An extensive craft bazaar, carriage rides, musical programs and home-style cooking add to the festivities. The celebration begins with candlelight tours on Saturday evening and continues with tours on Sunday afternoon.

Three out of the four Winterthur properties can be toured in any month except January and February. The **Wilson-Warner House,** the fashionable Georgian house built in 1769 by David Wilson, is one of the oldest historic house museums in Delaware. It is furnished to match an 1829 inventory. David Wilson was a prosperous merchant, but he suffered business reverses and had to sell his land, house and furniture. Years later the house returned to the family when it was purchased by his great-granddaughter Mary Corbit Wilson, who was also the granddaughter of William Corbit.

Grandfather **William Corbit** built his **home** between 1772 and 1774 when he was still in his twenties. Situated next door to his brother-in-law's, David Wilson's house, Corbit's is one of the finest examples of Georgian architecture in the state. Family furnishings reflect the gracious lifestyle the Corbits enjoyed from 1774 to 1818. Visitors note that young Daniel Corbit kept a penciled record of the family fortunes on the inside of his bedroom door.

When Daniel married, he brought his Quaker bride, Mary Wilson, to his family home. She was appalled by the rowdy behavior of the businessmen, ships' crews and farmers who stayed at the Brick Hotel across the street. It was a social center for the town, the place where news was gathered and opinions aired. Mary Wilson objected to the alcohol consumed at the hotel, and she launched what was ultimately a successful campaign to have its liquor license revoked.

Today the **Brick Hotel** serves as a gallery for exhibits on furniture making. The main collection of the gallery, another Winterthur property, is the work of John Henry Belter, a name synonymous with the 19th-century rococo revival-style of furniture. This is the country's largest collection of Belter furniture. The exhibit is called "Nature Tamed: Belter Furniture 1840–1860" because his designs utilized the Victorian theme of bringing the outdoors in, controlling nature by making it part of the design. You'll see how Belter, and his legion of copiers, fashioned their ornately carved furniture.

A fourth Winterthur property, the **Collins-Sharp House**, is not open for tours. It is used for special programs. The other three are open March through December on Tuesday through Saturday from 10:00 A.M. to 4:00 P.M. and on Sundays from 1:00 to 4:00 P.M. Admission is charged.

If you are a movie buff, plan to include a visit to a nearby boys' school where the 1989 hit *Dead Poet's Society* was filmed. Just outside Middletown, the lovely old stone buildings of St. Andrews School look like they have been transplanted from England. If you head into town you'll see the Everett Theater, which was also used in the film.

Directions: From the Beltway I-495/95 take Route 50 east across the Chesapeake Bay Bridge. Where Route 50/301 splits take Route 301-13 north to Odessa. To reach St. Andrews School take Main Street, Route 299, out of Odessa. After you cross Route 13 continue to the intersection with Route 442 and turn left. Route 422 dead-ends at the school entrance.

Paul Garber Facility

Hanging Around the Hangar

When you visit the **Paul Garber Facility** you feel you're on the set of *The Right Stuff* or *Top Gun*, particularly when you hear expressions like "the outside of the envelope" and "auger in." This aviation hot spot is popular with pilots and aviation buffs who know the lingo and the subject.

This huge complex is where the Smithsonian Institution stores and restores its priceless collection of planes. The enthusiastic docents who guide visitors tailor the two- to three-hour tours to the interests of the participants. They field the most basic or complex questions with equal ease.

One often-asked question is, "Who is Paul Garber and why is there a museum named for him?" Paul Garber started working at the Smithsonian Institute on June 1, 1920, and immediately made the early years of aviation his special area of interest. When the Air Force decided not to open its own air museum, Garber was in on the ground floor as the Smithsonian began to acquire the foreign planes the United States gained as war prizes at the end of World War II. On August 12, 1946, less than a year after the war ended, President Truman signed into law the act which established the National Air Museum. But it wasn't until 1980 that the collection housed in Prince George's County, Maryland, was named the Paul Garber Facility in recognition of Garber's work at the Smithsonian.

Perhaps the most frequent question is, "Can these planes fly?" The answer is that most can, but none do. Once the museum acquires a plane, they ground it to prevent any additional harm or deterioration. The work on these planes is painstakingly detailed, and in an average year they restore only two or three aircraft.

Some of the planes arrive at the Garber Facility in boxes, just pieces of once proud planes. Restoration is exacting and uses the original methods of construction. If the insignia was painted on with a brush, then a brush is used in the restoration process. On the Bellanca CF aircraft every screwhead on the wooden section is lined up just as it once was; this precise alignment was not for aesthetics but for safety. By lining up the screwheads a loose screw was easy to spot.

If the Garber Facility is unable to locate an original part they build a replacement. These parts are carefully labeled to show that they are not authentic. Airmen who once flew these old planes have commented that these restorations look better than the originals.

213

This degree of accuracy would be impossible were it not for the simultaneous development of aviation and photography. Almost every time a barnstorming ace flew into town a local photographer was on hand to capture the event. Even the earliest planes were meticulously photographed. From these pictures, restorers are able to draw the entire plane to scale. The parallel construction of airplanes helps in restoration work; if parts on one side survive they can be duplicated on the other side.

The Paul Garber Facility has roughly 140 aircraft, compared with approximately 75 at the National Air and Space Museum on the Mall. But the setting is bare bones; the planes line the hangars without fancy exhibit signs or sophisticated displays. For some, this behind-the-scenes look at aviation is even more intriguing than the Mall's more polished presentation.

Restorers have found some unusual messages from the past. Those working on the *Enola Gay*, the B-29 that dropped the atom bomb on Hiroshima, found one of the three original arming plugs for the bomb behind a heavy piece of equipment. It is intriguing to speculate on what was happening when the crew member dropped the plug.

Restorers found a faded piece of paper while working on a Chance Vought F4U Corsair, the U.S. Navy carrier-based fighter plane that first broke the 400 mph limit. The note, probably written by one of the 1940s' maintenance crew, read: "What in the hell are you looking for in here, you silly. . .?"

The stories are as interesting as the planes. Be sure to ask your guide why early pilots wore flowing white scarves, and why the Messerschmitts killed more friends than foes. Discover which airplane was on the military's inventory the day World War II started and the day it ended. These stories are as fascinating as any Hollywood fiction.

Certainly the Hemingway quotation spotted above one of the desks in the reception area could be dialogue from a hard-talking movie ace. It reads: "You love a lot of things if you live around them, but there isn't any woman and there isn't any horse. . .that is as lovely as a great airplane."

Free tours are by advance reservation Monday through Friday at 10:15 A.M. and 1:00 P.M. Wear walking shoes and keep in mind that the warehouses and hangars have neither heat nor air-conditioning. To arrange a tour you can call (202)357-1400 during working hours.

Directions: From the Beltway I-495/95 take Branch Avenue Exit 7B, Route 5, toward Silver Hill. Turn left onto Silver Hill Road and continue about a half mile to the Paul Garber Facility on the right.

Philadelphia

Philadelphia, Here We Come!

Philadelphia, the city of "brotherly love," is just over two hours from the Beltway (roughly 115 miles). It offers diversions for a day, a weekend or a week. (For a detailed visitor's information kit call (800)537-7676.)

The historical sites alone can keep you busy for an entire day. At the time of the American Revolution, London was the only city with a larger English-speaking population. It was in Philadelphia that leading patriots gathered, and their venerable ghosts are everywhere here.

It's easy to picture America's early leaders in the Assembly Room of **Independence Hall** where they met to draft the Declaration of Independence and the Articles of Confederation. The Assembly Room, considered the single most historic room in America, was the site of the First and Second Continental Congresses. In essence this was the birthplace of the American Revolution.

At the Visitor Center you can pick up a map and brochure for the 48-acre **Independence National Historical Park**. This downtown area comprises roughly 40 buildings and numerous parks all designed to bring alive the 18th century. The walking tour includes the Liberty Bell Pavilion, Franklin Court, the Second Bank of the U.S., Library Hall and Carpenters Hall as well as restored private homes with historic significance: Pemberton House, Bishop White House, Todd House and the Graff House, where Thomas Jefferson was boarding when he drafted the Declaration of Independence.

The Visitor Center has an interactive computer exhibit that focuses on the Constitution. "A Promise of Permanency," the phrase borrowed from Benjamin Franklin's description of the Constitution, lets you solve key constitutional cases dealing with such issues as civil rights and prohibition.

Visitors can follow in the founders' footsteps and enjoy lunch at City Tavern where delegates sought lodging and meals. They are still serving colonial selections at this tavern on Second Street between Chestnut and Walnut streets. It is advisable to make reservations for both lunch and dinner; call (215)923-6059.

If you spend a one-day visit seeing the historical sites, on another trip you can take in the city's eclectic museums. The wide Benjamin Franklin Parkway, modeled after the Champs-Elysees in Paris, is called "museum row." At one end of the parkway is the **Philadelphia Museum of Art**. Tourists and joggers run up and down the stately steps made famous, or infamous, by Sylvester Stallone in *Rocky*. It's worth a climb to see the view of **City Hall**.

215

If you have a special interest in sculpture don't miss the small **Rodin Museum** several blocks down the Parkway. Rodin's famous *The Thinker*, guards the gates to the museum, tucked away in a chateau-like building behind a curtain of greenery. This is the largest collection of Auguste Rodin's work outside of Paris. Renowned pieces like *The Burghers of Calais* and *The Gates of Hell* are part of this outstanding collection.

Among the museums along the Parkway there are two with special appeal for families. **The Franklin Institute of Science Museum** is a do-it-yourself, push-button museum that lets youngsters interact with the exhibits. Young and old visitors get involved, and it's a rare visit that isn't extended as the exhibits are entertaining and informative. The Institute's Fels Planetarium lets you travel through the solar systems on your one-day trip.

Just down the block is another popular family haunt, the **Please Touch Museum**. This is an ideal stop for families with young children (under 8) and handicapped children (under 13). Children of all ages will enjoy the animal habitats at the **Academy of Natural Sciences**, another nearby attraction. Simulated environments teach about the Chinese pandas, Alaskan brown bears and many other species.

For animal lovers, an enjoyable option is a stop at the **Philadelphia Zoological Park**, America's oldest zoo. The Safari Monorail transports visitors through the park. There are more than 1,000 residents in a naturalized setting extending over 42 acres. The free-flying birds in the tropical Hummingbird House are guaranteed crowd pleasers.

The zoo's exotic birds may be colorful, but they can't match the flamboyant feathers you'll see at the **Mummers Museum** at 2nd Street and Washington Avenue. Even the facade of this unusual museum is multi-hued with bright orange, blue and green tiles. For more than a hundred years there has been a New Year's Day Mummers Parade. The museum re-creates the sights, sounds and ambience of this festive event.

If you travel to Philadelphia during pleasant weather try to include a stop at **Penn's Landing**, the city's revitalized waterfront. This is where William Penn landed more than 300 years ago to found the colony of Pennsylvania. Today visitors can board the USS *Olympia*, which saw service in the Spanish-American War, and the USS *Becuna*, a World War II submarine. You also can tour the 10-story-high *Moshulu*, the largest all-steel sailing ship still afloat. Although it is in the water, it is permanently docked and now serves as a maritime exhibit.

Directions: From the Beltway, I-495/95, take I-95 north to Philadelphia. As you approach the city, signs indicate Front Street. From Front Street turn left on Lombard Street and right on Broad Street. Then make a left onto the Benjamin Franklin Parkway.

At Kennedy Plaza you will see the Philadelphia Tourist Hospitality Center. For Independence National Historical Park turn left off Front Street at Walnut Street.

Prince William Forest Park and Marine Air-Ground Museum

Your Own Walden Pond

If you enjoy hiking through an unspoiled natural setting, visit **Prince William Forest Park** across from the U.S. Marine Corps Base at Quantico. This woodland watershed, administered by the National Park Service since 1939, has more than 35 miles of trails winding along streams and through forest. The park has more than 85 varieties of trees and shrubs including Virginia pine, mountain laurel, holly and dogwood.

The park crisscrosses the north and south branches of Quantico Creek on land that was once farmed. Scottish farmers settled in the area around Dumfries, including the park land, in 1756. Poor agricultural practices resulted in soil erosion, which silted up the harbor at Quantico Creek rendering it unfit for navigation. Now the once open water is an impenetrable marsh, and whistling swans winter over along Quantico Creek in Dumfries.

In 1934 the park land was acquired by the federal government as the Chopawamsic Recreation Demonstration Area, and the Civilian Conservation Corps undertook the job of restoring it to its natural state. As you travel around the park you'll see a few reminders of the farms. There are overgrown cemeteries, building foundations and even an abandoned pyrite mine.

The park trails are so infrequently traversed that you're likely to spot some of the abundant wildlife: white-tailed deer, red and gray foxes, raccoons, opossums, squirrels, rabbits and beavers. If you don't see the shy beavers, you're sure to see the dams they build. Visitors with a fishing license can try their luck at catching the bass, bluegill, perch and catfish. The park ranger will provide information on obtaining a license. Numerous songbirds make their home in the park as do ruffled grouse, wild turkeys and several varieties of raptors. To catch sight of these elusive denizens you have to sit quietly and enjoy the special tranquility that comes from being close to the quiet world of nature.

Prince William Forest Park has three self-guided trails. The Pine Grove Forest Trail, which begins at the Pine Grove Picnic Area, is paved to make it accessible for strollers and wheelchairs. This trail has informative taped messages at audio stations to acquaint visitors with the flora and fauna. At the Oak Ridge campground, which has 79 campsites, there is a Farms to Forest

Trail, which points out how the land reverted back from culti-
vation to its natural state. The Crossing Nature Trail at Telegraph
Road Picnic Area concentrates on the natural and human history
of the park. Pick up a trail map at the visitor center for more
information.

Open daily during daylight hours, the park now has a $3-per-
car entrance fee, which is good for seven days. For frequent
visitors there is a $10 yearly pass. Those eligible can also obtain
free Golden Age and Golden Access passports. There are both
camping and picnicking facilities. Conducted hikes, illustrated
talks and other programs are frequently offered.

If time permits, stop at the **Marine Corps Air-Ground Museum**
across Route 1 from the park. Hangars at Quantico contain an
impressive array of Marine ground equipment, weapons and
aviation exhibits. Quantico's association with aviation began
during the Civil War when hot-air reconnaissance balloons were
launched in this region. In 1896 the country's first flying vehicle
took to the air over the Potomac River near Quantico. It was a
25-pound, 13-foot flying machine called a Langley model after
its inventor, Dr. Samuel Pierpont Langley, who attempted two
unsuccessful manned flights prior to the Wright brothers'
triumph at Kitty Hawk.

Early models of Langley's flying machine are displayed at the
Quantico museum (the 1896 model is displayed at the National
Air and Space Museum). The Marine Museum also has vintage
World War I planes as well as planes from the 20s and 30s. The
story of the Marine Corps' air-ground attacks and defense is told
in photographs, art and exhibits. Hours are Tuesday–Sunday 1:00
A.M.–5:00 P.M. from April through November. The museum closes
for Easter and Thanksgiving but is open on holiday Mondays.

Directions: From the Beltway I-495/95 take I-95 south to Prince
William Forest, Exit 50.

Sandy Point State Park

Bundle up for the Beach

If you want a change of pace, why not head for the beach? You'll
find it's fun to visit a spot in winter that you normally see only
in the summer. Pick a pleasant day and take a 40-minute drive
to **Sandy Point State Park** on the western shore of the Chesapeake
Bay.

The unpopulated beach with its lapping water and swaying
sea grass is peaceful and restorative. There may not be many
people there, but you will find a wide variety of birds. This is
one of the best vantage points on the western side of the bay for
you to spot shore birds and migratory waterfowl. Many birds

stop just briefly during their migration, but others winter over on the marshy ponds within the park. A walk along the shore provides the opportunity to see some of these hearty residents. You may even find a unique piece of driftwood or an unusual shell the winter winds have washed ashore.

In the spring when the wintering birds head north, you can substitute boat watching for bird watching. On breezy days colorful sailboats play on the bay, while children play in the sand along the water's edge. Being virtually deserted off-season, the wide expanse of sand is ideal for kite flying and frisbee throwing. Warm weather brings sunbathers and swimmers to the park; the calm water is safe for youngsters, but by mid-summer sea nettles may invade the bay waters.

Fishermen also like Sandy Point State Park, either fishing from shore or using the park's ramps to launch their own boats. A marina rents boats and sells bait and tackle.

There is no admission to the park during the winter months. A per-car fee is charged in other seasons, and this fee does increase in the summer months.

Directions: from the Beltway, I-495/95 take Route 50 east. Just before the Chesapeake Bay Bridge there will be a turn-off for Sandy Point State Park.

U.S. Naval Observatory

Star Light, Star Bright

If you've always known that cold, crisp nights were good for something, it will not surprise you to learn that stargazing is never better than on a clear winter's night. For a different scientific experience, take one of the **United States Naval Observatory's** Monday night tours. Near the first-quarter moon you may peer through the observatory's giant telescope. Guides will direct your attention to double stars, nebulae, star clusters and the planets.

Two telescopes are used for this nighttime observation: the 26-inch refracting telescope and the 12-inch Alvan Clark refracting telescope. The 26-inch telescope is the largest on the Washington D.C. observatory grounds. When completed in 1873, it was the largest telescope of its type in the world. Now the largest telescope owned by the Naval Observatory is the 61-inch reflecting telescope at its research station in Flagstaff, Arizona.

The primary use of the 26-inch telescope at the observatory in Washington is for observing multiple-star systems. The telescope is mounted so that it compensates for the rotation of the earth and thus is able to follow celestial objects as they move across the sky. The 45-foot observatory dome can be rotated so that the desired portion of the sky is visible. The observatory floor also changes positions. It can be raised or lowered to accommodate the user of the telescope. The way the floor and ceiling move up, down and around always delights first-time visitors.

The second telescope, the 12-inch refractor built in 1892, has been restored to its original appearance by astronomy volunteers. It has "star dials," no longer found on telescopes but once used to direct the telescope to the desired star.

On the night tours, in addition to scanning the skies, you will be able to see the displays and exhibits in the **Main Building** and learn about the work of the U.S. Naval Observatory You will discover that this is the only institute in the United States (and one of the few in the world) where the fundamental positions of the sun, moon and stars are continually observed. The astronomers work with a telescope called a Transit Circle.

The observatory regulates all Standard Time. It has a Master Clock for the United States as well as receiver equipment that monitors time signals from various navigational systems and commercial time reference stations. You will see an atomic clock on your tour. Researchers actually keep track of four kinds of time: sidereal time, based on the transit of the stars; mean solar time, founded on the period of rotation of the earth on its axis; ephemeris time, determined by the position of the moon in relation to the stars; and atomic time, a very accurate recording of time measured by atomic cesium-beam clocks, which use electromagnetic waves of a particular frequency that are emitted when an atomic transition occurs.

The observatory can handle only 110 visitors a night in its telescope domes, so 120 passes are handed out on a first-come, first-serve basis. Children under 14 are not permitted on this tour. There are always more visitors on sharp, clear nights when observation is best. Although observations cannot be made on cloudy nights, the tours are nevertheless conducted on schedule except during severe weather conditions.

From September through April the observatory's South Gate is open on Monday nights at 7:00 P.M. for the 90-minute tours. From May through August the gates open at 8:00 P.M. Be sure to check the recorded message, (202)653-1543, on the day you plan to visit to confirm the time.

Directions: The U.S. Naval Observatory is located inside the Beltway at 34th and Massachusetts Avenue, NW, in Washington, D.C. Parking is not available on the observatory grounds. You can park on Observatory Circle near the British Embassy.

Valley Forge National Historical Park

Forging the Nation's Will

At **Valley Forge** the toughest enemy the Continental Army fought was not the British but the elements. The weather was brutally cold, food was scarce and the shelter minimal. This crucible tested all who stayed here; Valley Forge was a battle of wills not bullets.

While it undoubtedly is more fun to go exploring on a brilliant, sunny day, Valley Forge is best visited on a cold, steely-gray day. A gun-metal sky is the proper backdrop to walk the fields where the men wintered. Under such conditions visitors can more fully appreciate the bravery and fortitude of the men who camped here.

Every school child recognizes the name Valley Forge, but a visit adds new perspective to the pages of history. Visitors leave inspired by the story of how the ragtag troops became a formidable army. The men arrived ill-clothed and ill-fed; they spent the long winter months in harsh conditions fighting off hunger and disease. During one week 4,000 men were listed as unfit to work, but they emerged from the experience a disciplined and trained force.

Defeat brought the Continental Army to Valley Forge. The Battle of Brandywine failed to stop General William Howe who moved with his army to comfortable winter quarters in Philadelphia. General Washington then moved his men 18 miles northwest of the British to Valley Forge. Twelve thousand men arrived on December 19, 1777; they left on June 19, 1778.

Within a week after their arrival the men built more than 2,000 rough huts. Washington, who had been sharing the hardships with his men, moved from his field tent to the fieldstone house that served as his headquarters for the rest of the winter. The house, now open for tours, is 80 percent original and furnished to look as it did when Washington was in residence. You'll see Washington's army coat and glasses in the room he used as an office. One of Washington's field tents is in the park's Visitor Center.

To understand what occurred during the six months the army wintered here, start with the 15-minute audio-visual program in the Visitor Center, then explore the 2,788-acre park. An excellent way to see the park is to join a bus tour; they're conducted from mid-April through October. A narrative tape provides background information as you drive around the park. You can get off the bus at the various historical points of interest and reboard the next bus to continue your tour. Another way to learn about the events that occurred here is to rent a tape and play it in your car as you drive through the park. A final option is to pick up a park map and follow it. Bicycle enthusiasts may want to bring along their bikes and ride the six-mile cycling trail through the park.

One essential stop is the **Grand Parade Grounds** where General von Steuben drilled the men. Von Steuben was with the General Staff of Frederick the Great's Army. Benjamin Franklin, a bit of a Mr. Fix-It, asked von Steuben to leave Europe for the colonies to train the novice recruits. In six months von Steuben's efforts resulted in a well-trained army, a remarkable achievement considering that von Steuben spoke little English. Working from dawn to dusk, the men—many farmers and laborers only months before—were soon executing maneuvers and moving together as a military unit.

Another park focal point is the **Muhlenberg Brigade**, the location of the troops quarters. During the summer months the park schedules living history at this site. The staff demonstrate various aspects of military life in the 1700s. Another interesting stop is the **Isaac Potts House**, which General Washington used as his headquarters. You also can tour the quarters of General Varnum.

A striking Memorial Arch honors the "patience and fidelity" of the soldiers who spent the winter of 1777 at Valley Forge. It's also worth stopping at the privately operated **Washington Memorial Chapel** within the park. Thirteen stained-glass windows capture pivotal moments in our early history. The 13 original states contributed the money to purchase the chapel carillon in the bell tower. Next door to the chapel is the extensive collection of the Valley Forge Historical Society. A nominal admission is charged for this museum.

You can dine in the historic elegance of the **Kennedy-Supplee Mansion**, (215)337-3777, located within Valley Forge National Historical Park. The house was constructed in 1852 by John Kennedy, a Pennsylvania limestone supplier who used his own supplies to create an elaborately molded plaster ceiling. J. Henderson Supplee purchased the house in 1911. He took great pains to preserve the graceful Italianate exterior. The mansion is on the National Register of Historic Places. Lunch is available Monday through Friday and dinner every night except Sunday.

Valley Forge National Historic Park is open daily 8:30 A.M. to 5:00 P.M. There is no admission to the park, but there is a nominal fee for touring the historic buildings.

Directions: Take the Beltway I-495/95 and continue on I-95 north toward Philadelphia. Before entering the city take I-76 west to the Valley Forge exit, then take Route 363 to the park.

Washington Dolls' House and Toy Museum

A Lot of Interest in a Little World

A delightful miniature world with authentically furnished houses, shops, schools, churches and other tiny buildings beckons from the **Washington Dolls' House and Toy Museum.** The private collection of Flora Gill Jacobs, noted author of *Dolls' Houses in America*, *History of Dolls' Houses* and *Victorian Dolls' Houses*, will fascinate young and old alike. Flora Jacobs began collecting antique doll houses after starting work on her first book. Her writing career and avocational interest continued to grow, and 30 years later her enormous collection of houses and toys prompted her to open this museum.

After entering the chic Washington townhouse, you'll pay your admission fee at an antique post office window and literally step into a Lilliputian world. A great portion of the museum exhibits dates from the Victorian era, including one of the most popular items—a six-story Victorian hotel, complete with guest rooms. There is also a small Victorian home with a widow's walk.

Another perennial favorite is Bliss Street, which also evokes the turn of the century. Gingerbread houses surround a town square that features a working water fountain. An antique trolley runs down Bliss Street, and the action includes a knicker-clad boy riding a go-cart and a piloted blimp floating serenely over the square.

The National Trust for Historic Preservation was so taken with the fanciful Queen Anne mansion, circa 1900, they used a photograph of it for their 1989 Christmas card. This ornate doll house with turrets, gables and other gingerbread touches was crafted in Germany.

The museum has many items from other countries including an 18th-century German kitchen, a French turn-of-the-century villa with its original furniture sewn onto the floor and an elaborately furnished Mexican mansion complete with its own chapel.

Closer to home are the five Baltimore row houses, a post-Civil War Southern mansion and an assortment of merchant shops including a grocery store, millinery shop and a butcher's shop.

The collection also focuses on antique toys, games and dolls. Be sure to pay close attention to the replica of Mount Vernon. You'll see George and Martha on the front lawn, but what is interesting is that they are wearing 19th-century clothes popular when the model was created. As if that weren't enough, note that the Washingtons are standing lifelike on the front lawn, while their tombs are in place behind the house. Another fascinating item is the 1884 replica of the United States Capitol that contains a moveable strip of interior views behind its litho-graphed paper-on-wood facade.

At the museum's gift shop collectors can purchase a whole world in miniature. Furnishings and doll houses are available for the beginner and the dedicated collector. The detail and work-manship on these tiny items are amazing; you can see bedecked bonnets and eye-straining miniature copies of *The New York Times*. Copies of Flora Gill Jacobs books, including her children's stories, *The Toy Shop Mystery* and *The Dolls' House Mystery*, are also available.

The Washington Dolls' House and Toy Museum, at 5236 44th Street, NW, is open Tuesday to Saturday from 10:00 A.M. to 5:00 P.M. and Sunday NOON to 5:00 P.M. Admission is charged.

Directions: The museum is inside the Beltway off Wisconsin Avenue near the Mazza Galleria.

Washington National Cathedral

Miracle on the Mount

George Washington had his own ideas about the country's capital city: one dream was "a great Church for national purposes." Legend has it that Washington and city designer Major Pierre L'Enfant rode out from the thriving port of Georgetown to Mount St. Alban. On this commanding hill, the highest point in the new city, they found an ideal site for the church they contemplated. The political climate of the Federal period, however, emphasized separation of church and state, so more than a century passed before Washington's dream was realized.

It wasn't until 1891 that Charles Carroll Glover, a prosperous Washington banker and civic leader, revived the idea of a national church. The task of building the church began in 1893 when Congress issued the Protestant Episcopal Cathedral Foundation a charter for "a house of prayer for all people."

On September 29, 1907, a cornerstone, formed from a small stone found in a field near Bethlehem set into a large piece of American granite, was laid. For this historic task officials used the silver mallet that George Washington used when he placed the U.S. Capitol cornerstone on September 18, 1793.

Washington National Cathedral was under construction from that time until 1990. Eighty-three years to the day after the laying of the cornerstone, the last stone, weighing 1,008 pounds, was hoisted into position atop the south tower's southwestern pin-nacle. The church's full name is the Cathedral Church of St. Peter and St. Paul, and the west towers are dedicated in their names.

This 14th-century English Gothic-style church offers services for many faiths in addition to the regularly scheduled Episcopal worship services. When Egyptian President Anwar Sadat died, an Islamic muezzin was found for the memorial services held at the cathedral. There have also been Jewish, Polish National Catholic, Serbian Orthodox, and Russo-Carpathian services. It was in this church that the Reverend Martin Luther King preached his last sermon. More than 1,500 services take place annually in the nine small chapels.

A tour of the cathedral reminds visitors of the great churches of Europe; truly this is America's Westminster Abbey. The vast nave, crossed by the transept, creates a cross that rises to more than ten stories at its apex. Towering arches and vibrant stained-glass windows add to the grandeur. One of the most popular windows has an encapsulated moon rock donated by the *Apollo 11* astronauts. The two rose windows are reminiscent of the windows in Paris's beloved Notre Dame.

Still other windows commemorate noted Americans. The Civil War windows depict scenes from the lives of Generals Robert E. Lee and Thomas "Stonewall" Jackson. Windows above the marble sarcophagus of President Woodrow Wilson reflect the themes of war and peace.

The cathedral is the final resting place for more than 130 famous Americans including Admiral George Dewey, Secretary of State Cordell Hull, Helen Keller and her teacher-companion Anne Sullivan Macy. Statues honor other noted Americans. The Washington Bay, according to sculptor Lee Lawrie, depicts ". . .not the soldier, not the president, but the man Washington, coming into Christ Church, Alexandria, pausing a moment before going down the aisle to his pew." The Lincoln statue captures a younger man than the traditional view.

There is still talk about the "life-size" stone statues commissioned from an Italian sculptor. When the group of saints arrived they all stood a scant five feet, one inch tall. The artist came to Washington to discuss his work, and when he arrived no discussion of "life-size" was necessary. He, himself, stood five feet, one inch tall.

The larger pieces may attract your attention, but take the time to search out the small gargoyles and grotesques. You may even want to bring binoculars for a close look at the highly individualized and detailed exterior carvings. These whimsical sculptures suggest the personalities of church patrons and personnel. Two figures are of the grandsons of one of the cathedral patrons. One young boy is shown with his hand in the cookie jar while the other stands beside a broken wagon. Each of the boys has a broken halo around his head.

Another fanciful creation shows the faithful dog of one of the headmistresses of the Washington Cathedral School for girls. The pugnacious canine has a piece of the groundskeeper's pants between its teeth. Carvings also show a dentist drilling a giant tooth, a golfer and one of the carvers who worked on the gargoyles blowing his top, obviously in frustration.

The **Pilgrim Observation Gallery** at the top of the cathedral offers another perspective from which to view the gargoyles and grounds. The gallery, at 490 feet above sea level, gives you a sweeping panorama of Washington and the countryside that lies west of the city. If the weather is good, clear-sighted viewers will be able to see the Catoctin and Blue Ridge Mountains far in the distance.

After surveying the interior and exterior of the cathedral you should take a walk through the **Bishop's Garden**. You enter the garden through an 800-year-old Norman arch, and it's like stepping into a 12th-century walled garden. You'll see small Norman courts, old sundials and carved stone panels. A small ivy-covered gazebo is built with stones taken from President Grover Cleveland's house. The extensive use of shrubbery and statuary makes this garden appealing in any season.

At the base of the Pilgrim Steps stands an equestrian statue of George Washington. He appears to be gazing up at the church built on the hill he chose so many years ago. This sculpture has an interesting postscript. The sculptor Herbert Hazeltine had just finished a statue of the racehorse Man-O-War when he did this piece. Those who have seen his rendition of the famous racehorse that stands at Lexington's Kentucky Horse Park claim that George Washington is riding Man-O-War.

Free daily tours of the cathedral take place in the morning and afternoon Monday through Saturday and on Sunday afternoons. Call for specific times (202)537-6200 or (202)537-6207.

Directions: The Washington National Cathedral is inside the Beltway at the intersection of Massachusetts and Wisconsin avenues, N.W., just above Georgetown.

Winter Calendar of Events

DECEMBER

Early:

Winter Festival of Lights—Watkins Regional Park, Upper Marlboro, MD (301)699-2407. Over 125,000 lights create special holiday exhibits that you can enjoy as you drive through the park.

Christmas Open House & Bazaar—Carroll County Farm Museum, Westminster, MD (410)848-7775. The Main House at this farm museum is decorated with garlands, wreaths and an old-fashioned Christmas tree. You can purchase handcrafted gifts and enjoy caroling and listening to Christmas music.

Holidays at Mount Vernon—Mount Vernon, VA (703)780-2000. Borrow decorating ideas from the Washingtons, their home is decorated in the 18th-century manner throughout the month. This is your chance to see the third floor of the mansion not customarily open to the public.

Civil War Christmas Open House—Fort Ward Museum, Alexandria, VA (703)838-4848. Find out what it was like to celebrate Christmas during the Civil War. Victorian decorations, refreshments, period music and costumed interpreters add to the festivities.

Traditional Christmas Celebration—Colvin Run Mill Park, Great Falls, VA (703)759-2771. Family celebrations of an earlier era are brought to life when you join in on the taffy pull, popcorn stringing, straw wreath making and singing of Christmas songs. St. Nick is on hand so children can visit with this guest of honor.

Brandywine Christmas—Brandywine River Museum, Chadds Ford, PA (215)388-7601. Decorations made of natural material and a working train model add to the year-long appeal of this museum's outstanding art collection.

Pageant of Peace—Ellipse, Washington, D.C. (202)619-7222. Near the White House you can see the giant National Christmas Tree. From early December until New Year's Day there are nightly choral performances, a Nativity scene, a burning yule log and trees from each state and territory in the U.S.

Child's Colonial Christmas—London Town Publik House, Edgewater, MD (410)956-4900. Young children can participate in traditional holiday crafts and enjoy Christmas entertainment. Reservations required.

Christmas Candlelight Tours—London Town Public House, Edgewater, MD (410)956-4900. The old ferry house at London Town is decorated with holiday greens. Music of the 18th century will entertain you as you tour by candlelight. Holiday greens are offered for sale.

Christmas Candlelight Weekend—Fredericksburg, VA (703)371-4504. Resembling a Currier & Ives picture, the streets of Fredericksburg echo with the sound of horse-drawn carriages, and the long, full skirts of the costumed docents brush against the sidewalks. The annual Christmas Walking Tour lets you explore a number of private homes as well as the many historic sites in Fredericksburg. The town is decorated and there are carolers and holiday music.

Christmas Madrigal Evenings—St. Mary's City, MD (301)862-0990. A Medieval feast is served at long tables in the Reconstructed State House. Madrigal singers, jesters and strolling musicians in the Renaissance and 17th-century style entertain and amuse diners at this family-style dinner. Wassail is served before dinner, and the customary yule log is burned. Everyone joins in as musicians play familiar Christmas favorites, and the evening ends convivially as the holly is thrown into the burning fire. Reservations are necessary.

Grand Illumination—Williamsburg, VA (804)220-7645. Fireworks begin the fortnight Christmas celebration of Colonial Williamsburg. The town and historic buildings are decorated, and there are special tours, workshops on how to create colonial finery, musical programs and feasting.

Scottish Christmas Walk—Alexandria, VA (703)549-0111. You're invited to join in this parade through Old Town Alexandria saluting the city's Scottish heritage. Taking part each year are bagpipers, Highland dancers, Scottish clans' members and eager onlookers. You can also purchase handcrafted items and fresh heather.

Winter Crafts Festival—Sugarloaf Mountain, MD (301)540-0900. A great place to do your holiday shopping from displays of more than 250 artists and craftspeople.

Old Town Christmas Candlelight Tour—Alexandria, VA (703)838-4200. Christmas decorations bedeck the historic attractions you will see on your walking tour. Period music, colonial dancing and light refreshments add to the festivities.

Candlelight Tour—Montpelier Mansion, Laurel, MD (301)953-1376. This colonial plantation house is decorated for the holiday season and serves refreshments after the candlelight tour. Thursday, Friday and Sunday.

Annual Christmas Open House—Maymont House, Richmond, VA (804)358-7166. A Victorian Christmas is celebrated at the lavishly decorated Maymont mansion. Bonfires, wassail, carolers, bell ringers, carriage rides and Father Christmas add to the fun.

Christmas in Odessa—Odessa, DE (302)378-4353.You can tour Winterthur's historic homes in this 18th-century community or the picturesque private ones that open their doors for this annual event. Crafts, home-cooking, musical programs and candlelight tours are also part of this weekend-long celebration.

Christmas Open House—Ladew Topiary Gardens, Jacksonville, MD (410)557-9570. The English manor house at Ladew is lavishly decorated with Christmas greens. Wreaths and greens are for sale as well as handcrafted items. Holiday music is featured on Friday evening of this weekend-long event.

Festival of Music and Lights—Washington Mormon Temple Visitors Center, Kensington, MD (301)587-0144. More than 80,000 twinkling lights create a holiday atmosphere enhanced each night by a Christmas program. This event runs throughout December.

Carols by Candlelight—Woodlawn Plantation, Alexandria, VA (703)780-4000. The candlelit tour of this historic house is highlighted by 19th-century decorations and Christmas madrigals. A burning yule log and wagon rides add to the festivities.

A Jamestown Christmas—Jamestown Settlement, Jamestown, VA (804)229-1607. The bleak hardship-laden Christmases at Jamestown are compared with traditional English celebrations of the 17th century.

Mid:

Christmas Display in Conservatory—Brookside Gardens, MD (301)949-8230. Beginning on the second Thursday in December hundreds of poinsettias, several poinsettia "trees" and other flowering plants create a floriferous holiday bouquet.

Candlelight Christmas Tours—Sully Plantation, Chantilly, VA (703)759-5241. Sully Plantation is decorated with 18th-century Christmas decorations and suffused in candlelight. Refreshments from the same period include hot mulled cider and old-fashioned cookies.

Christmas Open House at Rose Hill Manor, Frederick, MD (301)694-1648. The 19th century comes alive with kitchen exhibits and weaving looms that children can handle. Children will enjoy the old-fashioned decorations and Santa Claus's visit. There are sleigh rides when the weather permits.

Christmas Candlelight Tours—Surratt House, MD (301)868-1121. A Victorian Christmas tree and greenery decorate this historic old house. You can also see a collection of Victorian children's toys. Punch and cookies are served.

Christmas Celebration—Stratford Hall, Stratford, VA (804)493-8038. A candlelight tour of this gracious colonial plantation house is augmented by the Christmas decorations. There is also caroling and refreshments.

Christmas at the Miller House—Hagerstown, MD (301)797-8782. At this Federal period townhouse Christmas has been re-created as it was celebrated over 100 years ago. A giant tree is decorated with rare antique ornaments, and beneath are toys from the times.

Christmas at the William Paca House—Annapolis, MD (410)263-5553. The William Paca Hose is decorated with greenery and resounds with traditional music for this annual celebration. There are colonial cooking exhibits and refreshments are served.

Christmas Parade of Yachts—Spa Creek, City Dock, Annapolis, MD (410)280-0445. This is one of the most popular events in the month-long holiday celebration in Annapolis. It is held in mid-month on a Saturday night; call for complete schedule of events.

Christmas Conservatory Display–Longwood Gardens, PA (215)388-6741. Thousands of poinsettias and other seasonal plants are on display in this 3½ acres of conservatories. There are also a towering tree and holiday music programs plus an outstanding exterior light display.

Christmas Open House—Decatur House, Washington, D.C. (202)673-4030. Decorations at the Decatur House reflect two periods. Downstairs you'll see decorations from 1819-20, the period of Stephen Decatur's residency. Upstairs there are decorations from the 1870s, the Victorian era, when the table-top tree was popular.

Christmas at the Woodrow Wilson House—Washington, D.C. (202)673-4034. At the Woodrow Wilson House you see Christmas celebrated as it was in the 1920s. Trees were becoming more fashionable, and German glass ornaments were in vogue. Outdoor decorations include a Della Robia wreath.

Christmas at the Octagon—Washington, D.C. (202)638-3105. If you cannot schedule a Christmas visit to the White House, then plan instead to see the Octagon, where in 1814 at the nation's first temporary White House, the Madisons celebrated Christmas. Period decorations capture this early era.

Late:

Christmas Pageant—Washington National Cathedral, Washington, D.C. (202)537-6200. The Washington National Cathedral holds a Christmas Eve service for children in late afternoon as well as a later service in the evening and on Christmas morning.

Christmas Candlelight Tours of the White House—Washington, D.C. (202)456-2200. This annual after-Christmas event lets you get a look at the Christmas decorations adorning the President's house. Be sure to arrive early for these popular tours.

Reenactment of Washington Crossing the Delaware—Washington Crossing Historic Park, PA (215)493-4076. Colonial uniformed reenactment groups parade with fife and drum on Christmas Day. Then Washington addresses the men before they board the authentic replicas of Durham boats to commemorate the 1776 crossing of the Delaware River to attack the unsuspecting Hessians at Trenton.

Scottish New Year's Eve, Hogmanay—Alexandria, VA (703)838-4200. Like its Scottish founders, Alexandria annually celebrates Old Year's Night with Scottish food and entertainment. The evening culminates with a traditional "first footing" ceremony at midnight. Reservations required.

Happy New Year—Baltimore Inner Harbor, MD (410)332-4191. Music and fireworks at the Inner Harbor provide a novel way to welcome the new year.

New Year's Eve Celebration—Old Post Office Pavilion, Washington, D.C. (202)289-4224. Live entertainment, plenty of available food and the ceremonial lowering of the giant U.S. Postal Service Love Stamp from the Pavilion's Clock Tower at midnight.

JANUARY

Early:

Philadelphia Mummers' New Year's Day Parade, PA (215)636-3300. Every year since New Year's Day, 1901, the Mummers have paraded down Broad Street in Philadelphia. Each year in sequins and feathers thousands of marchers and string musicians take part in this 12-hour spectacular. It's a great way to start the year.

Winter Chores—Oxon Hill Farm, MD (301)839-1177. Although most visitors stop at the Oxon Hill Farm during the growing season, it is also interesting to observe the winter farm chores being done on crisp January days. Farm workers are involved in repairing the farm tools, clearing the fields and preparing them for the spring planting. They also groom the animals.

Baltimore on Ice—Rash Field, Inner Harbor Ice Rink, Baltimore, (410)837-4636. Variety of ice events geared to young and old provide winter fun at the Inner Harbor.

Pocono Winter Carnival—Pennsylvania Pocono Mountains, (717)424-6050. Downhill and cross-country ski events at this family skiing festival.

Mid:

Religious Freedom Day—Fredericksburg, VA (703)373-1176. Every year at the Thomas Jefferson Religious Freedom Monument in Fredericksburg, the drafting of the Statute of Religious Freedom is commemorated. Thomas Jefferson, who wrote this significant statement, asked that his tombstone inscription include the words, "Author of the Declaration of Independence, of the Statute of Virginia for Religious Freedom, and Father of the University of Virginia." This bill, written in Fredericksburg in 1777, was one of his most famous pieces of legislation. The commemoration includes an honor guard and wreath-laying ceremony at the monument.

January 19—Robert E. Lee's Birthday—Stratford Hall, VA (703)493-8038. The Lee family tree contains the names of many who influenced the course of history. One of the first was the patriarch of the family, Thomas Lee, who held the highest office in the colony of Virginia, as president of the King's Council. In 1720, Thomas Lee built the family estate, Stratford Hall, on the cliffs overlooking the Potomac River. Thomas Lee's sons, Richard Henry and Francis Lightfoot, were signers of the Declaration of Independence. His great-nephew, Lighthorse Harry Lee, married Matilda Lee, who had inherited Stratford Hall. It was here at this family home on January 19, 1897, that Robert E. Lee was born. Each year the 20-room mansion is open free on General Robert E. Lee's birthday.

Ski Races—Wisp Ski Resort, McHenry, MD (301)387-4911. Throughout the month a variety of ski competitions are held including snowboard and shalom races.

Late:

Lee Birthday Celebrations—Candlelight Tours of the Boyhood Home of Robert E. Lee and the Lee-Fendall House, VA (703)548-1789. Alexandria, which considers itself the Lee family hometown, annually holds a dual Lee family celebration at the two Lee homes. The Lee-Fendall House is dedicated to Lighthorse Harry Lee, whose birthday falls on January 29. Harry Lee never, in fact, resided at this house, but it was here that he wrote the moving farewell address to Washington from the citizens of Alexandria. Costumed guides tell many interesting anecdotes as they escort visitors through the house. Across the street at the Boyhood Home of Robert E. Lee, music of the period is part of this annual celebration. Robert E. Lee spent ten of his early years at this house, leaving at age 18 to attend West Point. His upstairs room with its view of the Potomac River has been carefully restored.

Welcome Spring Exhibit—Longwood Gardens, Kennett Square, PA (215)388-6741. If winter gets you down, get a jump on spring by spending a few hours in Longwood's conservatories where spring arrives early.

FEBRUARY

Early:

Black History Month—Martin Luther King, Jr. Memorial Library, Washington, D.C. (202)727-0321. Month-long events celebrate the contributions of Afro-Americans to American life. Events also occur at the Smithsonian Institution.

Groundhog Day—Gobblers Know, Allegheny National Forest, PA (814)938-7700. The tradition has continued for over 100 years, each year on February 2, Punxsutawney Phil predicts how many more weeks of winter the nation will have before spring arrives. This event occurs between 7:00 and 7:30 A.M.

Mid:

Victorian Valentine Display—Surratt House, MD (301)868-1121. At the Surratt House's annual antique Valentine display you can see more than 50 sentiment souvenirs from the 1840s through the 1890s. Reproductions of period Valentines are for sale.

Chinese New Year Parade—Washington, D.C. (202)724-4091. On H Street, NW between 5th and 8th Streets there is a traditional Chinese parade to celebrate the Chinese Lunar New Year. Parade features firecrackers, lions, drums and dragon dancers.

Revolutionary War Reenactment—Fort Ward Park, Alexandria, VA (703)838-4200. Re-created Revolutionary units annually reenact a typical Colonial and British clash at Fort Ward Park. Prior to the battle you can see an interpretation of camp life.

George Washington Birthday Parade—Alexandria, VA (703)838-4200. On the Monday designated for celebrating George Washington's birthday the nation's largest annual parade in honor of George Washington winds through the historic streets of Alexandria. He may be the "Father of his Country," but in Alexandria Washington is also a hometown boy who made good. Traditionally more than 100 units take part in this parade.

George Washington Birthday Celebration—Fredericksburg, VA (703)373-1776. Each year in Fredericksburg at the home of George Washington's mother a birthday celebration is held. Frequently the sponsors present a vignette capturing the pivotal role played by Mary Washington in her son's life. Other Fredericksburg attractions also celebrate the occasion.

White-Water Rafting

Most of us are cushioned from the elemental forces of nature, so for a thrilling adventure that tests nature's ferocity try white-water rafting. White-water trips offer tranquil periods when you can relax and enjoy the passing scenery, but there are also moments of breath-stopping excitement.

Raft trips are not really dangerous when supervised by trained outfitters. Novices, families with young children and senior citizens should start on rivers with little or no rapids. They can take comfort from the fact that the commercial rafting companies have outstanding safety records. In West Virginia alone more than 10,000 people raft each year, and in the last ten years there has been only one serious accident.

Most rafts hold between four and eight people including a trained staffer who will let you know what to do as you travel the river. White-water raft trips are participatory; you will be expected to paddle for most, if not all, of the trip. The most exciting position on board is at the very front where you will feel the full impact of the rapids and riffles. If you are a bit apprehensive, forego that thrill and sit towards the back. Many outfitters do not allow any passengers under 12, so be sure to check if you are planning to include younger children in your party. Some outfitters offer a rubber ducky, a one-man inflatable kayak, for advanced rafters.

Trips run regardless of the weather, and you should be prepared to be thoroughly drenched. Bring a complete set of dry clothes to change into after the trip. If you plan a trip during cool weather, check to see if the outfitter rents wet suits. If you bring your own covering, include either a wet suit or wool clothing. Wool retains your body heat even when you're wet.

Be sure to make reservations as far in advance as possible. Rafting has become increasingly popular and trips fill up fast. Weekends in the summer are, of course, the most popular times. Raft trips are cancelled only when the water is dangerously high or too low.

VIRGINIA OUTFITTERS

James River Runners, Inc.
Rt. 4, Box 106
Scottsville, VA 24590
(804)286-2338
Canoe and tubing trips on the James River. Class 1-3 rapids. Season
    March–October. Options include overnight canoeing and camping.

Downriver Canoe Company
Rt. 1, Box 256-A
Bentonville, VA 22610
(703)635-5526
Canoe trips on the Shenandoah River from April–October.

Front Royal Canoe Company
P.O. Box 473
Front Royal, VA 23630
(703)635-5440
Canoe and tubing trips on the Shenandoah River. Canoe season mid-
  March–October, tubing trips Memorial Day-Labor Day.

Richmond Raft Company
4400 East Main Street
Richmond, VA 23231-1103
(804)222-7238
Summer raft trips on the James River in Richmond, only raft trips in
  Virginia on the waterway of a major city.

New River Canoe Company
P.O. Box 100
Pembroke, VA 24136
(703)626-7189

MARYLAND OUTFITTERS

River and Trail Outfitters
604 Valley Road
Knoxville, MD 21750
(301)695-5177
Rafting on the Potomac and Shenandoah Rivers.

Precision Rafting
P.O. Box 185
Friendsville, MD 21531
(301)746-5290
White-water rafting on the Upper Yough.

WEST VIRGINIA OUTFITTERS

American Whitewater Tours (also called USA Whitewater)
P.O. Box 277-GC
Rowlesburg, WV 26425
(800)USA-RAFT
White-water rafting in Garrett County, MD. Trips run on the Potomac,
  beginning just 45 minutes from Deep Creek Lake, one and two
  person duckies; trips also run on the Upper Yough for the

experienced paddler; white-water trips run on the Cheat in West Virginia. Canoe and tubing trips on the New River between Claytor Lake Dam and Bluestone Dam run from April-October. Options include 1–5-day canoe trips with primitive camping.

Appalachian Wildwaters
P.O. Box 277
Rowlesburg, WV 26425
(304)454-2475 or (800)USA-RAFT
Runs raft trips on the New, Cheat, Gauley, Big Sandy, North Fork of the South Branch of the Potomac, Bluestone, Meadow, Greenbrier, and Shavers Fork.

Blackwater Outdoor Center
Box 325
Davis, WV 26260
(304)259-5117
Runs raft trips on the Cheat and on the North Branch of the Potomac.

Blue Ridge Outfitters
P.O. Box 650
Harpers Ferry, WV 25414
(304)725-3444
Runs raft trips on the Potomac and the Shenandoah.

Cheat River Outfitters
P.O. Box 134
Albright, WV 26519
(304)329-2024
Runs raft trips on the North Branch of the Potomac, Cheat and Shenandoah.

Expeditions, Inc.
P.O. Box 277 C
Rowlesburg, WV 26425
(304)454-2475 or (800)USA-RAFT
Runs raft trips on the Cheat and Gauley.

River Riders
Rt. 3, Box 1260
Harpers Ferry, WV 25425
(304)535-2663
Runs raft trips on the Shenandoah, Potomac and Greenbrier.

Rough Run Expeditions
P.O. Box 277 D
Rowlesburg, WV 26425
(304)454-2475 or (800)USA-RAFT
Runs raft trips on the Cheat and Tygart.

PENNSYLVANIA OUTFITTERS

Jim Thorpe River Adventures
Jim Thorpe
(717)325-2570 or (800)424-RAFT

Kittatinny Canoes
Dingmans Ferry
(717)828-2338 or (800)FLOAT-KC

Lehigh Rafting Rentals, Inc.
White Haven
(717)443-4441

Laurel Highlands River Tours
Ohiopyle
(800)472-3846 or (412)329-8531

Mountain Streams & Trails
Ohiopyle
(412)329-8810 or (800)245-4090

Ohiopyle Recreational Rentals
Ohiopyle
(800)249-4090 or (412)329-4730

Pocono White Water Rafting, Ltd.
Jim Thorpe
(717)325-3656

Riversport School of Paddling
Confluence
(814)395-5744

Scotty's White Water Rafting
Hawley
(717)226-3551

Tri-State Canoe Boat Rentals and Campgrounds
Matamoras
(717)491-4948

White Water Adventurers of Cheat River Canyon
Ohiopyle
(800)992-7238 or (412)329-8850

Whitewater Challengers
White Haven
(717)443-9532

Whitewater Rafting Adventures
Albrightsville
(717)722-0285

White Water Rentals
Ohiopyle
(800)992-7238 or (412)329-8850

Wilderness Voyageurs
Ohiopyle
(800)272-4141 or (412)329-4752

Youghiogheny Outfitters
Ohiopyle
(412)329-4549

Vineyards of the Middle Atlantic Region

Connoisseurs have elaborate rituals for choosing and tasting wines, but the rankest amateur may have a lot of fun and learn a great deal about wine by visiting the local vineyards. You can stroll through the vineyards, tour the cellars and taste the finished product. The Middle Atlantic offers a multiple of choices each with its own proud history, interesting stories and distinctive taste.

VIRGINIA

There are more than 40 wineries in Virginia. The state is divided into regions: Eastern, Northern, the Shenandoah Valley, Central and Southwest Virginia. Throughout the state grape logo signs direct you to nearby wineries. Listed below are those wineries easily accessible for day-trippers. To obtain a complete listing of Virginia wineries, with specific directions to each, and a rundown on state winery festivals call (804)786-0481 or write the Virginia Wine Marketing Program, VDACS, Division of Marketing, P.O. Box 1163, Richmond, VA 23209.

Eastern

Accomack Vineyards, P.O. Box 38, Painter, VA 23420. (804)442-2110. Virginia's only Eastern Shore winery.

Ingleside Plantation Vineyards, P.O. Box 1038, Oak Grove, VA 22443. (804)224-8687. Award-winning Northern Neck winery near George Washington Birthplace.

Williamsburg Winery, Ltd., 2638 Lake Powell Rd., Williamsburg, VA 23185. (804)229-0999. Winery housed in 17th- and 18th-century designed buildings.

Northern

Farfelu Vineyard, Rt. 1, Rox 23, Flint Hill, VA 22627. (703)364-2930. Small winery in Rappahannock County.

Hartwood Winery, 345 Hartwood Road, Fredericksburg, VA 22406. (703)752-4893. Winery close to the area's historic sites and battlefields.

Linden Vineyards, Rt. 1, Box 96, Linden VA 22642. (703)364-1997. Winery is near Skyline Drive and Shenandoah National Park.

Loudoun Valley Vineyards, Rt. 1, Box 340, Waterford, VA 22190. (703)882-3375. Winery visits can be combined with a walkthrough quaint 18th-century Quaker village.

Meredyth Vineyards, P.O. Box 347, Middleburg, VA 22117. (703)687-6277. Vines at this highly regarded vineyard are grown on the slopes of the scenic Bull Run Mountains.

Naked Mountain Vineyard, P.O. Box 131, Markham, VA 22643.
(703)364-1609. (703)364-1609. Classic European grapes are grown
on the east slope of the Blue Ridge.

Oasis Vineyard, Hwy 635, Box 116, Hume, VA 22639. (703)635-7627.
Winery near Skyline Drive facing the scenic Blue Ridge Mountains.

Piedmont Vineyards & Winery, P.O. Box 286, Middleburg, VA 22117.
(703)687-5528. This former dairy barn now houses a winery, tasting
room and gift shop.

Swedenburg Winery, Middleburg, VA 22117. (703)687-5219. Loudoun
County winery on Valley View Farm.

Tarara, Rt. 4, Box 229, Leesburg, VA 22075. (703)771-7100 or for
Metro Washington (703)478-8161. Vines are grown along the
Potomac River outside historic Leesburg.

Willowcroft Farm Vineyards, Rt. 2, Box 174-A, Leesburg, VA 22075.
(703)777-8161. Winery is in rustic barn on top of Mt. Gilead,
overlooking the Blue Ridge.

Shenandoah Valley

Deer Meadow Vineyard, HC-34, Box 4763, Winchester, VA
22601.(703)877-1919 or (800)752-1746. This winery has a fishing
pond and picnic area.

Guilford Ridge Vineyard, Rt. 5, Box 148, Luray, VA 22835. (703)778-
3853. Small winery between the Blue Ridge and Massanutten
Mountains.

Mount Herman Vineyard, P.O. Box 94, Basye, VA 22810. (703)856-
2196. A new small winery.

North Mountain Vineyard & Winery, Rt. 1, Box 543, Mauertown, VA
22664. (703)436-9463. This winery offers hayrides in the
fall.Shenandoah Vineyards, Rt. 2, Box 323, Edinburg, VA 22824.
(703)984-8699. Award-winning 40-acre vineyard.

Winchester Winery, HC34, Box 5243, Winchester, VA 22601.
(703)877-2200 or (703)877-1275. Tasting room overlooks the wine
cellar at this vineyard.

MARYLAND

There are 11 wineries in Maryland, a state with one of America's
oldest wine-making traditions. In the 17th century settlers were
producing wine from their harvest of grapes, apples, berries and
even dandelions. For a complete listing of the state's wineries
that gives details on tours and tastings call (800)237-WINE or
write: Association of Maryland Wineries, P.O. Box 277, Glen
Arm, Maryland 21057.

Boordy Vineyards, 12820 Long Green Pike, Hydes, MD 21082.
(410)592-5015. The oldest and largest winery in Maryland. Wine
festivals are frequently hosted in and around the 19th-century
fieldstone barn.

Montbray Wine Cellars, Ltd., 818 Silver Run Valley Road, Westminster, MD 21157. (410)346-7878. This Carroll County D Fwinery was the first in America to produce a varietal wine from the French hybrid Seyve-Villard.

Berrywine Plantations/Linganore Wine Cellars, 13601 Glisans Mill Road, Mt. Airy, MD 21771. (301)831-5889. This family vineyard produces vintage-dated estate wines, fruit wines and flavored wines.

Byrd Vineyards and Winery, Church Hall Road, Myersville, MD 21773. (301)293-1110. This winery produced the first wines in the Catoctin viticulture area in western Frederick County.

Ziem Vineyards, Rt. 1, Box 161, Fairplay, MD 21733. (301)223-8352. This is Maryland's westernmost vineyard. It's located in a 200-year-old stone house with a spring house and bank barn.

Elk Run Vineyards, 15113 Liberty Rd., Mount Airy, MD 21771. (301)775-2513. The wine shop is in the summer kitchen of anhistoric 1750s house.

Catoctin Vineyards Winery, 805 Greenbridge Road, Brookville, MD 20833. (301)774-2310. The closest Maryland vineyard to D.C.

Woodhall Vineyards and Wine Cellar, 15115 Wheeler Lane, Sparks, MD 21152. (410)771-4664. This winery is the closest one to Baltimore.

Loew Vineyards, 14001 Liberty Road, Mt. Airy, MD 21771. (301)460-5728. More than the grape varieties owe an allegience to Europe; a European family tradition of winemaking has been transplanted to Maryland.

Fiore Winery, MD Rt. 136, 3026 Whiteford Rd., Pylesville, MD21132. (410)836-7605/1860. Vines grow along the Susquehanna River in Harford County's first winery.

Basignani Winery, 15772 Falls Rd., Sparks, MD 21152. (410)472-4718. A new winery just north of the village of Butler in Baltimore County.

PENNSYLVANIA

America's first commercially successful vineyard was in Pennsylvania just northwest of Phildelphia. Several wineries in the state were started in the early 1800s. There are six regions in the state, only two are convenient for Washington day-trippers, the Southeast and Southcentral region. For additional information on Pennsylvania wineries call (717)927-6192 or write the Grape Industry Association, P.O. Box 35, Brogue, PA 17309.

Southeast Region

Buckingham Valley Vineyards, Rt. 4113, Box 371, Buckingham, PA 18912. (215)794-7188.

Calvaresi Winery, Bernville-Shartlesville Roads, R.D. 3, Bernville, PA 19506. (215)488-7966.

Clover Hill Vineyards, R.D. 2, Box 340, Old Route 222, Breinigsville, PA 18031. (215)395-2468.

Fox Meadow Farm, R.D. 2, Box 59, Chester Springs, PA 19425. (215)827-9731.

In & Out Vineyards, 258 Durham Road, Newtown, PA 18940. (215)860-5899.

Peace Valley Winery, P.O. Box 94, Chalfont, PA 18914. (215)249-9058.

Twin Brook Winery, 5697 Strasburg Rd., Rt. 2, Box 2376, Gap, PA 17527. (215)442-4915.

Southcentral Region

Adams County Winery, 251 Peach Tree Rd., Orrtanna, PA 17353. (717)334-4631.

Allegro Vineyards, R.D 2, Box 64, Brogue, PA 17309. (717)927-9148.

Stephen Bahn Winery, R.D.1, Box 758, Brogue, PA 17309. (717)927-9051.

Hunter's Valley Winery, R.D. 2, Box 326D, Liverpool, PA 17045. (717)444-7211.

Naylor Wine Cellars, R.D. 3, Box 424, Ebaugh Rd., Stewartstown, PA 17363. (717)993-2431.

Nissley Vineyards, R.D. 1, Bainbridge, PA 17502. (717)426-3514.

Pumpkin Patches

Halloween can become more than a time for children to dress in costumes and go trick or treating; it can mean a festive family outing to a nearby pumpkin patch. Visiting a farm on a crisp autumn day and hand-picking a pumpkin can become a tradition.

Picking the pumpkin is just the beginning of the fun. You display it uncut until the weekend before Halloween, then design and carve a jack-o-lantern. Pumpkins come in all sizes and shapes. The traditional favorite seems to be a jolly round one, though the original Jack was certainly not happy. Legend has it that the first Jack was an Irish miser who was not welcome in either heaven or hell. Instead, he was forced to walk the earth until Judgment Day carrying a lantern to light his way.

Once you carve your pumpkin it will last only a few days. Before carving it, scoop out the pulp and use for pies and bread. You can also toast the pumpkin seeds in the oven for a tasty snack. It is easier to carve the pumpkin if it is hollowed to a one-inch thickness.

First draw a design on the pumpkin with a felt-tip marker before you begin carving. If you have a lot of confidence, or a lot of experience, you can omit this step. But outlining the features gives you a chance to get the family input before you begin cutting. Woe betide the carver who creates a scary visage when a happy one was envisioned! Pumpkin carving can be simple or complex. You can either make a few large cutouts or create a more expressive face with small, thin, line cutouts.

To enhance your pumpkin face use an assortment of fruit and dried natural embellishments. Acorns, walnuts and Indian corn can be used for eyes and teeth. Noses and tongues are often formed from gourds. Try adding leaves, dried grasses or corn husks for hair.

If you plan to burn a candle inside the pumpkin, you should cut a wedge out of the lid so the smoke can escape. If you do not, the inside will dry out faster and you will notice the smell of burning pumpkin.

There are many pumpkin patches to visit in Maryland and Virginia. To obtain a complete listing for Maryland write the Marketing Research & Development Group, Maryland Department of Agriculture, Annapolis, MD 21401 or call (410)841-5770. For the Virginia Apple & Pumpkin Guide call (804)786-5867 or write the Virginia Department of Agriculture and Consumer Services, Office of Domestic Marketing, P.O. Box 1163, Box 1004, Richmond, VA 23209.

MARYLAND

Anne Arundel County
Pumphrey's Home Grown Vegetables
8326 Rt. 3 North
Millersville, MD 21108
(410)987-0669

Howard County
Larriland Farm
2415 Rt. 94
Woodbine, MD 21797
(410)854-6110
Also hayrides, scarecrow workshop, straw maize, hot apple fritters
and tours by appointment

Montgomery County
Becraft's Farm Produce
14722 New Hampshire Avenue
Silver Spring, MD 20905
(301)236-4545

Butler's Orchard
22200 Davis Mill Road
Germantown, MD 20876
(301)972-3299
Hayrides and pumpkin festival on weekends in October

Homestead Farm
15600 Sugarland Road
Poolesville, MD 20837
(301)977-3761
Wagon rides and hayrides by appointment

Rock Hill Orchard
28600 Ridge Road
Mt. Airy, MD 21771
(301)831-7427
Hayrides by appointment, honey, jams and jellies

Prince George's County
Darrow Berry Farm
Bell Station Road
Glen Dale, MD 20769
(301)390-6611
Pumpkinland, farm animals and hayrides

Cherry Hill Farm
12300 Gallahan Road
Clinton, MD 20735
(301)292-4642/1928
Wagon rides to petting zoo or orchard

Miller Farms
10140 Piscataway Road
Clinton, MD 20735
(301)297-5878/9370

E.A. Parker & Sons
12720 Parker Lane
Clinton, MD 20735
(301)292-3940
Hayrides and bonfires by appointment

Queen Ann Farm
1800 Central Avenue
Mitchellville, MD 20716
(301)249-6475
Hayrides and petting zoo

Robin Hill Farm Nursery
15800 Croom Road
Brandywine, MD 20613
(301)579-6844

VIRGINIA

Fairfax County
Chantilly Farms
Rt. 2, Box 238B
Leesburg, VA 22075
(703)378-7113 or 777-4831
Pumpkin patch located at farm stand, hayride tours, farm zoo and
  hay maze

Fauquier County
Hartland Orchard
Rt. F 284
Markham, VA 22643
(703)364-2316

Stribling Orchard
Rt. 688 south
Markham, VA 22643
(703)364-2092/3040

Frederick County

Rinker Orchards
Rt. 631
Stephens City, VA 22655
(703)869-1499
Over-size pumpkins available on select-your-own basis

Virginia Farm Market
Rt. 522
Winchester, VA 22601
(703)665-8000
Select-your-own from 3 oz. to 100 lbs., pumpkin land with storybook
    characters

Choose-and-Cut Christmas Trees

Charles Schultz's *Peanuts* cartoon, hits a responsive chord in many American homes with his story of Charlie Brown trying to find a real Christmas tree among the aluminum trees ones sold everywhere. If you feel nostalgic at Christmas time, visit one of the choose-and-cut tree farms in Maryland and Virginia and cut your own tree.

The custom of bringing a live tree into the house reportedly began in 16th-century Germany. The Eastern Orthodox Church celebrated the Feast Day of Adam and Eve on December 24th with the tradition of decorating a fir tree with apples. When Prince Albert of Germany married England's Queen Victoria he introduced the custom of decorating a tree in the home to Great Britian. German immigrants who came to the colonies introduced the practice in America.

Traditionalists prefer live trees, but nowadays too many trees are cut too early. Hasty harvesting results in brittle trees and lost needles. Nearly everyone has heard horror stories of needleless trees on Christmas Eve. Disappointments of this type have prompted many people to turn to artificial trees, but choose-and-cut tree farms offer another alternative. You can cut the tree when you want and be sure it is fresh. You don't even have to hold the trees up; nature does that. Your problem will be getting it down.

A number of Christmas tree farms offer four choices: cut your own tree, buy one already cut, buy a live tree that is balled and ready for planting or dig up your own tree.

The more the farm hands do for you the more the price goes up. Cutting your own tree is the most economical. Be sure to bring a saw or an ax. Some farms supply cutting tools, but most do not. Be sure to protect the tree from the drying wind if you have to carry it on top of the car by wrapping it with cloth or plastic. Otherwise the wind created by your moving car will cause the needles to dry. When you get your tree home, cut off an inch and place in warm water, then cut off another inch before you bring the tree inside to decorate. If you plan to plant your Christmas tree keep it inside only a short time. A week is considered ideal. You might want to dig your hole ahead of time as the ground is often frozen by late December. Cover both the hole and the dirt you remove with leaves to keep the area from becoming too hard.

In this region you can usually find Scotch pine, white and Austrian pine, Douglas fir and Norway, blue and white spruce. Call ahead before you drive to a Christmas tree farm to make sure they have an ample supply of the variety you prefer.

To obtain a complete Virginia Christmas Tree Guide call (804)786-5867 or write: Virginia Department of Agriculture and Consumer Services, Division of Marketing, P.O. Box 1163, Suite 1004, Richmond, VA 23209. To obtain a copy of the Maryland guide write Agricultural Development Group, Maryland Department of Agriculture, 50 Harry S. Truman Parkway, Annapolis, MD 21401.

VIRGINIA

Beech Hill Farm
Rt. 1, Box 281
Remington, VA 22734
(703)439-8287
Hours: 9:00-4:30 December weekends
Selection: white and Scotch pine, Norway spruce
Services: bring your own saw

Beverly and Hug Heclo
Box 220
White Post, VA 22663
(703)837-1240
Hours: call anytime after Thanksgiving
Selection: white and Scotch pine, blue spruce
Services: you choose, they cut, you carry

Blair Farms
Windeyedge
Rt. 2, Box 186-A
Woodstock, VA 22664
(703)893-7760
Hours: weekends from Thanksgiving to Christmas
Selection: Scotch pine, Virginia and white pine, Norway and blue
    spruce
Services: they supply handsaws

Calamus Creek Christmas Trees
Rt. 1, Box 2065
Front Royal, VA 22630
(703)635-7763
Hours: 9:00–5:00 daily after Thanksgiving
Selection: white and Scotch pine
Services: saws, twine, baling and assistance available

Chestnut Hill
Rt. 1, Box 770
Amissville, VA 22002
(703)937-5461
Hours: 9:00–4:30 daily after Thanksgiving to 12/23
Selection: white and Scotch pine, Norway spruce
Services: twine and saws available, no digging, you cut or they cut

Clemmer's Choose & Cut Christmas Tree Plantation
Rt. 8, Box 443
Winchester, VA 22601
(703)667-0807
Hours: 9:00–dark weekends, 3:30-dark weekdays
Selection: Scotch and white pine, Norway spruce and fir
Services: saws, vexar wrap and twine, you cut or fresh-cut tree

Glengary Christmas Tree Farm
Rt. 1, Box 270
Viewtown, VA 22746
(703)937-4751
Hours: 8:00–dark daily
Selection: white, Scotch and Austrian pine, Colorado blue spruce,
   Douglas fir
Services: choose and cut

Glen Manor Christmas Tree Farm
Rt. 1, Box 767
Front Royal, VA 22630
(703)635-2569
Hours: weekends 10:00–5:00
Selection: white pine
Services: handsaws, twine, hay and horsedrawn wagon rides

Gooney Creek Tree Farm
Rt. 1, Box 170A
Browntown, VA 22610
(703)893-9784
Hours: 10:00–dark daily
Selection: Scotch and white pine, balled and burlapped spruce
Services: saws, tree netting, twine and assistance available, hay
   wagons

Great Hickory Farm
Rt. 726
Rixeyville, VA 22737
(703)675-3175
Hours: 9:00–5:00 weekends
Selection: white and Scotch pine, blue and Norway spruce, Fraser fir
Services: tree baling, twine and saws, hayride

Greene Meadows Tree Farm
Rt. 1, Box 296
Stanardsville, VA 22973
(804)985-3226
Hours: 9:00–5:00 weekends, selected Fridays
Selection: white pine
Services: cut or dig your own, saws, rope and baling

Hapdogs's 1st Tree Farm
First Street
Berryville, VA
(703)955-2144
Hours: 8:00–5:00 Saturday, 12:30-5:00 Sunday
Selection: sheared white and Scotch pine
Services: cut your own, pre-dug, saws and twine

Hapdog's 2nd Tree Farm
Rt. 625
Millwood, VA
(703)955-2144
Hours: 8:00–5:00 Saturday, 12:30–5:00 Sunday
Selection: sheared white and Scotch pine
Services: cut or dig your own, pre-dug, saws and twine

Hendershott Farm
Rt. 340, north of Rt. 7
Berryville, VA
(703)768-5762
Hours: 10:00–5:00 December weekends
Selection: Scotch and white pine
Services: tree baling at extra charge, saws

Jacobson's Tree Farm
Rts. 15 & 658
Lucketts, VA 22075
(703)777-9534
Hours: 9:00–5:00 Friday–Sunday
Selection: Scotch and white pine, Douglas fir, Norway and blue
    spruce
Services: saws, shake and bale, live balled and burlapped trees

Loudoun Nursery-Bellwether Plantation
Rt. 716
Purcellville, VA
(703)882-3450 or 338-2770
Hours: 9:00–4:30 weekends in December
Selection: Scotch and white pine, balled and burlapped white pine
    and blue spruce
Services: bow saws, vexar baling

Loudoun Nursery-Gilberts Corner Farm
Rt. 860
Arcola, VA
(703)882-3450 or 327-6586
Hours: 1:00–4:30 weekdays, 9:00–4:30 weekends
Selection: Scotch and white pine
Services: cut or pre-cut, bow saws and vexar baling

Loudoun Valley Christmas Tree Farm
Rt. 1, Box 77
Purcellville, VA 22132
(703)882-3394
Hours: 9:00–5:00 weekends
Selection: white and red pine, Norway spruce, white fir
Services: cut or balled, free baling

Lowelands Farm
Rt. 1, Box 98
Middleburg, VA 22117
(703)687-6923
Hours: 9:00–5:00 weekends
Selection: white and Scotch pine, Fraser fir
Services: gift shop, free greenery, handsaws, tree baling, twine,
    hayrides, you cut or they cut, refreshments

Lugar's Tree Farm
Rt. 623
Woodstock, VA
(703)971-5473 or 459-4893
Hours: 10:00-dark Thursday–Sunday
Selection: Scotch and white pine
Services: cut or pre-cut, baling and saws

Middleburg Christmas Tree Farm
P.O. Box 1256
Purcellville, VA 22132
(703)554-8625
Hours: 9:00–4:30 weekends
Selection: white and Scotch pine, Norway and Colorado blue spruce
Services: saws and baling, free greenery

Mill Creek Christmas Tree Farm
Rt. 2, Box 20A
Mt. Jackson, VA 22842
(703)477-2310 or 237-2164
Hours: 9:00–5:00 Friday–Monday in December
Selection: white pine
Services: choose and cut

Milltown Creek Tree Farms
Rt. 1, Box 212
Lovettsville, VA 22080
(703)822-5428
Hours: 9:00–4:00 weekends, Friday 2:00–5:00
Selection: white and Scotch pine, Norway and blue spruce, Douglas
   fir
Services: saws, baling and twine, cutting assistance, refreshments

Moose Hill Farm
Rt. 1, Box 104A
Sperryville, VA 22740
(703)987-8271
Hours: 9:00–dark weekends
Selection: white pine
Services: saws, baler, twine, shovel, burlap, assistance, refreshments

Oakland Tree Plantation
Rt. 340
Berryville, VA 22611
(703)955-4495
Hours: 9:00–5:00 daily
Selection: white and Scotch pine, Norway spruce
Services: cut or pre-cut, refreshments, hayrides, baling, twine, saws,
   Santa's Shop

Oak Shade Farm
Rt. 2, Box 170-A
Rixeyville, VA 22737
(703)937-5062
Hours: 9:00–5:00 daily
Selection: white pine
Services: you cut or they cut

Pinehill Christmas Tree Farm
Rt. 9, Box 132
Winchester, VA 22601
(703)877-1643
Hours: 9:00–5:00 daily
Selection: Scotch and white pine
Services: saws, twine, vexar wrapping, picnic area and pond

Pinetop Tree Farm
170 Hawthorne Drive
Winchester, VA 22601
(703)858-3381 or 662-8356
Hours: 9:00–5:00 Friday–Sunday
Selection: white and Scotch pine
Services: tree baling and saws, assistance

Shenandoah Countryside
Rt. 2, Box 370
Luray, VA 22835
(703)743-6434
Hours: 9:00–dark daily early December to mid-month
Selection: white and red pine, Norway spruce
Services: saws and twine, will cut and load trees

Shenandoah River Christmas Trees
Rt. 1, Box 184
Gore, VA 22637
(703)858-2825
Hours: 10:00–4:30 Friday–Sunday until mid-December
Selection: sheared white pine
Services: handsaws, baling twine, assistance

Shepherd's Hill Farm
Box 464
Bowling Green, VA 22427
(804)633-5487/5133
Hours: 9:00–5:00 weekends
Selection: white, Virginia and Scotch pine, Norway spruce
Services: saws, baling

Sherwood Christmas Tree Farm
HU1, Box 300
Cross Junction, VA 22625
(703)888-3597/3061
Hours: 8:00–5:00 Friday–Sunday
Selection: white and Scotch pine
Services: tree baling and saws

Sipe's Christmas Tree Farm
Rt. 1, Box 38
White Post, VA 22663
(703)837-1496
Hours: 8:30–4:30 daily
Selection: white, Austrian and Scotch pine, Norway spruce
Services: you choose, they cut, Christmas shop

Skyline Evergreen Farm
P.O. Box 86
Bentonville, VA 22610
(703)635-4366
Hours: daylight hours
Selection: Scotch pine, Norway spruce
Services: saws and assistance

Snickers Gap Tree Farm
P.O. Box 215
Bluemont, VA 22012
(703)554-8323
Hours: 9:00–dark weekends
Selection: white pine, Norway spruce, Douglas fir
Services: saws, baling, twine, assistance

Spring Hill Farm
Rt. 622 North
Washington, VA 22747
(703)987-9414
Hours: daylight daily
Selection: white pine
Services: free tree wrapping, refreshments

Spring Valley Farm
P. O. Box 495
Delaplane, VA 22025
(703)364-2129
Hours: 9:00–5:00 weekends
Selection: white pine, Norway spruce
Services: you cut or they cut

Stonehearth Christmas Tree Farm
Rt. 631
Leon, VA
(703)547-2576 or (301)384-6215
Hours: 8:30 A.M. to dark Thursday–Sunday
Selection: Scotch, Virginia and white pine
Services: you cut or they cut

Ticonderoga Farms
RR 1, Box 405
Chantilly, VA 22021
(703)528-4620
Hours: 8:00–dark Monday–Saturday, 9:00–dark Sunday
Selection: white and Scotch pine, Norway spruce, cedar
Services: cut your own and pre-cut and balled, greenhouse,
    refreshments

Valley View Nursery
3170 Arrowhead Road
Harrisonburg, VA 22801
(703)433-3016
Hours: 9:00–dark weekends
Selection: white and Scotch pines, Norway spruce
Services: cut or balled and burlapped, assistance

White Oak Farm
Rt. 1, Box 256
Middleburg, VA 22117
(703)687-6121/3433
Hours: 10:00–4:30 weekends
Selection: white pine, spruce, cut Fraser firs
Services: free hot cider

MARYLAND

Anne Arundel County
Coulter Farm
Double Gate Road
Davidsonville, MD
(410)261-4869
Hours: daily 9:00–5:00 from 2nd week in Dec to 12/23
Selection: white pine, Douglas fir

Friendship Trees
Route 778
Friendship, MD
(410)262-8514
Hours: daily 9:00–4:30
Selection: Scotch, white and Virginia pine, Norway and blue spruce

Hilltop Farm
Mallard Lane
Upper Marlboro, MD
(410)855-8431
Hours: weekdays 10:00–4:30, weekends 9:00–4:30
Selection: Scotch, white and Virginia pine, Douglas fir

Mas-que Farm
Spa Road
Annapolis, MD
(410)757-4454
Hours: weekends 8:00–4:00 from 2nd week of Dec to 12/23
Selection: Scotch and white pine, Norway spruce

Nicholson Tree Farm
Little Road
Deale, MD
(410)855-8388/8389
Hours 7:00–5:00 daily
Selection: Scotch, white and Austrian pine, Douglas fir, Norway and
    white spruce
Services: balled and burlapped trees and greenery also available

Carroll County

I. W. Davidson Farm
Emory Church Road
Reisterstown, MD
(410)374-2348 or 239-6556
Hours: daily 9:00–5:00
Selection: Scotch and white pine, Douglas and Fraser fir, Norway and
blue spruce

Feldhof Farm
Neudecker Road
Westminster, MD
(410)848-5526
Hours: Thursday–Sunday 10:00–5:00
Selection: Scotch and white pine, Norway, gray, blue, Serbian spruce,
Douglas fir
Services: balled and burlapped and pre-cut trees, greenery

JCK Christmas Tree Farm
Mayberry Road
Westminster, MD
(410)346-7597
Hours: daily 8:00–5:00
Selection: Scotch and white pine, Norway spruce
Services: balled and burlapped trees and pre-cut trees, greenery

Pine Valley Farm
Fannie Dorsery Road
Woodbine, MD
(410)795-8314
Hours: 9:00–5:00 daily
Selection: Scotch, white and Austrian pine, Douglas, Fraser and
Concolor fir, blue and Norway spruce
Services: bow saws, greenery, refreshments

Silver Meadow Farm
Davis Road
Mt. Airy, MD
(410)829-9198
Hours: weekdays 1:00–5:00, weekends 9:00–5:00
Selection: Scotch and white pine, Douglas fir
Services: bow saws available

Thomas Tree Farm
Rt. 30
Manchester, MD
(410)374-9538/9589
Hours: 9:00–5:00 daily
Selection: Scotch and white pine, Norway, white and blue spruce,
    Douglas fir
Services: trees baled, rope, greenery

Owl Pine Farm
Carter Road
Elkton, MD
(410)398-2821
Hours: weekend only 9:00–4:00
Selection: Scotch and white pine, Norway spruce

Frederick County

Clemsonville Christmas Tree Farm
Clemsonville Road
Libertytown, MD
Hours: daily 10:00–5:00
Selection: Scotch and white pine
Services: dig your own, pre-cut or dug-to-order, greenery

Franz Tree Farm
Route 80
Damascus, MD
Hours: weekdays 11:00–5:00, weekends 9:00–5:00
Selection: Scotch and white pine, Norway spruce
Services: greenery

Hardee Farms
Renner Road
Woodsboro, MD
(301)384-6576/9455
Hours: weekdays 9:30–4:30, weekends 9:00–4:30
Selection: Scotch and white pine, Douglas and Concolor fir, Norway,
    Austrian and blue spruce
Services: greenery, refreshments

Mayne's Tree Farm
Rt. 85
Frederick, MD
(301)662-4320 or 874-2665
Hours: daily 9:00–5:00
Selection: Scotch and white pine
Services: greenery

Owl Hollow Tree Farm
Kimmel Road
New Market, MD
(301)829-1254 or 831-5591
Hours: weekdays 1:00–dark, weekends 9:00–dark
Selection: Scotch, white and red pine
Services: greenery

Woodville Forest Farm
Peddicord Road
Mt. Airy, MD
(301)829-1478
Hours: weekends 9:00–4:00
Selection: Scotch and Virginia pine, white, blue and Norway spruce,
    Douglas fir
Services: balled and burlapped trees and some large trees 12–20 feet

Howard County
Kyme Nursery & Tree Farm
Forsythe Road
Sykesville, MD
(410)442-2088
Hours: Monday–Saturday 8:00–5:00, Sunday 9:00–5:00
Selection: Scotch and white pine, Norway and blue spruce, Douglas
    fir
Services: balled and burlapped, container trees, greenery

Larriland Farm
Route 94
Lisbon, MD
(410)854-6110
Hours: daily 9:00–5:00
Selection: white pine, Douglas fir
Services: balled and burlapped and pre-cut trees, greenery, jams and
    jellies

Prince George's County
Enchanted Forest
Baden-Westwood Road
Westwood, MD
(301)579-2238
Hours: Saturday 7:00–5:00 and Sunday 9:00–5:00
Selection: Scotch, white and Virginia pine, Norway and blue spruce,
    Cedar, Fraser fir
Services: greenery

GROWER-OWNED RETAIL LOTS

Anne Arundel County

Hunter's Meadow Mountain Trees
Papa John's Farm Market
New Cut Road
South Glen Burnie, MD
(410)255-2683
Hours: weekdays 9:00–9:00, Saturday 8:30–10:00
Selection: Scotch and white pine, Douglas and Fraser fir, blue spruce
Services: greenery

Montgomery County

Sundback's Christmas Tree Farm
6400 Wisconsin Avenue
Bethesda, MD
Hours: daily 9:00–9:00
Selection: Scotch pine, Engleman and blue spruce, Fraser, Douglas
and Concolor fir
Services: greenery

Sundback's Christmas Tree Farm
Colesville Road at Dale Drive
Silver Spring, MD
Hours: daily 9:00–9:00
Selection: Scotch pine, Fraser, Douglas, Concolor fir, Engleman and
blue spruce

Topical Cross Reference

ARTS AND CRAFTS
Chadds Ford, 20
Ellicott City, 137
Fallingwater, 139
Georgetown, 31
Glen Echo Park, 90
New Hope, 76
Peddler's Village, 77
Torpedo Art Center, 181
Union Station, 194

GARDENS
Brookside Gardens, 168
Dumbarton Oaks, 32
Franciscan Monastery, 89
Hershey, 96
Hillwood Gardens, 197
Kenilworth Aquatic Gardens, 100
London Town Publik House and Gardens, 37
Longwood Gardens, 39
Morven Park, 41
National Arboretum, 43
Nemours, 44
Norfolk Botanical Gardens, 47
President's Park, 52
Oatlands, 42
White House Rose Garden, 53
William Paca Gardens, 182
Winterthur, 61

HISTORICAL
Alexandria, 179
Annapolis, 181
Belair Mansion, 19
Cedar Hill, 209
Chestertown, 23
Clara Barton House, 91
Colvin Run Mill, 25
Decatur House, 209
Ford's Theatre, 194
Fredericksburg, 27
Gunston Hall, 92
Hagley Museum, 33
James River Plantations, 34
London Town Publik House, 37

CHILDREN (Attractions with special appeal to the young)
Baltimore Orioles Museum, 16
Capital Children's Museum, 186
C&O Canal Boat Trips, 80
Flying Circus, 88
Glen Echo Park, 90
Hersheypark, 97
Land of Little Horses, 144
Maryland Science Center, 198
National Zoological Park, 107
Oxon Hill Farm, 105
Washington Dolls' House and Toy Museum, 223
Wheaton Regional Park, 168

MILITARY
Anderson House, 84
Antietam National Battlefield, 69
Arlingon National Cemetery, 127
Gettysburg National Military Park, 149
Harpers Ferry National Historic Site, 94
Military Bands Summer Series, 120
NASA's Goddard Space Flight Center, 199
Navy Yard Museums, 205
Norfolk Naval Base, 46
U.S. Army Ordnance Museum, 160
Valley Forge National Historical Park, 221
Virginia Air and Space Center, 164
Yorktown, 171

RELIGION
Ephrata Cloister, 137
Franciscan Monastery, 89
Lititz, 102
National Shrine of the Immaculate Conception, 204
People's Place and Amish Farms, 113
Washington National Cathedral, 224

TRANSPORTATION
Baltimore and Ohio Railroad Museum, 17
Chesapeake & Ohio National Historical Park, 80
College Park Airport Museum, 82
C&O Canal Trips, 80
Flying Circus, 88
National Capital Trolley Museum, 203
Paul Garber Facility, 213
Strasburg Rail Road, 154
Union Station, 194

INDEX

TO HELP PLAN YOUR TRAVEL IN THE MID-ATLANTIC AREA

THE WALKER WASHINGTON GUIDE   **$8.95**
The seventh edition of the "Guide's guide to Washington,"
completely revised by Katherine Walker, builds on a 25-year
reputation as the top general guide to the capital. Its 320
pages are packed with museums, galleries, hotels, restaurants, theaters, shops, churches, as well as sites. Beautiful
maps and photos. Indispensable.

INNS OF THE BLUE RIDGE   **$11.95**
More than 125 country escapes in six mountain states,
Virginia to Georgia, all personally visited. Selections include country manors, farmhouses, hunting lodges,
B&Bs—a complete range from the luxurious to the laid-
back. Nuts and bolts info tells the what, where, how much
and other details to help make the right choice. Maps and
photos.

MARYLAND ONE-DAY TRIP BOOK   **$10.95**
From boiling rapids and rugged trails high in the western
mountains to frontier forts, horse country, Baltimore's urban
treasures, the Chesapeake Bay and the plantations and preserves of the Eastern Shore, Maryland is more than you can
imagine!

PHILADELPHIA ONE-DAY TRIP BOOK   **$8.95**
And you thought Independence Hall and the Liberty Bell were
all Philadelphia had to offer? Norman Rockwell Museum,
Pottsgrove Mansion, Daniel Boone Homestead, Covered
Bridges and Amish Farms are among 101 exciting one-day
trips featured.

ONE-DAY TRIPS THROUGH HISTORY   **$9.95**
Describes 200 historic sites within 150 miles of the nation's
capital where our forebears lived, dramatic events occurred
and America's roots took hold. Sites and arranged chronologi-
cally starting with pre-history.

THE VIRGINIA ONE-DAY TRIP BOOK   **$8.95**
Jane Ockershausen Smith, one of the most experienced travel
writers in the Mid-Atlantic area, admits to being surprised by
the wealth of things to see and do in the Old Dominion. With
101 sites divided into seven geographic regions, this is the
perfect guide for anyone who is anywhere in Virginia.

NORTH CAROLINA ONE-DAY TRIP BOOK $11.95

150 excursions throughout the Tarheel State that beckon day-trippers of all ages and interest. The state slogan says "The beauty only begins with the scenery"—we've organized all of it into seven geographic regions for easy planning, supplemented with maps and seasonal information.

Also:

Florida One-Day Trips (from Orlando). What to do after you've done Disney. **$7.95**

Call it Delmarvalous. How to talk, cook and "feel to hum" on the Delaware, Maryland, and Virginia Peninsula. **$7.95**

A Shunpiker's Guide to the Northeast. Wide open routes that shun turnpikes and interstates between Washington and Boston. Maps and directions included. **$9.95**

Footnote Washington. Tracking the engaging, humorous and surprising bypaths of capital history by one of the city's most popular broadcasters. **$8.95**

Walking Tours of Old Washington and Alexandria. Paul Hogarth's exquisite water-colors of grand old buildings, lovingly reproduced and arranged in seven guided walking tours. **$24.95**

Order Blank for all EPM books described here. Mail with check to:

EPM Publications, Inc.
Box 490, McLean, VA 22101

Title	Quantity	Price	Amount	Shipping
_____	_____	_____	_____	_____
_____	_____	_____	_____	_____
_____	_____	_____	_____	_____
_____	_____	_____	_____	_____

Subtotal _____

Virginia residents add 4 1/2% tax _____

Orders totaling up to $15 add $2.50 shipping/handling _____

Orders totaling more than $15 add $3.50 first item, $1 ea. add'l _____

Name _____

Street _____

City _____ State _____ Zip _____

Total _____

Remember to enclose names, addresses and enclosure cards for gift purchases.
Please note that prices are subject to change. Thank you.

About the Author

Jane Ockershausen began writing in the early 1970s as a means of sharing new discoveries she made while traveling in and around Washington with her young daughter. Her first book was the original edition of *The Washington One-Day Trip Book*. Since then she has written One-Day Trip Books on Virginia, Maryland, North Carolina, and Philadelphia and the best-selling guide to historic sites in and around the capital city entitled *One-Day Trips Through History*.

Jane was a correspondent for *The National Geographic Traveler* for several years. For three years she wrote a weekly regional column for *The Washington Times*, and for six years she has written a regular feature in *AAA World, Potomac Magazine*.

Her byline has appeared in *The Washington Post, The Baltimore Sun, The Chicago Tribune, The Buffalo News, The Dallas Times Herald, The Oregonian* and *The Pittsburgh Press*. She has also written for *The Washingtonian, Mid-Atlantic Country* and *Historic Preservation Magazine*.

Jane is a member of the Society of American Travel Writers and the American Society of Journalists and Authors.